AMERICA IN THE GILDED AGE

SEAN DENNIS CASHMAN

AMERICA IN
THE GILDED AGE

FROM THE DEATH OF LINCOLN
TO THE RISE OF THEODORE ROOSEVELT

NEW YORK UNIVERSITY PRESS
NEW YORK & LONDON

Library of Congress Cataloging in Publication Data

Cashman, Sean Dennis.
America in the Gilded Age.

Bibliography: p.
Includes index.
1. United States—History—1865–1901. I. Title.
E661.C38   1983   973.8   83-14610
ISBN 0-8147-1386-6 (alk. paper)
ISBN 0-8147-1387-4 (pbk.)

c 10 9 8 7 6 5 4 3

Manufactured in the United States of America

Clothbound editions of New York University Press books are Smyth-
sewn and printed on durable and acid-free paper.

FOR
PIERS MACKESY

CONTENTS

ILLUSTRATIONS

PREFACE

THIS BOOK, intended as an introduction to the Gilded Age and Industrial America, offers a general account of the industrial and economic, social and political history of the period from 1865 to 1901. It is a work of synthesis, drawn from recent scholarship and from some primary sources. It gives pride of place to the amazing developments in industry—for many people the most original and distinctive feature of the period—and then describes the complementary social history of immigration, urbanization, and labor unions. The second half of the book concentrates on the political stories of Reconstruction and party politics and the rise of dissent culminating in the Populist Revolt. It concludes with accounts of imperialism and progressivism at the turn of the century. The book aims at a clear, concise presentation of essential facts but it does not attempt to record the history of high society nor of the complex and diverse stories of education and religion, arts and letters, and considers westward expansion briefly. It is designed both for those who want to read about Reconstruction and the years to 1877 in general and those who, instead, prefer to begin in 1876 or 1877. It places some emphasis on the life stories and personalities of the principal protagonists and includes illustrations.

I began this book in the spring of 1981 at the suggestion of Colin Jones, and I completed it in the fall of 1982 during a study-leave from my duties as lecturer in American history at Manchester

University in England. I thank my colleagues and especially Professors Peter Marshall and Dennis Welland for making this possible. During fall semester of 1982 I was the guest of the American Studies Program at the George Washington University, Washington, D.C. I thank the Director, Professor Howard Gillette, for making arrangements for my visit, and Professors Bernard Mergen of GWU and Wilcomb Washburn of the Smithsonian Institution for inviting me to teach in their classes. Professor David Reimers of New York University offered constructive advice on the structure and content of the book, particularly on immigration. Ms. Mary Ison of the Library of Congress was most helpful in the selection of illustrations. Mrs. Eileen Grimes typed the manuscript.

SEAN DENNIS CASHMAN
WASHINGTON, D.C.
NOVEMBER 1982

INTRODUCTION

T HE ASSASSIN who ended the life of Abraham Lincoln extinguished the light of the Republic. On April 14, 1865, after the president argued in the cabinet for generous treatment of the South, vanquished in the war between the states, he went to the theater. It was Good Friday and there was a conspiracy afoot to kill him. During the third act of the play at Ford's Theatre in Washington, actor John Wilkes Booth, a fanatical partisan of the southern cause, stole into his box and shot him in the head at close range. Lincoln never regained consciousness and died early the next day. Until his death Lincoln had been a most controversial president—yet his secretary of war, Edwin Stanton, could justly claim, "Now he belongs to the ages." The transfiguration of the murdered president cast a long shadow over American history from 1865 to 1901. The period that begins with the assassination of one president is divided by the assassination of another, James Garfield, in 1881, and ends with the assassination of a third, William McKinley, in 1901.

These were formative years. The Industrial Revolution and the development of commercial monopolies, Reconstruction and the New South, the settlement of the West and closing of the frontier—all brought to the fore of politics a cast of characters that was very different from the statesmen, soldiers, and slaves of the Civil War. This was the heyday of the robber barons. Perhaps the most damaging accusation against Lincoln after his assassination was that to win the war he had been ready to sacrifice the ideals of the Republican party to spoilsmen and profiteers. Progressive journalist Lincoln Steffens observed that in England politics was a sport, in Germany it was a profession, but in the United States it was a business—and a corrupt one at that. Yet, in the absence of strong executive leadership during a prolonged period of social, industrial, and economic growth, Lincoln's reputation soared ever higher. At the end of the century New England intellectuals criticized the cult of idolizing Lincoln in an anecdote about an American traveler to England who visited Oxford University. Confused by the architectural similarity between two of the colleges in Turl Street—Jesus and Lincoln—he exclaimed, "I can't tell the difference between Lincoln and Jesus!" A passing student remarked that it was the same with all Americans. The allusion and the confusion were understandable. Lincoln had, after all, saved the Union in war, whereas his successors came close to losing the peace.

The West was settled at a fatal cost to the American Indian. The South was tied back to the Union at a humiliating cost to the American black. There were two depressions, in 1873 and 1893, each with devastating effects on the economy. The amazing industrial expansion of the United States was accomplished with considerable exploitation of factory artisans. The splendors of the new cities rose amid the squalor of industrial slums. The most damning indictment of this postwar American society was attributed to the future French prime minister Georges Clemenceau, who lived for a time in New York and New England. Noting its undoubted problems, he could claim the United States had gone from a stage of barbarism to one of decadence without achieving any civilization between the two.

Mark Twain paid a different but no less censorious tribute to the aspirations, autocracy, and affluence of the new American plutocracy of industrialists, financiers, and politicians in his utopian satire, *The Gilded Age* (1873). The title takes its cue from Shakespeare. King John is dissuaded from a second superfluous coronation with the argument, "To gild refined gold, to paint the lily,/ . . . Is wasteful and ridiculous excess." And Lady Macbeth implicates King Duncan's sleeping attendants in his murder by daubing them with blood from the dagger Macbeth used to do the

The murder of President Abraham Lincoln was a political disaster of the first magnitude for the United States at the end of the Civil War. The deed cast its dark shadow over Reconstruction and posterity has agreed with Mark Twain that what should have been an age golden with industrial opportunity turned out, instead, to be gilded, guilded, and guilt-ridden. The photo by Alexander Gardner was one of a series taken on April 10, 1865. (Library of Congress).

deed. "I'll gild the faces of the grooms withal," she says, "For it must seem their guilt." Mark Twain took this grotesque pun of gold and crime a stage further. His title was to become a triple pun. To gilt and guilt were added guilds in the sense of interest groups, labor unions, and monopolies. Twain's epithet, approved by his collaborator, Charles Dudley Warner, has survived as the most apt description of the period.

If the age had a motto it might well be, "The ayes have it," not only for the celebrated interest in voting stock, but also for the eyes that rejoiced in the glitter of gold, and the I's that define many of the pervasive social themes. Society was obsessed with invention, industrialization, incorporation, immigration, and, later, imperialism. It was indulgent of commercial speculation, social ostentation, and political prevarication but was indifferent to the special needs of immigrants and Indians and intolerant of black Americans, labor unions, and political dissidents.

Whereas the Gilded Age had no predecessors, we may discern in two subsequent periods some of its features—notwithstanding the very considerable differences between them. The first is the 1920s; the second, the period from 1945 to 1960. These were periods of predominantly (but not exclusively) Republican administrations that, in the 1870s, 1880s, and 1920s, were led by ineffective presidents. The government as a whole in each period was conservative. Accusations of nefarious links between politicans and businessmen and of widespread corruption in public life were rife. The presidency of Ulysses S. Grant is usually represented as a nadir of political probity. But the excesses of so-called carpetbaggers as well as of Congress and the administration in the 1870s pale in comparison with those of the Watergate burglars and some White House staff during the presidency of Richard M. Nixon in the early 1970s. Yet, the profligacy of the Ohio gang in the 1920s and the Republican chant of K1C2 (Korea, communism, and corruption) against the Democrats in 1952 have also remained a notorious part of the legend of the periodic corruption of public life in America.

Each period benefited from a boom in transportation—after 1865, the railroad; in the 1920s, the mass production of the automobile; in the late 1940s, the widespread commercial use of the airplane. Each enjoyed a revolution in communications—in the Gilded Age, telegraph and telephone; in the 1920s, motion pictures and radio; in the 1950s, television. Innovations in transportation and communications together worked for a more homogeneous culture and a more informed citizenry, as well as having undisputed industrial and commercial significance in their own right.

Each period followed a war that left many Americans disillusioned, bitter, and confused. Their hostility to changed circumstances and the residue of hate engendered by the war but not yet expended partly account for the founding of the racist Ku Klux Klan after the Civil War and for its startling revival during the 1920s. This hostility was also vented against suspect ideologies. In the 1870s and 1880s labor unions were tainted by presumed association with anarchism, and the Haymarket anarchists of 1886 were tried without justice. The Great Red Scare of 1919 and the Palmer raids on radicals expressed genuine if exaggerated anxiety about the dangers of a communist revolt, which was confirmed in the 1920s by the prejudicial treatment of the anarchists Sacco and Vanzetti. In 1950 Senator Joseph McCarthy lent his name to another wave of anticommunist hysteria that had been growing with the cold war.

In one respect, however, the political and economic profile of the Gilded Age was unlike those of its successors. In the most literal sense of the word it was gilded: politics and economics were bound by bars of gold. And what should be the true basis of the currency—whether gold, silver, or credit—became the most enduring controversy of the period. It tarnished presidents and Congress, Supreme Court and stock market, and both major parties. It was the eye of the hurricane of depression in 1873 and 1893 and the heart of the new Greenback and Populist parties. Though the tide of arguments about an expanded or contracted currency seemed to ebb and flow over the years it was swelling inevitably to a climax in the election of 1896.

The controversy had its origins in the Civil War. Not satisfied with other ways of raising additional revenue to pay for the war, the federal government resorted to printing extra money. In the Legal Tender Act of February 25, 1862, Congress authorized the

Treasury to issue $150 million in paper notes—greenbacks. There were, therefore, three kinds of money in circulation—gold, silver, and paper dollars. Paper dollars included both national bank notes and the new government greenbacks. By the end of the war the administration had given way to the temptation of easy finance. Of perhaps $1.08 billion in circulation altogether greenbacks accounted for $433.16 million. Their value fluctuated but in 1865 it stood at a ratio of $157 in greenbacks to $100 in gold coin.

Notwithstanding the national emergency of the war, conservative financial thinking cherished a classical theory of finance according to which the value of money was determined by the amount of gold bullion (uncoined ingots) held in the Treasury as security. After the war the government concurred with this school of thought. Secretary of the Treasury Hugh McCulloch (1865–69) proposed resumption, a return to the gold standard—hard money as it was called. He proposed to contract the money supply by eliminating greenbacks. In 1866 Congress authorized him to withdraw $10 million in notes immediately and, thereafter, to retire up to $4 million in notes each month. As a result of this policy by February 1868 McCulloch had eliminated some $45 million in greenbacks.

This deflationary policy was to the advantage of certain classes such as businessmen who believed a stable currency was essential for industry and commerce. It also appealed to those who had supported the war effort by buying government bonds. They had done so with a depreciated currency and now stood to make a handsome profit if the bonds were redeemed in gold. But resumption imposed an additional handicap on debtors such as farmers who had borrowed depreciated money to buy homesteads during the war. If the value of the currency were revised upwards they would have to repay their loans at a higher rate of interest.

In February 1868 Congress reversed the postwar policy of contraction. Alarmed by economic recession, it forbade further retirement of paper money. It did so on the assumption that some sort of controlled inflation would stimulate the economy. During a more serious depression in 1873 the cry for inflationary policies became ever more insistent, especially in the West. Secretary of the Treasury William A. Richardson (1873–74) had, as undersecretary in 1872, reissued $5 million of the greenbacks that had, by now, been retired. He continued to introduce more greenbacks into circulation. By 1874 he had issued $26 million, making a total of $382 million altogether.

Another complicating factor in the history of the coinage was the fate of gold and silver as minerals. Before the Civil War the traditional relative value of gold and silver for the purposes of currency was 15.98 ounces of silver to one ounce of gold. But in 1861 the yield of silver mines was so low that silver was worth more than that on the commercial market. Thus silver miners sold silver commercially instead of to the Treasury which bought only gold for coins. However, in the process of opening up the trans-Mississippi West after the war, prospectors discovered ever richer veins of silver. In 1873 the value of silver mined was the same as that of gold at $36 million. But the following year the value of silver began an irreversible slide below the official ratio of 16 to 1. It was now more advantageous for investors and miners alike to sell silver to the Treasury at the official rate rather than on the commercial market where they would get less for it. Of course, the government was reluctant to buy silver at an inflated price. And in the Coinage Act of 1873 Congress withheld the customary provision for minting silver dollars. Thus there would be no new silver coins. Silver investors considered themselves cheated of future prospects and denounced the act as "the crime of '73."

In 1875 Congress went further and returned to a policy of contraction. It passed a Resumption of Specie Payment Act. It declared that for every $100 issued in new national bank notes the Treasury would withdraw $80 in greenbacks. More important, it set a time limit for the withdrawal of greenbacks. Payments in specie were to be resumed by January 1, 1879. This was achieved by Secretary of the Treasury John Sherman (1877–81).

The coinage was clearly a most controversial subject. It is, therefore, somewhat surprising that economic debate played such a small part in the two congressional elections following the depression. The inflationists' principal political vehicle, the Greenback or Independent National Party, polled only 81,737 votes in the election of 1876. Even in 1880 its presidential nominee, James B. Weaver, took only 308,578 votes, 3.4 percent of the total. However, in the 1880s the torch of inflation was passed from the green-backers to the silverites.

It was quite natural that silver mining interests should continue to press the case for minting silver since they stood to gain financially. But their arguments also appealed to many without a direct financial stake in silver. Bimetallism, currency of silver as well as gold, represented a sort of middle ground between radical and conservative theories. It was not as radical as paper money, which was based on nothing more substantial than trust, nor was it as unyielding as gold. The new school of thought believed that it was the duty of the federal government to regulate money in the interests of the whole of society and not just a particular class. It declared that money should represent credit rather than bullion. It maintained there was not enough gold to provide as large or flexible a currency as was required by a nation expanding its industry, its territory, and its population as rapidly as was the United States. By tying the entire monetary system to gold, argued the bimetallists, the government was giving hostages to the varying fortunes of gold production.

The agricultural depression of the late 1880s and early 1890s prompted farmers to champion the silver cause with greater fervor. In 1890 their lobby succeeded in persuading Congress to pass the Sherman Silver Purchase Act. It required the Treasury to buy 4.5 million ounces of silver per month. But the Sherman Act failed to maintain the price of silver, failed to increase the money supply, and failed to stop the fall in crop prices. In 1890 the value of silver stood at 19.76 ounces of silver to 1 ounce of gold. As the supply of silver increased so the value fell. In 1893 it was 26.49 ounces of silver to 1 ounce of gold. By June 1893 the gold value of a silver dollar was less than 60 cents. Whereas "goldbugs" concluded that the only proper course was a return to the gold standard silverites could not accept that their remedy was a failure. Instead, they concluded that compromise was futile and argued for unlimited coinage of silver at the ratio of 16 to 1. If only the federal government would exchange gold for silver at the traditional ratio then the market price of silver would surely rise to that level. To the goldbugs this was throwing good money after bad.

Moreover, the United States was now in the grip of a major industrial depression. President Grover Cleveland (1893–97) believed he must restore business confidence and to do this he had to eliminate monetary uncertainty by getting Congress to repeal the Sherman Silver Purchase Act. He recognized that many western Democrats were committed to silver on account of their constituents' interests. He realized that his proposal would divide the party. Undeterred, he used his patronage to persuade enough Republicans and Democrats to support repeal in the fall of 1893. Repeal, however, had minimal economic consequences. Politically, it was momentous, dividing the Democrats and opening nationwide debate on the merits of bimetallism.

In the election of 1896 both the Democrats and the new party of Populists, representing farmers and silverites in South and West, came to focus their policies on a reform of the currency by the use of silver as well as gold on a ratio of 16 to 1. For their part the Republicans and their rich industrial and commercial allies came out for gold. The "Battle of the Standards" in the election was the climax of a protracted struggle for control of government and economy between the industrial interests of the Northeast and the agrarian forces of the West and South. The Republicans and their presidential candidate, William McKinley, defeated the Democrats and Populists. After the discovery of more gold in Australia and Alaska the United States returned formally to the gold standard in an act signed by McKinley on March 14, 1900. In future gold was to be the sole standard of currency. It seemed the dominant plutocracy would not allow its cloth of gold to be made threadbare by a more even distribution of wealth throughout society. So potent was the appeal of the myth of rags to riches—that an individual could, by his own efforts, rise from obscurity to great wealth—that the majority concurred.

CHAPTER ONE

THE SIGHT AND SOUND OF INDUSTRIAL AMERICA

D URING THE Gilded Age natives and immigrants alike were more interested in the stars in their eyes than the stripes on their backs. The promise of American life lay in its industrial future. As early as 1871 Congress resolved that in the centennial of 1876 Americans should appraise their achievements, "the natural resources of the country and their development, and of its progress in those arts which benefit mankind, in comparison with those of older nations." The exhibition, which opened on the banks of the Schuylkill River outside Philadelphia for five months beginning on May 10, 1876, was conceived in a very different spirit from the celebrations for the bicentennial in 1976. Instead of political achievement, it emphasized America's mastery in the appliance of science. As such, it constituted an industrial revelation of America to the rest of the world.

Memorial Hall in Philadelphia was built in modern Renaissance style to exhibit American arts and culture. But nearby was Machinery Hall, a more austere yet more inviting building. It was guarded by a huge breech-loading cannon, the symbol of war, and by the Corliss steam engine. This enormous 1,400-horsepower machine, designed to furnish power to all the exhibits inside Machinery Hall, astonished the 9,910,966 visitors that summer. It weighed nearly 1.7 million pounds and yet ran without vibration

The giant Corliss engine in Machinery Hall was a star attraction of the 1876 Centennial Exhibition outside Philadelphia and taken as a symbol of American industrial progress. After the exhibition closed it was used to drive machinery in the Pullman works outside Chicago. The illustration first appeared in *Harper's Weekly* on May 27, 1876. (Library of Congress).

or noise. Here was a new symbol of peace and progress. Inside the hall inventions in the fields of agriculture, transportation, and machinery were given special prominence. By its display of drills, mowers, and reapers, of lumber wagons and Pullman sleeping cars, of sewing machines and typewriters, of planes, lathes, and looms, the United States demonstrated its preeminence in mechanics. As the *Times* of London reported on August 22, 1878, "the American mechanizes as an old Greek sculptured, as the Venetian painted." Novelist William Dean Howells gave his verdict to the *Atlantic Monthly* of July 1876. It was in engineering, rather than in art, that "the national genius most freely speaks: by and by the inspired marbles, the breathing canvases . . . [but] for the present America is voluble in the strong metals and their infinite uses." Industrial development was America's destiny.

Between 1865 and 1901 the American Industrial Revolution transformed the United States from a country of small and isolated communities scattered across 3 million square miles of continental territory into a compact economic and industrial unit. Thus, the rural Republic of Lincoln and Lee became the industrial empire of Roosevelt and Bryan. The United States already had the prerequisites for such a transformation. It was fabulously rich in minerals, possessing about two thirds of the world's coal; immense deposits of high-quality iron ore; great resources of petroleum; and, in the West, a natural treasury of gold, silver, and copper.

Although in 1860 the United States was still a second-rate industrial power, by 1890 it led Britain, France, and Germany. The value of its manufactured goods almost equaled the total of the others. The accompanying table, adapted from *Historical Statistics of the United States* (1975), shows increases in the production of raw materials between 1860 and 1900. It was precisely because the base of industry before the Civil War was so narrow that its advance seemed so spectacular later on.

From the middle of the century to the 1890s the railroads were the basis of the new industrial economy. They made possible the development of new areas of commerce as well as that of steel, iron, coal, and other industries. But in the 1890s it was the complex, varied urban market with its demand for a wider range of

Commodity	1860 (millions)	1900 (millions)	Increase (%)
Anthracite coal (short tons)	10.9	57.3	525
Bituminous coal (short tons)	9.0	212.3	2,358
Crude Petroleum (barrels)	.5	45.8	9,160
Pig iron (long tons)	.8	13.7	1,713
Crude steel (short tons)	.01	11.2	11,227
Wheat (bushels)	173.1	599.0	339
Wheat exported (bushels)	4.0	102.0	2,550
Corn (bushels)	838.8	2,662.0	301
Cotton (bales)	3.8	10.1	261

refined materials and manufactured goods that replaced the railroads as the principal stimulus of the economy as a whole. In the 1890s American cities were modernized, and steel was the essential medium used for building bridges, piping water and sewage, transmitting gas and electricity, and constructing ever higher buildings.

Iron replaced wood; steel replaced iron; and electricity and steam replaced horsepower. In 1870 agricultural production surpassed industrial production by about $500 million. Both were increasing year by year. But by 1900 manufacturing had increased by more than four times. Thus, industrial production now exceeded agricultural production by $13 billion to $4.7 billion. In every decade the levels of production increased in the oil refineries of Ohio and Pennsylvania; the iron and steel mills of Michigan, Illinois, and Pennsylvania; the meatpacking plants of Cincinnati and Chicago; the clothing and shoe factories of New England; and the breweries of Chicago, St. Louis, and Milwaukee. The number of people engaged in manufacturing was 2¼ times as great in 1890 as in 1870; in mining 2½ times as great; in transportation and public utilities 2½ times; in construction 2 times.

Industrial growth and westward expansion were assured by the revolution in transportation and the revolution in communications. There was a spectacular growth in population, from 35,701,000 in 1865 to 77,584,000 in 1901. Yet these widely dispersed people felt part of a unified whole. A transcontinental railroad network brought farm and factory, country and town closer together. Telegraph and telephone, electricity and press increased public knowledge, business efficiency, and political debate.

By their aptitude for invention and their ability to harness the inventions of others to their own purposes Americans acquired a facility for turning raw materials into finished industrial products. Between 1860 and 1890 as many as 440,000 patents were issued for new inventions. During the Gilded Age the most significant American inventions, whether new or improved, were those that could hasten and secure *settlement*: the steam boilers of Babcock and Wilcox; the electric lamp of Thomas Alva Edison; the telephone of Alexander Graham Bell; the telegraph stock ticker of E. A. Callahan; linoleum; the elevator of Elisha G. Otis; machine tools of Pratt and Whitney; the elixirs of John Wyeth; the newspaper linotype compositer of Ottmar Mergenthaler; and the typewriter of Christopher Sholes. The fundamental principles behind many of these and other inventions had long been understood. But not until technology could fashion tools of great delicacy could they be put into practice. Thus, the inventions depended on improved technology, and they in turn transformed that technology making possible ever more inventions of still greater refinement.

EDISON AND BELL

In the field of scientific invention the best prizes fall to those who see the need and find the means to meet it. The American inventors Thomas Alva Edison and Alexander Graham Bell saw the need to transmit light and sound and found the incandescent light bulb and the telephone, the motion picture and the phonograph. They were, perhaps, the only authentic heroes of the age. They transformed the society into which they were born by an astute blend of inventive genius and technological knowledge. Their fame was spread by the communications they devised. They seemed like heroes because they combined technical expertise in the new field of communications with the sort of traditional pioneer spirit that had the tenacity to see a novel idea through from start to finish. The American humorous magazine *Puck* of July 1880 explained why such a man as the boastful but enterprising Edison should be taken as a symbol of national optimism in industrial progress: "Edison is not a humbug. He is a type of man common enough in this country—a smart, persevering, sanguine, ignorant show-off American. He can do a great deal and he thinks he can do everything."

Edison and Bell were strict contemporaries—both were born in 1847—and their talents were as complementary as melody and harmony are in sound. However, both of them recognized in silence a golden opportunity. Bell's mother and his wife were both deaf, and he became a teacher of deaf-mutes. Edison went deaf. They thus acquired special insight into the world of communication that they were determined to expand. Their inventions were not the happy result of accident and intuition but of back-breaking trial and error in painstaking experiments carried out night after night for months—and sometimes for years. In fact, Edison's most famous remark was, "Genius is 1 percent inspiration and 99 percent perspiration." They regarded science, not as an absolute, but as an infinitely expanding world in which to seek was to find. Thus, they were perfectly equipped for the competitive worlds of business and industry when business and industry were putting a special premium on increasing efficiency by improving communications. Indeed their careers were governed by the priorities of business.

What industrialists and businessmen wanted was a better telegraph. The electric telegraph, first made practical by the English inventors Sir William Cooke and Sir Charles Wheatstone, had already been instrumental in winning the Civil War. The states of the Union were linked together by thousands of miles of overhead wire. But although there were 37,000 miles of wire in 1865, this was nothing compared with the 215,000 miles in existence by 1900 through which millions of short and long pulses of electricity flowed each day. As with other inventions in communication, telegraphy was, necessarily, a matter of commerce. During the 1870s and 1880s various attempts were made to bring it under the control of the federal government. But the backers had not the force of the major company, Western Union, organized by Hiram Sibley of Rochester, New York, and Ezra Cornell, who were determined to consolidate the service as a private monopoly. By the end of the century Western Union owned about 90 percent of all telegraph lines. However, with the amazing expansion of business and industry the telegraph was being required to deliver more than Western Union's system, the automatic, was capable of doing. The automatic was economical for use over short lines with heavy traffic. But its speed decreased over greater distances— transmitting no more than 80 or 90 words per minute, far less than the 1,000 words it claimed. Edison, Bell, and other inventors were in feverish competition with one another to devise improved means of communication by telegraph or some alternative to it.

Thomas Alva Edison, born in Milan, Ohio, was the youngest of seven children of a feckless Canadian immigrant and a mother who made herself a martyr to her husband's bizarre life-style before she slid into madness and an early death. Edison was a sickly child who suffered from periodic bronchial infections and had little formal schooling. At sixteen he became a telegraph transmitter and receiver and worked in various northern and southern cities. For several years he led the life of a rolling stone gathering neither moss nor morse but increasing deafness of the middle ear, caused by scarlatina, was concentrating his mind wonderfully. When he was twenty-one he bought a copy of Michael Faraday's *Experimental Research in Electricity* and found the English scientist's accounts of his experiments so lucid and compelling that he determined to perform them himself. Previously, his exploration of chemistry and electricity had been haphazard. Now he spent much of his monthly salary of $120 on books, chemicals, and electrical equipment. At a time when it seemed that every telegrapher was trying to make a duplex—an apparatus to send two messages, one in either direction, on the same wire simultaneously—he claimed to have invented one. After repairing the telegraphic gold price indicator at the gold exchange in New York in 1869 he acquired the reputation of being able to eliminate bugs and was made supervisor of the machine. He won the confidence of financiers, who commissioned him to make an improved stock ticker, and in January 1871 he created the Edison Universal Stock Printer, an automatic machine capable of transmitting between 200 and 300 words a minute and far superior to any in use before.

With the continuing support of his investors the twenty-four-

Thomas Alva Edison, the most prolific inventor in history, with one of his early phonographs in 1878. His inventions in the field of communications provided the sinews for the transformation of America from an agrarian to a complex industrial and urban society. (Library of Congress).

year-old inventor set himself up in Newark, New Jersey, as an independent manufacturer of stock tickers with two other scientists, English immigrant Charles Batchelor and Swiss immigrant John Kruesi. They had the scientific training Edison lacked. He would conceive a plan that Batchelor would turn into an exact drawing and from which Kruesi would make the model. In 1873 Edison devised both the diplex and the quadruplex telegraphs. The diplex could send two different messages together on one wire in the same direction. The quadruplex could send two in both directions at once, so that only one wire was now required instead of four, as previously. The quadruplex was sold to financier and railroad entrepreneur Jay Gould.

In 1876 Edison established the world's first industrial research laboratory at Menlo Park, twelve miles south of Newark, a prototype of company laboratories of the future. To say that he was prolific is to make an understatement. That summer he worked on the electromotograph, acoustic telegraph, autographic telegraph, speaking telegraph, electric pen, and mimeograph; and, in the fall, on the electrical dental drill and an electric sewing machine.

Both Western Union and its rival, Atlantic and Pacific, for whom Edison worked, claimed rights to the quadruplex. Their legal battle led to a sensational trial in the spring of 1877 that made Edison's name widely known. The *Telegrapher* of March 25, 1876, had already called him "the professor of duplicity and quadruplicity." But the rival companies settled out of court and agreed to share the income from the new system.

It was Edison's natural serendipity that led him to invent the phonograph in 1877. What he was searching for was a way to record messages for commercial purposes. What he found was a new world of entertainment. He discovered that he could retain sound by attaching a stylus from an embossing telegraph to a telephone speaker and shouting into it while running a band of paraffined paper rapidly underneath the speaker. The paper could be replayed with the stylus; and the sound, if indistinct, could be recorded. He continued to experiment with alternate means of recording—cylinder, disk, and paper bands. He tested the new toy with cheeky rhymes, such as:

Mary has a new sheath gown,
It is too tight by half.
Who cares a damn for Mary's lamb,
When they can see her calf!

Edison disclosed his new invention to the National Academy of Sciences in Washington on April 18, 1878, and the excitement was such that two women fainted. President Rutherford B. Hayes got his wife out of bed in the middle of the night so that they could hear it at a midnight matinee at the White House.

Having found a way to record sound, Edison now decided to find a way to retain light. By the 1870s various types of electric arc lamps were available, but because of the enormous power they supplied and the gases they gave off they were suited only to large halls or open spaces. However, a consortium of New York financiers, including banker John Pierpont Morgan, believed that Edison could invent a more practical electric lamp and, in November 1878, subsidized his newly formed Edison Electric Light Company. The crucial breakthroughs in the search for a practicable electric lamp were the invention of a special generator (the long-waisted Mary Ann), and the carbon-filament lamp. Edison discovered that carbon remained stable in a nearly perfect vacuum. But he was unable to bake carbon wire in spiral form. It was only when his associate, Charles Batchelor, shaped the wire into a horseshoe that the first viable incandescent lamp was realized. It burned for sixteen hours on November 17, 1879.

Edison understood the significance of publicity and realized that it was important to have his system of electric lighting accepted in London and Paris as soon as possible. He thus made installation in these capitals a priority in the summer of 1881 before laying the mains for a central power station in New York at Pearl Street at the end of the year. Supported by Morgan, he moved his Edison Illuminating Company to New York; and there, on September 4, 1882, he switched on electric lights in the "House of Morgan," the New York Stock Exchange, the *New York Times*, the *New York Herald*, and other buildings in lower Manhattan. By 1883 Edison had 246 plants making electricity for 61,000 lamps. Artificial light could continue day and night, thereby increasing the industrial potential of factories, the commercial potential of offices, and the social life of city and home. It was a case of many lights make hands work.

Edison's plant used direct current. Electricity could be transmitted long distance only by first increasing and then lowering the voltage in alternating current. George Westinghouse of Pittsburgh devised a transformer in 1886 that could transmit high-voltage alternating current over long distances. In 1888 a Hungarian immigrant and engineer, Nikola Tesla, invented an alternating current motor that converted electricity into mechanical power. Westinghouse and Tesla subsequently worked together to improve their inventions. They used alternating current to light the Columbian Exposition in Chicago in 1893. The inventions of Westinghouse and Tesla suggested the future use of hydroelectric power, and by the end of the century Niagara Falls was harnessed for electric power.

The use of electric motors in manufacturing made electricity the cleanest and most convenient form of industrial power yet known. Electric power was being used widely in transportation by the 1890s. Frank J. Sprague introduced the first electric street railway in Richmond, Virginia, in 1888. His invention, affording cheap, rapid, and clean transportation, was soon adopted by other cities anxious to free themselves from the pollution and risk of fire of steam trains.

Edison, who always plowed back his money into new research, opened a new laboratory of grand design at West Orange, New Jersey, in 1887. He now employed 120 research assistants; eventually the laboratory was surrounded by an industrial estate of 5,000 people making goods from his inventions.

Despite the fact that many of his inventions were worth millions of dollars, Edison's career was plagued by financial insecurity. He had no professional skills as a businessman, turning over his affairs to successive financiers in exchange for ready cash and subsequently quarreling with them when he thought himself badly treated. A compulsive spender on equipment and research, he could not bring himself to balance income and expenses. He made and lost several fortunes. His business dealings had taught him to trust nobody and to expect the worst from human nature. But his newfound ruthlessness was so ill concealed that he alienated his associates and damaged himself commercially. This partly explains how he lost control of his own company. In February 1892 the General Edison Electric Company merged with its great rival, Thomson-Houston. The new corporation, capitalized at $50 million, was named, quite simply, General Electric. It had a new president, Charles Coffin. But for Edison the unkindest cut was the exclusion of his name from the company's name. Edison eventually sold many of his shares. He squandered the $4 million he had gained from the electric lamp on a mistaken and foolhardy attempt to mine, or mill, iron ore magnetically.

However, he recovered his personal fortune in the two revolutions he started in the world of entertainment. By 1899 the sales of the spring-motor phonograph amounted to $500,000, although the mass production of records as disks did not begin until February 1902, after Eldridge Johnson had organized the Victor Talking Machine Company in 1901. Edison also introduced a mutation of the phonograph that completely transformed entertainment. From Eadward Muybridge, an English immigrant who produced still photos of nudes for stereoscopic projection that he called "Animal Locomotion," Edison conceived the idea of moving, talking pictures. Ever since 1878, when he won a bet for Governor Leland Stanford of California that a horse in full gallop had all four feet off the ground, Muybridge had been widely recognised as an expert in sequential photography. Four years earlier he had scored a success de scandale by killing his wife's lover and persuading a jury to acquit him of murder.

Using celluloid film produced by George Eastman of Rochester, New York, Edison devised a kinetoscope that cast separate still photos on a screen one after the other so rapidly that the pictures seemed to be moving. It was the first invention that Edison fully developed before putting on the market. The first public showings were on New York City's Broadway in kinetoscope parlors of slot machines that charged ten cents for a program lasting sixteen seconds. The subjects were violent and included lynchings, scalpings, and beheadings.

The transformation of these hole-in-the-corner affairs into large-screen exposures was the work, not of Edison, but of little-known inventor and realtor Thomas Armat of Washington. Edison's backers knew that the new invention would have more appeal to the public if it carried Edison's name. Accordingly, when the Amazing Vitascope was shown to the press on April 3, 1896, it was described as "Thomas A. Edison's latest marvel." Armat was initially quite content to forgo the credit and take the cash. A renegade Edison associate, William Dickson, developed a camera taking pictures eight times larger than Edison's. He filmed the *Empire State Express*; and when his show opened at Hammerstein's Theater on October 12, 1896, the sight of the great train hurtling along was so realistic that the alarmed audience stampeded for the exits.

Whereas Edison became the most prolific inventor in the history of the world, holding patents for over a thousand inventions, his equally great rival, Bell, held patents for only eighteen. He had, however, just as fertile an imagination as Edison and preferred to concentrate on what he regarded as his true profession, teaching the deaf. Alexander ("Graham") Bell was the second of three sons of Alexander Melville Bell, a noted professor of elocution in Edinburgh and London who invented a universal phonetic alphabet called visible speech. The three sons were to continue the work of the father. But, after two died of tuberculosis, the family emigrated to Canada, and settled in Brantford, Ontario, in 1870. Alexander Melville Bell had good reason to believe that visible speech would be better received in the New World than in the Old where phoneticians had resisted his progressive ideas.

Alexander Graham Bell began teaching deaf-mutes in Boston in 1871 where he met Gardiner Greene Hubbard, an affluent businessman and philanthropist. One of Hubbard's daughters, Mabel, had been deaf from scarlet fever since the age of five. She became one of Bell's pupils. He fell in love with her and they were married. Bell was very sensitive to the psychological plight of children imprisoned by their physical disability. He had an extraordinary capacity for reclaiming recalcitrant children and gained the support of Sarah Fuller, a prominent Boston teacher of the deaf. He became interested in multiple telegraphy as a means of communication and tried to make an instrument for transmitting sound vibrations. His father had seen two sons fall victim to overwork and die as

Alexander Graham Bell, the inventor of the telephone, with his wife, Mabel, and daughters, Elsie (left) and Marian ("Daisy"), in 1885. Like his great rival, Edison, Bell was one of the few genuine heroes of the Gilded Age. He seemed to combine stunning expertise in the rapidly expanding world of communications with the traditional pioneer spirit. (Gilbert H. Grosvenor Collection of Alexander Graham Bell Photographs. Library of Congress).

a result of his ambitions for them and for his own progressive methods and begged him to give up the attempt. In the early days he regarded Alec's obsession with the telephone as a needless distraction from teaching that, far from making his fortune, would, instead, damage his ability to earn a living.

Bell's considerable reputation as a teacher led Lewis Monroe, dean of the School of Oratory of the recently formed Boston University, to offer him a chair in vocal physiology and elocution there in 1873. This provided him with a permanent base from which he could pursue his research. Bell was the first person to realize that the electrical transmission of the human voice was physically possible and commercially practicable and conceived the idea of the telephone in July 1874. The caller would speak into vibrating plates or reeds, thus inducing a continuous fluctuating current that would carry the exact amplitude and frequency of his voice along a wire. At the receiver an electromagnet would transform the current into pulses or undulations of magnetic force that would then act on another array of tuned reeds to reproduce the original sound.

Gardiner Hubbard was greatly excited by the idea. He was opposed to Western Union because it was a monopoly and favored a United States Postal Telegraph Company. On March 7, 1876, Bell obtained patent number 174,465 for the telephone despite his competitors, who included Edison, Elisha Gray, and Paul La Cour of Copenhagen. On March 10, 1876, he and his assistant, Thomas Watson, had their first intelligible conversation by telephone from adjacent rooms. The new invention in an imperfect state was demonstrated to a large audience at the Massachusetts Institute of Technology on June 23 and, on June 25, 1876, at the instigation of Hubbard, to three judges at the Philadelphia Centennial Exhibition. The judges pronounced Bell's telephone "perhaps the greatest marvel hitherto achieved by the electric telegraph." The interest of Emperor Pedro II of Brazil who attended these demonstrations was decisive. His prestige ensured the sort of full publicity for the new invention that the press might not otherwise have conferred.

Bell obtained a second patent, number 186,787, for an improved model on January 30, 1877. However, a host of detractors tried to transfer the honor from Bell to one of his rivals, such as Gray or Philipp Reis. Western Union, threatened in its monopoly of communications, brought together a motley collection of rival claimants to dispute Bell's authorship and impugn his character.

Hubbard organized the Bell Telephone Company and secured the outstanding services of Theodore N. Vail as its president who had it incorporated in July 1878. Western Union established a rival in December 1878, the American Speaking Telephone Company, but not before the Bell Company had sued for an injunction in Massachusetts against Western Union's agent, Peter Dowd, for renting out telephone transmitters illegally. The case was first heard on January 25, 1879. Western Union claimed that Elisha Gray had first invented the telephone and that Amos Dolbear had perfected it. Bell produced a letter from Gray to himself of March 5, 1877, acknowledging Bell's prior claim, and this crucial piece of evidence was taken as positive proof that Bell had conceived, made practical, and patented the telephone before anyone else had. The Dowd case was resolved on November 10, 1879, when Western Union agreed to forfeit its telephone business and to assign all its telephone patents to the Bell Company in return for 20 percent of telephone rental receipts for seventeen years.

The first commercial telephone switchboard was established in New Haven, Connecticut, in 1878. By March 1880 there were 138 exchanges and some 30,000 subscribers. In 1887 there were 743 main and 444 branch exchanges and over 150,000 subscribers. In 1880 the various companies were reorganized as the American Bell Telephone Company; then, in 1885, as the American Telephone and Telegraph Company. In 1900 there was, however, on average only 1 telephone for every 66 people.

The complementary work of Edison and Bell had led to different solutions to the problems of increasing and improving communications. The electric light, telephone, telegraph, phonograph, and motion picture all had a profound effect on society. As historians Dexter Perkins and Glyndon Van Deusen explain, "Ease of communication was forging tighter bonds to unify the country and to make Americans more and more conscious of their common past, their common association, their common interest, and their common destiny." This new facility was increased by an expansion in the rail network on such a scale that it amounted to a revolution in transportation.

The railroad, which had been in existence for three decades before the Civil War, was transformed out of all recognition in the thirty years that followed. The iron-and-steel rail network extended some 35,000 miles in 1865; in 1870 it was 53,000 miles; in 1880, 93,000 miles; in 1890, 164,000 miles; in 1900, 193,000 miles. American rail mileage was greater than that in Europe, and almost the whole population lived within the sound, if not the sight, of a locomotive. The American Industrial Revolution depended on the ability to move raw materials, agricultural produce, and manufactured articles quickly from site to city. American railroads carried 10 billion tons of freight per mile of track in 1865 and 79 billion tons per mile in 1890. Moreover, the real cost of shipping freight fell steadily in the late nineteenth century, from an average of 2 cents a mile for every ton in 1865 to about .75 cents in 1900.

The story of how the great railroad lines were built is epic, encompassing the physical qualities of energy, enterprise, and endurance, all the virtues from courage to conviction, and all the vices from avarice to anger. These were heady days of achievement that seemed romantic to the generation involved. Young ladies were compared to locomotives because they also drew trains and transported males.

Congress gave as much attention to the railroads as to any economic or social problems, recognizing that the railroads were the sinews of industrial development. Between September 1850, when Congress made its first land grants to the Illinois Central and Mobile and Ohio railroads, and March 1871, when it made its last grant to the Texas and Pacific, the federal government had made more than 170 million acres available to more than 80 different railroad companies. Half of them never laid the lines, and some 35 million acres were returned. Land grants were the basis of easy credit in the initial stages of construction. Some roads sold off this land. The Union Pacific disposed of extra land in Nebraska to farmers at prices ranging from $3 to $5 an acre in the 1870s. They

Laying the track of the Pacific Railroad. The construction of the first transcontinental railroad, completed in 1869, was an epic adventure which included daring enterprise and audacious deceit. This romantic interpretation of white advance with red consent is a wood engraving from a drawing by Arthur Lumley which was first published in *Our New West* (1869). (Library of Congress).

thus advanced settlement and ensured business. In these different ways federal land grants defined the site of railways and made them financially sound.

It was the railroads that made possible both the settlement and the development of the West. The opening of the first transcontinental railroad in 1869 was as significant an event for Americans as was the contemporary completion of the Suez Canal for Europeans, and far more so than the landing of men on the moon a century later. The pioneer of a transcontinental line was Theodore Dehone Judah of the Central Pacific who was not content with dreaming about a railroad across the Sierra Nevada but actually worked out a possible route and founded a company to carry it out. He managed to capture the imagination of Leland Stanford, governor of California, who was able to provide proper political support for the project. When the Central Pacific Railroad was organized in June 1861, it was as a private enterprise. But it would have collapsed without public funds. Both Sacramento and San Francisco became stockholders. And in 1864 the California legislature displayed its confidence in Stanford, recently retired as governor, by agreeing to underwrite the interest on the company's bonds at a rate of 7 percent. Judah, the original founder of the Central Pacific, also enticed an unscrupulous businessman, Collis P. Huntington, to act as his agent in the East. It was Huntington's task to procure and dispatch necessary supplies. Associated with them was construction manager Charles Crocker. He had no practical training or skills but he was a born leader of men.

The Pacific Railroad Act, signed by Lincoln on July 1, 1862, authorized the Central Pacific to extend eastward from Sacramento, California, and the Union Pacific to extend westward from the Missouri River. The Union Pacific had been created by federal charter with a capitalization of $100 million. The federal government was to grant it 10 (later 20) alternate sections of public lands for each mile of track laid. So eager was the federal government to unite the country by rail that the act of 1862 contained essential and generous loan provisions. Central Pacific and Union Pacific were loaned $16,000 per mile for construction costs over the easiest part of the route; $48,000 per mile over the most difficult mountainous section, the Rockies and Sierras; and $32,000 per mile on other areas.

Construction of the Central Pacific began in Sacramento in January 1863, but at first progress was so slow that only 18 miles were laid in 1863 and only 12 miles in 1864. Even after the company began to employ conscientious Chinese immigrants the line moved at a snail's pace. Crocker's engineer did not dare use the new steam drill, and his men nibbled at rocks with pickaxes and dug tunnels with their bare hands. Work was sometimes interrupted by avalanches and blizzards. Consequently, the laborers spent half of their time clearing the completed line of boulders and snow.

The Union Pacific, moving from the East, faced different but equally dramatic difficulties: attacks by marauding Indians. Construction gangs lived in squalid shantytowns that became ghost towns after a section of the line was completed. When the two lines met at Promontory Point, near Ogden, Utah, on May 10, 1869, the Central Pacific had completed 689 miles of track; the Union Pacific had laid 1,086 miles. The honor of driving home the final golden spike was shared between Thomas C. Durant and Leland Stanford for the two roads. As the telegraph tapped the news across the country celebrations began in Chicago, Washington, New York, and San Francisco.

Despite the fact that physically the railroad was a daring achievement in financial terms the entrepreneurs and their private promoters had risked little. The federal government had lent its prestige, authority, and resources to the enterprise. Thus private backers, intent on a fat buck if not a fast one, were assured of high returns. They awarded the most profitable contracts to their own construction companies and supply firms. If they could not be paid in cash they took kind: railroad bonds. Their profits, like their innermost motives, remain obscure. The great enterprise had its share of shady episodes. Thomas Durant, vice president of the Union Pacific, and his friends bought up a Pennsylvania firm, Crédit Mobilier, that was licensed for a whole range of fund raising activities. The men in charge of Union Pacific voted construction contracts to dummy companies that awarded them to Crédit Mobilier. Thus, they were able to raise unnecessarily large funds for building the road and then to divert these monies into their own pockets. It was said that Crédit Mobilier showed profit of 100 percent on the original investment. The scandal following exposure in 1872 and 1873 had significant political repercussions (q.v.).

The panic of 1873 and the ensuing depression delayed but did not halt construction of other transcontinental lines. The Northern Pacific was completed in 1883, the Atchison, Topeka and Santa Fe in 1883, and the Great Northern in 1893.

Besides astonishing growth railroads benefited from a whole series of technological advances that led to a more efficient and better integrated system across the country. The most significant was the introduction of steel rails, more capable of carrying the heavier locomotives and longer trains of the Gilded Age than the old prewar iron rails. In 1872 the United States manufactured 809,000 tons of iron rails and only 84,000 tons of steel rails. In 1877 more steel rails were made than iron rails. By 1895 iron rails were no longer being made, and 88 percent of railroad tracks were made of steel.

Because there was no uniform gauge across the country in 1865, at that time freight could move neither quickly nor freely. Movement was impeded by delays caused in coupling or braking cars manually, differences in time between adjacent areas, and the hazards of inadequate train control. By 1880 older railroads in the East and Midwest adopted a uniform track gauge of 4 feet 8½ inches. On the mistaken assumption that a different gauge could deter invasion, much of the South was laid with a wider gauge of 5 feet. In the West, to minimize the dangers of mountain traffic, many roads laid very narrow tracks. But connection was the essence of commerce and communication. When the change to a regular standard came, it came quickly. Much of the South accepted the standard gauge on May 31, 1886, and by 1890 it was uniform in all regions.

Another improvement was the adoption of standard times. In the first years after the Civil War trains did not always run on time. They would stop at an isolated house to pick up only a few passengers or a package for a town. The Old Colony Railroad in

Massachusetts used to stop at Wheat Sheaf Lane every day to collect eggs from an old woman. Once she told the engineer there that she only had eleven eggs and persuaded him to wait until the hen laid the extra egg to make up the full dozen. Such practices did not increase industrial efficiency or public esteem. The Delaware, Lackawanna and Western Railroad, or D, L & W, was known as the Delay, Linger, and Wait. The Newburgh, Dutchess and Connecticut, or N, D & C, was the Never Did and Couldn't.

Railroads compounded their problems by measuring time according to the local time of their major stations. The B & O used Baltimore time on its eastern routes, Columbus time for Ohio, and Vincennes time for the West. Thus, the station at Buffalo had three clocks and the station at Pittsburgh had six, each showing a different time. Once widely separated communities were brought into the same commercial basin such differences caused endless confusion. Therefore, William F. Allen, secretary of the General Time Convention, devised a scheme of four time zones across the country: Eastern, Central, Mountain, and Pacific. Their times were based on the mean sun time on the meridians near Philadelphia (75th), Memphis (90th), Denver (105th), and Fresno (120th). In October 1883 the railroads agreed to accept it, and they put the plan into effect at noon on Sunday, November 18, 1883. The impact of this decision was truly revolutionary. As the *Indianapolis Sentinel* proclaimed in a much quoted passage:

People will have to marry by railroad time, and die by railroad time. Ministers will be required to preach by railroad time, banks will open and close by railroad time, in fact the Railroad Convention has taken charge of the time business, and the people may as well set about adjusting their affairs in accordance with its decree.

However, people were as much concerned with the dangers of rail travel as with the time it took. Accidents, sometimes involving heavy loss of life, were common. The most disastrous were at Revere, Massachusetts, in 1871 when two trains collided; at Ashtabula, Ohio, in 1876 when a fire broke out after a train crashed through a bridge; and at Chatsworth, Illinois, in 1887 when more than eighty people were killed. The causes were inept management, inadequate bridges, and insufficient fire precautions.

American inventors found the means to improve safety and lessen the risk of accident with new couplers, brakes, and signals. In 1868 Confederate veteran Eli H. Janney devised a coupler that worked like the hooked fingers of two hands. It was adopted first by the Pennsylvania Railroad, and by 1887 it was being used throughout the country. George Westinghouse invented the air brake in 1869 when he was only twenty-two. He got the idea of stopping trains with air after reading how French engineers cut tunnels into rock with compressed air. The railroad commissioner for Iowa, Lorenzo S. Coffin, persuaded the state assembly to pass laws requiring trains in the state to use the new brakes and couplers. Coffin and other state railroad commissioners called for federal legislation, and Congress finally passed a Railroad Safety Appliance Act in 1893. By 1900, 75 percent of locomotives had been fitted with air brakes and 96 percent had automatic couplers. Safety was also improved by better signaling, such as the block-signal control invented by engineer Ashbel Welch, the closed electric track signal circuit, and the electric compressed air switch.

Still not satisfied, passengers wanted comfort as well as safety. In 1867 George Pullman of Chicago founded the Pullman Palace Car Company and introduced the hotel car, a combination sleeping and dining car. In the next year the deluxe dining car, the Delmonico, went into service on the Chicago and Alton Railroad. It was an immediate success. This was the turning point in the fortunes of his company, which was commissioned to turn out sleeping, parlor, and dining cars by the thousands during the following years. Many were private cars for businessmen and industrialists who wanted to outdo one another in extravagance and luxury. In the 1880s George Pullman's sleeping and dining cars became so common that the term "Pullman" was synonimous with first-class rail service. However, there was no pleasing some people. Comedian De Wolf Hopper told a New York audience in 1900 that he had returned to Broadway revue to escape railway sleeping cars. After a picturesque account of the hazards of traveling by rail he concluded, "When I finally reached Washington and a stationary bed, I had to hire two men to shake the bed all night and pour cinders down my neck."

Railroad development provided the sinews of the American Industrial Revolution. Its expansion and contraction were largely responsible for the financial health of the economy. For example, the root cause of the depression of 1873 was railroad collapse. And the railroads collapsed because they were overextended. Railroad construction had already doubled from 35,000 to 70,000 miles since the Civil War. Two thirds of the increase had been in the West, which was sparsely populated. Thus, most railroads there had little business and were unprofitable. For instance, in 1872 no more than a third of the 350 railroad companies could pay their stockholders any dividends.

The failure of a leading investment bank, Jay Cooke and Company, precipitated a general panic. Cooke was financing the Northern Pacific Railroad, the second transcontinental line across America. In 1873 Cooke was funding its construction in the Northwest and underwriting 7–30 bonds at a price to guarantee dividends of 8.5 percent. But the railroad was already so overextended that it could yield no dividends at all. Cooke and other bankers had already allowed railroads like the Northern Pacific excessive credit. But when money became tight, they were not able to continue the process by selling more bonds. Money deposited in Cooke's New York branch was siphoned away to the West to pay for seasonal crop shipments there. On September 18, 1873, Cooke's bank failed, and its branches in New York and Philadelphia were closed.

Until then no one had doubted the probity of Cooke and Company. In Philadelphia a newsboy who cried the story was arrested for slander. But it was true. People panicked. They wanted to trade in their stocks and shares for cash. In the headlong rush the value of stocks fell dramatically. The New York Stock Exchange closed for ten days from September 20. Railroads were the worst hit. Eighty-nine defaulted on their bonds. Construction ceased. By 1874, 500,000 men were out of work. Breadlines were becoming a regular feature of city life. But that was only one part of the story. Supply industries—iron, steel, lumber, glass, upholstery—also suffered. So did industries that relied on railroads to carry their goods. By the end of 1873 there were 5,000 commercial failures. The total investment lost was $775 million.

The hopes that died with the depression revived at the end of the decade, however. New farming areas in the West had come into production by 1879, and agricultural production was twice as high as it had been in 1873. The resulting increase in railroad traffic brought renewed interest and investment in railroads until 1882. Thus, in three years—1880, 1881, and 1882—more than 28,000 miles of railroad were laid, each creating new opportunities for agriculture and industry, especially in the West and South (q.v.).

ROBBER BARONS

The way railroads were established and fortunes made from their operation has colored most interpretations of the Gilded Age according to which sharp practice became standard practice in commerce and politics. Whereas English historian Thomas Carlyle called the entrepreneurs of the Industrial Revolution "captains of industry," they were known more commonly in America as robber barons. The term was first conferred by disgruntled farmers in Kansas specifically on railroad magnates in 1880.

There were in fact two distinct types, or generations, of robber barons. Strictly speaking, the first were not industrial entrepreneurs at all but rogue financiers. Many had made fortunes in the war and were still anxious to make a killing, especially in railroads and public utilities. It did not matter to them that the cost might be economic or political stability. To this category we can assign the unholy trio of Jay Gould, Jim Fisk, and Daniel Drew. Their nefarious activities spread through whatever aspects of public life they could penetrate and defile. "His touch is death," exclaimed Daniel Drew of Jay Gould. The most notorious act of Gould and Fisk was not in railroads but gold. On Gould's advice, President Ulysses S. Grant appointed one Gen. Daniel Butterfield as head of the subtreasury. What he did not realize was that Butterfield was involved with Fisk and Gould in a scheme to make a killing on the New York gold market by hoarding gold. Because of their gold corner, the price of gold rose from 132 to a peak of 162. By September 24, 1869, "Black Friday," scores of Wall Street bankers faced ruin. The corner collapsed when Grant and Secretary of the Treasury George S. Boutwell began to sell $4 million of government gold to depress the market. In the process they unintentionally harmed hundreds of businessmen, especially importers.

The trio became railway kings en route to untold fortunes. For example, Jay Gould controlled in succession the Erie, the Union Pacific, and the Wabash. Eventually he owned Western Union, and the Manhattan Elevated and Texas Pacific railroads. His associate, Jim Fisk, was soon known as the Prince of Erie for being there "first in the pockets of his countrymen."

The most common device for making money out of corporations, whether railroad or industrial, was to overcapitalize them—to launch stocks and shares beyond the true value of the business. It was said of any company that was overcapitalized that it had "watered stock." The term originated with Daniel Drew in his early days as a cattle drover. His cattle were kept thirsty throughout the drive from Putnam County, in upstate New York, to New York City, fed with salt, and were allowed water only immediately before they arrived at the Third Avenue drovers' market where they appeared bloated and, therefore, beefy enough to buy.

The later generation of robber barons was no less ruthless than Gould, Fisk, and Drew. But they were providing the public with some sort of service. They aimed for monopoly control of a product or market, but not simply to control prices. They determined to replace fierce industrial competition with sound commercial order. From 1890 financier John Pierpont Morgan, for example, strove to secure profitable symmetry in the overextended railway system.

Between these two generations of robber barons were a few transitional figures, rapacious men capable of criminal acts for commercial gain but who nevertheless worked within the letter (if not the spirit) of the law. Such a pivotal man was Cornelius Vanderbilt, the founder of a railroad dynasty. Furthermore, it was the opulent life-style of his gregarious and extraverted family that gave the Gilded Age much of its well-deserved reputation for display in high society.

Cornelius ("Commodore") Vanderbilt was born at Stapleton, on Staten Island in 1794, the fourth of nine children of a subservient ferryman and his aggressive, acquisitive wife. At seventeen he could not persuade his father to expand the family business of ferrying and market gardening and cajoled his mother into loaning him the money to start a rival ferry service. From these small beginnings, and taking advantage of such crises as the War of 1812, the gold rush of 1849, and the Civil War, he built up a profitable steamboat operation worth perhaps $11 million by 1862. During the Civil War, however, he realized that it was on land rather than sea that the United States' destiny lay. Only the railroad could follow armies in the field and penetrate the empty interior of the West.

Vanderbilt plowed his war profits into the great railroad boom. He determined to acquire control of a crucial route for passengers and freight alike, that from New York to the Great Lakes. In 1862 he began investing in two rival railroads, the New York and Harlem and the New York and Hudson, and in 1867 he took over a third, the New York Central. He and his eldest son, William Henry, persuaded the state assembly to allow them to combine these properties into the New York Central and Hudson River Railroad. He had himself voted a bonus of $20 million in watered stock and a bonus of $6 million in cash.

The main competitor of the New York Central was the Erie, a railroad controlled by Daniel Drew, James Fisk, and Jay Gould. Vanderbilt fought a rate war against the Erie. He once cut the rate for cattle between Buffalo and New York on the New York Central to $1 a head as part of the battle. However, his rival, Jim Fisk, did not retaliate in kind. He took advantage of Vanderbilt's cheap fares by buying beef in Buffalo that he then shipped on the New York Central. He thus made a profit on the price of beef in New York City while at the same time weakening the Vanderbilt system, which had to accommodate extra freight below cost.

Between 1864 and 1872 Gould, indulging in his usual practice of watering the stock, increased the nominal value of Erie common stock from $24 million to $78 million. Vanderbilt now intended to buy the Erie and have done with the competition. He began acquiring the new stock. But as fast as he did so the unholy trio issued more with the blessing of the state assembly at Albany. Even Vanderbilt's great fortune was insufficient to buy out his rivals. He admitted defeat gracelessly, complaining that "it never pays to kick a skunk." The reputation of the Erie was ruined, however. To investors it was "the scarlet woman of Wall Street." It paid not a single dividend between 1873 and 1942.

Gould and Drew quarreled and Gould ousted Drew, who lost his fortune in the panic of 1873. In 1872 Gould himself was forced to resign. Fisk's brilliant career came to an even more abrupt end. He discovered that one man's folly was another man's wife. He was shot and killed by one of the other suitors of his mistress, Josie Mansfield.

When Cornelius Vanderbilt died in 1877 at the age of eighty-three, he was the richest man in America. The bulk of his fortune of at least $70 million went to his eldest son, William Henry, whom he thought the one competent and obedient member of his family who could keep the empire united. William lived to enjoy the family fortune for only another eight years. By ruthless manipulation of capital and labor alike he increased it, so that when he died in 1885 he was the richest man in the world. His brutal handling of strikes made him one of the most unpopular men in America, and to him was attributed the notorious declaration, "The public be damned!" In fact, he had put his trust in the financier John Pierpont Morgan, who was about to take the best railroad prizes for himself.

John Pierpont Morgan was born in Hartford, Connecticut, in 1837, the son of a small-town businessman, Junius Morgan. In 1854 Junius became a partner of an American financier living in London, George Peabody, and John Pierpont, a robust child struck down by rheumatic fever that left him with one leg shorter than the other, was then sent first to a Swiss school on Lake Geneva and later to the University of Göttingen to complete his education. He subsequently managed his father's affairs in New York. During the Civil War his reputation was tarnished by damaging allegations about his part in the Hall carbine affair whereby faulty breech-loaders were sold back to the army for six times their original price. It did not help matters that he had the first telegraph wire on Wall Street installed so that he could receive news from the battlefields immediately and speculate in gold according to the fortunes of the North.

Morgan and his partners in the new firm of Drexel, Morgan and Company, formed in 1871, were determined to bring order to the chaotic jumble of competing, superfluous, and inefficient railways. In 1878 as a first step they acquired the Long Island Railway. They also persuaded the new Vanderbilt heir, William Henry, to sell 250,000 shares of the New York Central to English investors and to combine the Central with the Wabash. Morgan's aims were threefold: to secure real support from overseas investors, usually financiers associated with his father; to eliminate price-cutting and alternative routes and thus raise profits; and to assume indirect control through ownership rather than direct control by administration.

In the East competition was internecine and began to involve other industries when steel magnate Andrew Carnegie supported the Vanderbilt lines against the Pennsylvania and its ally, George Pullman, in the 1880s. This intense struggle was resolved only by the intervention of Morgan who, after careful planning, invited the warring factions to a peace conference aboard his yacht, the *Corsair*, in New York Harbor in July 1885. They paid him a cool million for acting as honest broker and abandoned additional competitive railroad projects.

The House of Morgan had a uniform policy to all the insolvent companies it penetrated. It dried out the old stock, issued new bonds at a lower rate of interest, and insisted on consolidation or collusion with rivals. Once it had achieved a maximum of voting stock, it persuaded shareholders to surrender their duties to Morgan or his nominees on the board. This reputation for organizing himself and his staff into various interlocking directorates led to him and his junior executives being called "Pierpontifex Maximus and his Apostles" and "Jupiter Morgan and his Ganymedes." The titles were apposite. Morgan, who loved the high life and had put on the flesh of success, was much seen in the company of actresses. Twice married and with three children, he nevertheless liked to gaze at a former Harvard football star, Robert Bacon, whom he had made his most trusted assistant. The way robber barons like Morgan flaunted their wealth, wining and dining with actresses, gave rise to this anecdote of 1900 that, perhaps, also pays tribute to Morgan's florid countenance and bulbous nose: "I got a pearl out of a fresh oyster at Shankley's," remarked one chorus girl to another. "That's nothing," said her friend. "I got a whole diamond necklace out of an old lobster."

By the close of the century Morgan was in control of the South Atlantic, the Erie, the Reading, and the Northern Pacific railroads, and exercised some control of the Baltimore and Ohio, and the Atchison, Topeka and Santa Fe. However, one magnate always resisted his external magnificence and challenged the myth of his necessity. That was Edward H. Harriman. Harriman predicted that Morgan would fail to reform the Erie and the Union Pacific, worked against him behind the scenes, and was proved right. Morgan and his associate, James Hill, decided to buy Harriman's road, the Chicago, Burlington, and Quincy, and began to acquire shares in secret. When he discovered what was happening, Harriman retaliated by buying himself into a Morgan road, the Northern Pacific. Their confrontation led to a panic on the market on May 9, 1901—"Blue Thursday." Hill devised a face-saving compromise whereby the roads would be linked in a holding company, the Northern Securities Company, capitalized at $400 million, which was registered in New Jersey on November 13, 1901.

The improvement of the telegraph and the invention of the telephone had rendered time no object to industry and commerce. The expansion of the railroad had reduced the significance of distance. Morgan now held the keys to time and place and would make new fortunes from them both. Time and place were less important than money.

Having achieved sufficient lines with enough capacity for current traffic in the period to 1893 railroad construction declined thereafter. Individual roads no longer needed to compete with one another for business with the old ferocity. There was not the same urge to expand in order to anticipate the moves of a rival. Further expansion would simply cost more than any resultant savings from a more comprehensive and efficient network. However, the railroads had been the first modern companies to find the route to effective management of large scale industry. Whereas early industries had been local, based in one particular region, railroads now spanned the whole country, employing tens of thousands of men across thousands of miles of track. The only contemporary precedent for enterprise on such a scale was the Union army during the Civil War—another public bureaucracy with a hierarchical structure. Thus it was from the army that the railroads took their particular form of corporate structure. Each giant railroad, like an army, was composed of several divisions led by an area manager who was accountable to a general staff at headquarters. These local divisions, in turn, were composed of a series of lesser units each asigned specific tasks, such as engineering, maintenance, or administrative duties. Here was a peacetime army with its regiments, battalions, companies, and platoons. In the railroad companies and, later, the industrial corporations a chain of command extended from individual section leaders at the base of a pyramid to the company president and board of directors at the apex. Moreover, there could only be a proper coordination of activities between the widely separated component parts of these corporations if the company adhered to some sort of schedule and this could only be defined and maintained by a standard system of timekeeping. As we have observed, it was the railroads that first recognized standard times. In short, the new form of enterprise grew out of the new technology in industry.

The early robber barons not only learned from the Union army during the Civil War and the railroads afterwards but also from the panic of 1873. The collapse of overextended companies taught them the necessity of economy in terms of both financial expense and physical structure. As Morgan and others realized, unless the management and materials of a company were well deployed, with a minimum of waste, it was vulnerable to all sorts of external economic pressures. In addition, as we shall see in the next chapter, the most astute entrepreneurs, such as John D. Rockefeller in oil and Andrew Carnegie in steel, took full advantage of the depression as part of their strategy towards monopoly control of their industries. First they acquired their weaker competitors at bargain prices and then they began to remodel them in the interests of greater efficiency. But the monopolies were not simply a federation of autonomous companies. In theory, individual companies still operated as independent enterprises. In practice, the stronger companies ran the various tiers of production, distribution, and administration across their different subsidiaries as if they were part and parcel of the same cohesive network, agreeing on common supportive policies in buying and manufacturing, pricing and marketing.

As important in the new system as the robber barons themselves were their salaried managers. It is a matter of argument whether the robber barons were exploitive or not. But their hierarchy of managers had very different goals from the most rapacious robber barons. Their economic survival depended on the permanence, power, and growth of the hierarchy itself. Thus, for instance, they preferred policies that would ensure the continuing stability of the company rather than excessive, short-term profits. They were selected and then proved themselves on the basis of their training, experience, and performance rather than on account of some financial investment in the firm or, more crudely, nepotism. Their priority was the survival of the institution whatever the fate of individuals within it. In large scale enterprises with a maximum of technological innovation, such as refining oil or manufacturing steel, they appropriated from the natural market control of production, distribution, and sale of goods and services in the interests of their particular class. Until recently their contribution to the industrial revolution was undervalued. They went unrecognized years later just as they were unnoticed, or even invisible, in their own time. The reason is not hard to find. Unlike their most famous masters they were not ostentatious.

AN AMERICAN RENAISSANCE

Robber barons were accountable to no one. Their control was always autocratic, their life-style frequently opulent. They flaunted their wealth, painting the gilded lily. E. L. Godkin, founder of the *Nation*, described the United States in 1866 as a "gaudy stream of bespangled, belaced, and beruffled barbarians. . . . Who knows how to be rich in America? Plenty of people know how to get money; but . . . to be rich properly is, indeed, a fine art. It requires culture, imagination, and character." The extravagance of robber barons and politicians in their employ gave the Gilded Age much of its character. Not since the heyday of the Venetian Republic had successful merchant families indulged themselves in such ostentatious displays of wealth. To enrich their homes and give society notice of their new status robber barons acquired paintings, sculptures, and manuscripts of great cultural value. The sophistication they could not achieve within themselves by education they could amass for themselves by possession. The absolute distinction was ownership of a unique object.

The Vanderbilt family were the quintessential American patrons of art and architecture in the Gilded Age and beyond. Before World War I they had built seventeen large houses, each costing more than $1 million, and one—Biltmore at Asheville, North Carolina—costing $5 million. From 1879 to 1881 William Henry had architects Charles B. Atwood and the Herter Brothers build an Italianate mansion in New York on Fifth Avenue between Fifty-first and Fifty-second streets. His sons competed with him and with one another. William Kissam commissioned architect Richard Morris Hunt to build a mansion on the northwest corner of Fifth Avenue and Fifty-second Street between 1877 and 1881. It was in the style of châteaux of Francis I and built of Caen stone imported from France.

From 1878 to 1882 architect George B. Post built a château for Cornelius II in the style of Henry IV on the west side of Fifth Avenue between Fifty-seventh and Fifty-eighth streets. Post allowed his contributor artists considerable freedom within his grand design. The result, according to contemporary critic Mary Gay Humphreys, was "the most important example of decorative work yet attempted in this country." Its special features were the dining and watercolor rooms by John La Farge and Augustus Saint-Gaudens. The dining room was forty-five feet long. The walls were paneled in oak and embossed leather. The coffered ceiling had twenty panels, of which six were in opalescent glass studded with jewels. The oak beams were inlaid with mother of pearl. At the corners were mahogany panels with scenes of Apollo and cupids in repoussé bronze. At the door were carved panels of green marble representing *Hospitalitas* and *Amicitia*, decorated in iridescent ivory, metal, and mother of pearl. When the house was remodeled in 1895, the decorations were moved to a billiard room.

Such houses were designed for great receptions, of which the most notable was the housewarming of William Kissam. He and his wife threw a costume ball costing $75,000. He appeared as the duc de Guise, his wife as a Venetian princess. His brother, Cornelius II, came as Louis XVI, and his wife as an electric lamp, wearing not incandescent bulbs but iridescent diamonds. The

The Great Hall of what is now called the Thomas Jefferson Building of the Library of Congress, Washington, D.C. Originally designed by Smithmeyer and Pelz and completed in 1897, it was the costliest public library yet built and remains one of the most striking neo-classical buildings of the American Renaissance inspired by the Paris Opéra of the nineteenth century and Italian palaces of the fifteenth with towering marble columns, murals and mosaics, statues and stained glass. (L. C. Handy, Library of Congress).

highlight of the evening was a hobbyhorse quadrille for which the guests donned hunting pink and danced inside artificial horses made of real horsehair.

A spirit of noblesse oblige pervaded the families of the robber barons, who believed that it was their duty to found such major cultural institutions as museums, libraries, and opera houses. Thus, Cornelius Vanderbilt was prompted by his second wife to found Vanderbilt University in Nashville, Tennessee—an act of generosity and philanthropy that was otherwise quite out of character. The Metropolitan Opera was conceived by the Vanderbilt family and their associates and opened in 1883. Appropriately enough for a house that was to become known as the "Diamond Horseshoe," the first work was *Faust* with its famous jewel song. However, it was not sung in the original French but in Italian thus giving rise to a gross word play about the "foul song from *Just.*"

The centennial of 1876 had not only awakened Americans to the potential of the Industrial Revolution but had also rekindled their interest in previous cultures. The displays of paintings, sculptures, and photographs alerted them to the origins of their culture in other nations. For many artists, architects, and scholars there followed an American Renaissance comparable with the Italian Renaissance of the fifteenth and sixteenth centuries. It extended beyond the distinguished paintings of John Singer Sargent, Winslow Homer, and Thomas Eakins to all the visual arts. First defined in the journal *Californian* in July 1880, it was encouraged academically by new periodicals such as the *American Architect and Building News* (1876) and artistically by the formation of new societies such as the Society of American Artists (1877). It reached its height of achievement in the World's Columbian Exposition of 1893 in Chicago.

The American Renaissance was not simply for the elite of high society. It extended to the masses. Thus, the Boston Public Library, built between 1887 and 1895, was a large Renaissance palazzo in pink Milford granite designed by rising architect Charles McKim. Contributing artists included Bela Pratt, Augustus Saint-Gaudens, Daniel Chester French, Frederick MacMonnies, and John Singer Sargent. The scale and magnificence of the library put

Detail of the Great Hall of the Library of Congress with statue of Minerva
by Philip Martiny. (L. C. Handy, Library of Congress).

it on a par with great monuments of the past. The Brooklyn Institute of Arts and Sciences designed by McKim, Mead and White, which opened in 1893, was then the largest museum in the world, with 1.5 million square feet of floor space.

But although architects and artists in the Gilded Age were inspired by the glory that was Greece and the grandeur that was Rome, their patrons never let them forget the priorities of the present. It was their task to celebrate the confidence of accumulated capital. They had chosen as symbol of America's new prosperity, not silver or lead, but gold. As society hostess Elizabeth Drexel Lehr explains in "*King*" *Lehr and the Gilded Age* (1935):

It merited its name. There was gold everywhere. It adorned the houses of men who had become millionaires overnight, and who were trying to forget with all possible speed the days when they had been poor and unknown. . . . Gold was the most desirable thing to have because it cost money, and money was the outward and visible sign of success.

CHAPTER TWO

THE WORLD OF THE
ROBBER BARONS

BUSINESS MONOPOLIES were the inextinguishable flame of economic life in the Gilded Age. The expansion of industry and improvement of technology increased the possibility and need for commercial consolidation. A common myth about American industry before the Civil War is that it was a harmonious system of individual family businesses. In fact, before the Civil War competition was almost nonexistent over vast stretches of the United States. Where it did exist, it was local rather than regional or national. What in retrospect was regarded as the good old society of free competition was, in reality, a stagnant society with next to no competition at all. Limitations in transportation and communications left the local boss in politics and business in monopoly control. Postwar developments in transportation and communications broke up this complacent world once and forever. At the same time, business rivalry was intensified by scientific, industrial, and technological developments. In addition, nationwide corporations were replacing regional firms. In certain fields, such as public utilities and mining, they became common. There is plenty of statistical evidence to show this. For instance, in 1899, 66.7 percent of all manufactured goods were made by corporations.

The essence of corporation management was the exact ordering of the three stages involved in manufacturing: extraction (of materials), production, and distribution. In certain industries the economic advantages of large-scale production were considerable. This was certainly the case in the manufacture of such machines as combine harvesters and other farm implements, sewing machines, bicycles, and typewriters, and in the refining of steel, sugar, and oil. Those firms that took advantage of improvements in technology expanded rapidly at the expense of those that did not. Some advantages of size had nothing to do with efficiency but more with costs. A large company could more easily obtain credit, more readily get raw materials at a cheaper rate, and deploy its resources on research.

The story of industry in America in the Gilded Age is not, however, one of continuous growth. Demand for most products was subject to random changes in booms and slumps. For twenty-five years beginning in 1873 excess capacity was chronic in most industries, especially oil and steel. Industrialists thus did not seek combination simply for the sake of expansion. They wanted to protect themselves against oscillations in the business cycle. As economist John Tipple explains, giant corporations had greater control and a larger share of the market. They could, therefore, dictate prices and terms to everyone. Vertical integration that reached up or down to other stages of production led to the creation of a firm that could compete more effectively because it increased efficiency by reducing costs. Horizontal integration— the creation of a firm with several plants each at exactly the same stage of the industrial process—was less likely to be efficient. It was, however, possible to dictate prices to plants at different stages if the horizontal control was a true monopoly.

The first businessman's remedy for commercial problems was the pool, a gentlemen's agreement between rivals to divide trade and share profits. More formal association was sought through rings in the 1870s and then through trusts in the 1880s. The prototype was the oil trust of Standard Oil formed in 1882. Trusts under other names were formed in cottonseed oil (1884), linseed oil (1885), lead mining and refining (1887), whiskey distilling (1887), sugar refining (1887), and cord manufacture (1887). The most successful were in refining and distilling.

Such corporations had considerable economic consequences.

Cornelius ("Commodore") Vanderbilt, pioneer in transportation on sea and land, and founder of a powerful railroad dynasty. (Library of Congress).

They divorced the owners, who were the stockholders, from the chores of management. Stockholders were rarely interested in running the business. All they cared about were their dividends. Indeed, one reason for the formation of trusts was to inflate the value of companies so that greater dividends could be claimed. Exaggerated prices were put on stocks and shares when corporations were capitalized, that is, when the money was raised to launch them.

The interaction of various economic forces and the prevalent religious faith in progress had, as we noted in chapter one, produced a new type of entrepreneur peculiar to the United States and particularly suited to developing its resources. This entrepreneur was ready to put his faith in the collective security of a corporation. These robber barons were the new rich, an opulent and ostentatious plutocracy. In 1892 two New York newspapers, the *World* and the *Tribune*, competed with one another to see which could find the most American millionaires. The *World* discovered 3,045, but the *Tribune* outdid it with 4,047. John D. Rockefeller in oil, Andrew Carnegie in steel, Gustavus Swift in meat, Charles Pillsbury in grain, Henry Havemeyer in sugar, Frederick Weyerhauser in lumber, and John Pierpont Morgan in railroads and finance were altogether more influential figures than the principal actors on the political stage. Unlike the politicians who specialized in words without deeds, the robber barons said little but did much. The secret of their success lay in their acumen that amounted to vision, their avarice that was transformed into commercial foresight, and their attack that was equal to military strategy.

It is a myth that the captains of industry and commerce rose from rags to riches. In fact, most of them came from business and industry or one of the professions. Indeed, 65 percent of those from the upper classes had been to college. Yet—and this partly explains the supposed rise from obscurity to opulence—most of them worked their way up in the business in which they made their fortune. They claimed they were self-taught. Perhaps, in everything that really mattered, they were. Many came from New England or the North Atlantic states. The bulk were native-born, Protestant, and Republican. By birth Collis Huntington and John

Pierpont Morgan and by descent the Jays Cooke and Gould were Connecticut Yankees. Andrew Carnegie and James J. Hill were Scots.

The public persona of the self-made man was based on a cult of outward modesty and respectability. As a rule, robber barons were puritanical, parsimonious, and pious. Only Jim Fisk, the son of a Vermont tin peddler, spent his youth sowing his wild oats among the fleshpots. Thus, the majority were continuing an established tradition. Historian Matthew Josephson emphasizes that the original colonists were English Protestants devoted to business as if it were a religion. Money was the sole means of attaining power. Benjamin Franklin was held up as a paragon of virtue and thrift. After all, it was he who coined the succinct aphorism, "Time is money." When Rockefeller claimed, "God gave me my wealth," he was speaking in the spirit of Cotton Mather.

Businessmen, however, usually preferred the myth that they had made their money by the sweat of their brow. Railroad baron Cornelius Vanderbilt even claimed that he made a million dollars every year of his life but that it was worth "three times that to the people of the United States." Steel tycoon Andrew Carnegie agreed. In *The Empire of Business* (1902) he said, "Under our present conditions the millionaire who toils on is the cheapest article which the community secures at the price it pays for him, namely, his shelter, clothing, and food." It is certainly true that, consumed with ambition, many worked to excess, damaging their health in the process. Most suffered from chronic stomach complaints. Morgan's face was often a rash of spots and Rockefeller was a victim of premature hair loss. Public opinion preferred to believe that special privilege rather than personal virtue had enabled robber barons to transform abundant natural resources into a profitable preserve. Behind every great fortune was crime. John Reagan, congressman from Texas, advised his constituents in 1876: "There were no beggars till Vanderbilts and Stewarts and Goulds and Scotts and Huntingtons and Fisks shaped the action of Congress and molded the purposes of government. Then the few became fabulously rich, the many wretchedly poor . . . and the poorer we are the poorer they would make us." While it was true that individuals might rise or fall by special merits or particular defects, it was equally true that whole classes could not change places.

However, a new philosophy, Social Darwinism, justified the robber barons and their methods. The leading proponent of Social Darwinism was an English journalist, Herbert Spencer. As early as 1850, nine years before Charles Darwin published his revolutionary theory of evolution, Spencer's *Social Statics* propounded an extreme form of laissez-faire economics akin to monetarism. The appearance of Darwin's *The Origin of Species* in 1859 strengthened Spencer's case. It was Spencer who in two articles of 1852 first coined the phrase "survival of the fittest," which Darwin later used to describe the mechanism that propelled evolution. Spencer's *Social Statics* mixed laissez-faire economics and biology. Its premise was that the pressure of subsistence on the human race had had a beneficent effect. It had led to social progress by putting a premium on intelligence, self-control, and skill. Spencer opposed state aid to the poor, whom he regarded as unfit and candidates for elimination. By the same token, he disapproved of tariffs to aid agriculture or industry, state banking, and governmental postal services.

It is hardly surprising that the robber barons found Social Darwinism congenial. They were being told what they wanted to hear—how a political system that claimed all men were equal could also encompass economic inequality. Moreover, the new philosophy denied any need for social reform. Between 1864, when his *Social Statics* was published in New York, and 1903, 368,755 volumes of Spencer's works were sold in the United States—probably a record for books on sociology and philosophy. It was ironic that a hypochondriac like Spencer should tell society who was and who was not fit. His lasting success was proof of the old adage that a puny, sickly reputation will outlive more robust characters. In the fall of 1882 at the peak of his popularity Spencer toured the United States. The effusive tributes paid him at banquets everywhere showed that the origins of species had been turned into the origins of speeches.

Spencer's most ardent supporter was William Graham Sumner, who held the chair of political and social science at Yale for over

thirty years from 1872. Sumner insisted on the beneficence of social struggle: "If we do not like the survival of the fittest we have
only one possible alternative, and that is the survival of the un-
fittest. The former is the law of civilization, the latter is the law
of anti-civilization." Such ideas were supported at a popular level
by the children's books of Horatio Alger, Unitarian chaplain to
the Newsboys' Lodging House in Manhattan. Alger extolled the
virtues of self-improvement and propounded the myth of rags to
riches in a variety of tales such as *Ragged Dick* (1867), *Luck and
Pluck* (1869), and *Tattered Tom* (1871). Each was the first in a
series which sold over 20 million copies.

The world of the robber barons was a vast human caricature of
the Darwinian struggle in which the two pivotal entrepreneurs
were John Davison Rockefeller and Andrew Carnegie. Each faced
similar problems in his search for monopoly control. Their solutions were different but complementary. Carnegie had political,
cultural, and philosophical breadth. Rockefeller was narrow. And
this difference defined their careers and, after their retirement, their
philanthropy. By tracing their careers we can learn something of
the industries they led, the techniques of management they established, and their significance in the Gilded Age.

ROCKEFELLER AND OIL

It was generally thought that John Rockefeller's product went well
with his personality. The mixture was oil and vinegar. He gave
his ear freely to most; his voice rarely and to few. Rockefeller's
habitual secretiveness is usually ascribed to the shame inflicted on
his family by his father, William. Once indicted for rape but never
brought to trial, William Rockefeller lived in bigamy from 1855
until his death in 1906 with a woman twenty-five years younger
than himself. He had taken an assumed name, Dr. William Lev-
ingston. John Rockefeller had continued to support him in secret.

In 1858 George H. Bissell, Edwin L. Drake, and others began
to drill oil from deep inside the ground in Titusville, Pennsylvania.
There followed a spectacular oil rush and a fever of speculation
for the liquid that could lubricate machines and light homes,
streets, and factories. To the *Boston Commonwealth Bulletin* of Jan-

uary 21, 1865, it must have been petroleum that lit Aladdin's lamp. If that were so, it was Rockefeller who became the genie of both lamp and ring. Rockefeller achieved almost complete control of oil refining in four stages: initial establishment of his own companies between 1862 and 1870; manipulation of transportation for his own advantage; ruthless elimination of competition; and an interlocking trust to unify his empire. Expressed geographically, he attained national control by securing first Ohio, then Pennsylvania, and finally New York.

In 1862 Rockefeller, then a bookkeeper living in Cleveland, Ohio, made an initial investment of $4,000 in a new oil and kerosene refinery of two English immigrants, Samuel Andrews and Maurice Clark. In retrospect, Rockefeller's decision looks like common sense. At the time it was foolhardy. As a business, oil refining was as risky as gambling, and almost as disreputable. Bankers were so conservative that they treated the new industry with caution, not to say prejudice. They were wary of making credit easily available. It was their reluctance to do so that convinced Rockefeller to cast his net deep rather than wide. His goal was control of a particular industry, and he first explored the idea of vertical integration, the control of everything he needed—barrels, warehouses, tankers, pipelines—from start to finish.

Mrs. Mary Ann Rudd, Rockefeller's younger sister, recalled later how when everyone else was talking of the Civil War, Rockefeller and his associates, Andrews and the Clark family, "were talking oil all the time. . . . They didn't seem to care for anything else." The secret of his company's early success was its refusal to deal with intermediaries. It was independent of jobbers, coopers, and drayers, so that none of the profits were diverted to others. To help as much as he could Rockefeller pitched in with his partners and did all the dirty jobs. Waste was eliminated. By drying the barrels in kilns before transportation they cut down the costs of transportation. Samuel Andrews ensured that nothing was lost in the refining process. Even the sulfuric acid was recovered and used again. Benzene, gasoline, paraffin, petrolatum (Vaseline), and other lubricating oils became by-products. The initial period of financial hardship not only taught Rockefeller the benefits of stringent economies but also the necessity of streamlined management in the interests of maximum efficiency.

Rockefeller and various associates reorganized the company as the Standard Oil Company of Ohio on January 10, 1870, at a capitalization of $1 million made up of 10,000 shares of $100 each. The name, which came from one of their refineries, the Standard Works, was meant to suggest the sale of standard oil, oil of good quality. There were 250 refineries in the United States, and Standard Oil then had about 3 or 4 percent of the refining business. Because Rockefeller was not able to realize his preferred goal, vertical integration at this time, he concentrated on horizontal integration and acquired a monopoly of a crucial stage of the oil industry—refining.

Rockefeller's main strategy to this end was to acquire control of transportation. Cleveland was farther from the oil lands than other cities with oil refineries, such as Pittsburgh, and also farther from the national center of commerce, New York. If Rockefeller and his associates were to compete effectively with oil companies in Pennsylvania, they had to ensure that railroad rates for shipping oil undercut those charged to their rivals. They did, however, have an advantage over companies in Pittsburgh. Pittsburgh was served by only one railroad, the Pennsylvania. Cleveland was served by two, the Atlantic and Great Western (part of the Erie Railroad) and the Lake Shore Railroad (part of the New York Central). They could play off one against the other.

The word "rebate" is derived from the French *rebattre*, which means "to beat again." In business it came to mean a refund. Rockefeller found a system of rebates and discriminations in existence and became its master. He bought the loyalty of railroad bosses by outright, if secret, bribes. Railroad entrepreneurs such as William H. Vanderbilt became stockholders of Standard Oil and received dividends. Accordingly, they acquired an interest in the company that they resolved to protect. Rockefeller was not breaking the law by gaining concessionary fares, since no laws existed on the subject. The published rate was a basis for barter. Long haul was usually cheaper than short haul. Long-distance, "through" rates were governed by competition and often set below the rate at which they would pay. Local lines had a monopoly. They could charge customers what they liked to make up the difference.

In his *Reminiscences* (1909) Rockefeller explains away the Standard's reliance on railroad rebates. In his version, instead of the railroads doing him a favor, it is the other way around. It was the Standard that was providing the railroads with special services:

It offered freights in large quantity, carloads and train loads. It furnished loading facilities and discharging facilities at great cost. It provided regular traffic so that a railroad could conduct its transportation to the best advantage and use its equipment to the full extent of its hauling capacity without waiting for the refiner's convenience. It exempted railroads from liability for fire and carried its own insurance. It provided, at its own expense, terminal facilities which permitted economies in handling. For these services it obtained special allowances on freight.

Standard Oil received favorable rates from the Erie Railroad as a contract of June 5, 1868, shows. Rockefeller and his associates also acquired a quarter interest in the Allegheny Transportation Company, the pipeline owned by the Erie Railroad. According to the contract, the ATC would receive from the Erie $5 for every carload of oil of another company moving west from Cleveland and $12 for every car shipped east. This payment or fine was called a drawback. In yet another contract of March 19, 1870, Standard Oil was to receive a rebate of 5 cents per barrel on its own oil bound for Cleveland provided it used an Erie road, the Atlantic and Great Western, exclusively. Moreover, through its part ownership of ATC, Standard Oil shared in rebates on oil shipped by other refineries.

The system worked so advantageously for the Erie Railroad that it was soon accepted by other railroads, including the Lake Shore, whose managers believed that a steady flow of through trains carrying one commodity, refined oil, would save them time and money. Rockefeller's concern was to keep the price down for Standard Oil but up for its rivals. Thus, he could first undersell them, then eliminate them, and finally establish Standard Oil as an overshadowing monopoly. Once the railroads began to do business with Rockefeller on his terms, however, they were in his power.

John D. Rockefeller achieved a nationwide monopoly in oil refining by rigid economies, cutthroat competition, and manipulation of transportation to his own ends. He unified his various companies in the first trust and became the most widely hated entrepreneur of the Gilded Age. (Library of Congress).

Simon Sterne, counsel to the Hepburn committee of 1879, derided railroad executives who ingratiated themselves with Rockefeller as "foolish, shortsighted people not to have foreseen that such a monopoly when created would eventually dictate terms to the railways and become a modern Frankenstein, a monster that would plague its inventors."

Public disquiet about Rockefeller's methods burst open when Thomas A. Scott, manager of the Pennsylvania Railroad, engaged in a general scheme to favor Rockefeller's companies and discriminate against others. This was the "South Improvement Plan" of 1872. The secret creation of a common cartel of big oil companies and great railroads produced a public uproar when the press published the news on February 26, 1872. No small refinery was in the scheme. None could compete with the new rates. Thousands of people in small firms would be ruined. For the first time Rockefeller was reviled in the press. He was now the "Mephistopheles of Cleveland." The universal opprobrium showered on his company and all who dared to do business with it forced him to give up the scheme on April 8. He had lost a battle. What he learned from his experience enabled him to win the war.

In the meantime Rockefeller, now thirty-two, had taken over 21 of Cleveland's 26 refineries. Standard Oil was reorganized on January 1, 1872, its stock increased to 25,000 shares and its capitalization to $2.5 million. He had all the trump cards—refineries, railroads, and banks. One by one his remaining competitors were forced to sell out. Isaac Hewitt, the commission merchant who had first engaged Rockefeller as a bookkeeper, had to accept 50 cents on the dollar of the book value of his firm, Alexander Scofield and Company. For a refinery on which they had spent $120,000 they were paid only $65,000. The sequence of events in this crucial year left Standard Oil ready and poised to seize the American oil refining industry. By 1879 it was producing only a fiftieth of the nation's oil, but it was refining nine tenths of the whole and dictating the price of it all.

Technological improvements that the larger refineries could afford and that the smaller refineries could not contributed to strengthening the former at the expense of the latter. To make matters worse for small refiners, the price of oil fell along with everything else in the panic of 1873. It was only 13 cents a barrel in December 1873, and by November 1874, was as low as 11 cents. The smaller companies fell to Rockefeller because they could not compete in his markets. His railroad rebates allowed him to undersell. Sometimes they could not even hire tank cars for shipping oil because the railroads were letting Standard Oil use their entire fleet. Other refiners could not buy barrels to distribute their oil. J. N. Camden, a Rockefeller agent, persuaded the timber merchant of Cincinnati who supplied Pittsburgh coopers with staves for barrels to sell his entire surplus stock to Standard Oil. The cooperage business fell apart in Pittsburgh, and independent refiners could only buy barrels from elsewhere at ruinous prices. They had no option except to sell out.

Most notorious of all was Rockefeller's war with the Pennsylvania Railroad in 1877. At that time the "Pennsy" was the world's biggest carrier of freight. But it was allied to a rival pipeline and refinery, the Empire Transportation Company. Rockefeller determined to crush both by withdrawing Standard Oil business from his old ally, the Pennsy, just as it was suffering incalculable damage in the Great Railroad Strike of 1877 (q.v.). The Pennsy's share of eastbound oil freight fell from 52 percent to 30 percent. The fight was too expensive for Tom Scott. On September 17, 1877, at the St. George Hotel, Philadelphia, he agreed to sell the Pennsy's assets to Standard. The Empire Transportation Company was acquired by Standard for $3.4 million.

THE STANDARD OIL TRUST

Having reduced competition, Rockefeller now sought ways of conferring form and unity on his vast empire. A corporation in Ohio could not hold stock in another company except by particular legislation sometimes passed for the benefit of railroads. Thus, when Rockefeller acquired another company, he did so secretly and by subterfuge. He had the stock of the newly acquired company turned over to an officer of Standard Oil acting as trustee for the stockholders of Standard Oil. But this method left open the possibility that a trustee would act independently, and it would be a danger to the whole system if an important trustee died. The change in the technology of transportation from railroads to pipe-lines finally forced Rockefeller to find a solution to these problems. In the late 1870s the laying of independent pipelines threatened to bring down the whole pack of cards of railroad control. The so-lution to the problem was the Standard Oil Trust.

Authorship of the trust is usually credited to Rockefeller lawyer Samuel C. T. Dodd. In April 1879, at Dodd's suggestion, the individual trustees of companies that had been taken over, the thirty-seven stockholders, and the Standard Oil Company of Ohio entrusted the stock of the subsidiaries to dummy trustees who were to manage the stock on their behalf. The fiction was that the subsidiaries were no longer the property of Standard Oil but of the trustees. Their function was, of course, to serve Rockefeller. The fact was a monopoly by which 95 percent of American re-fineries were part of Standard Oil. But the arrangement was full of discord. The State of Pennsylvania threatened to tax the entire capital of any corporation doing business within its boundaries. Dodd therefore recommended an expansion of the existing trust, and, on January 2, 1882, it took its definitive form.

The three trustees, the stockholders (who numbered forty-two), and Standard Oil of Ohio now entrusted all the stock to nine trustees including John Rockefeller, his brother William, Henry B. Payne, Henry Flagler, and John D. Archbold. The new com-bination had neither name nor charter. It was, in common law, a trust. In place of their shares stockholders received twenty trust certificates representing portions of the total holdings. The trust was capitalized at the comparatively modest sum of $73 million. Its annual earnings were at least $10 million. Rockefeller had al-most a quarter of the shares. Thus, his total wealth was $18 mil-lion. In addition, he was paid a salary for managing the trust.

The trust included fourteen companies that it owned com-pletely. First and foremost was Standard Oil of Ohio at $3.5 mil-lion. Twenty-six companies were partially owned by the trust, of which the largest was National Transit in which the trust owned 85.4 percent of the shares. National Transit was capitalized at $30 million. In the course of the 1880s transportation beat refining into second place as the main source of income for the trust. In 1885 it provided 53 percent of earnings, whereas refining yielded 36 percent.

From 1884 the Standard's central office was at 26 Broadway, New York. There Rockefeller organized the trust through a series of committees, and the executive committee, which he chaired himself, met every day. It conferred unity on a system always in danger of dissolving into its component parts. Here the genius of Rockefeller for tiered management had maximum effect. The lesser committees dealt with specific areas such as transportation and export, manufacturing and lubricating, and led to a synthesis of ideas. The individual companies were run as autonomous units except in one crucial particular. They did not compete in selling.

Within three years the trustees had reduced the Standard's number of refineries from fifty-three to twenty-two. They proceeded to consolidate the buying of crude oil and from that to control of the domestic and foreign market. At the turn of the century the Rockefeller companies produced an astonishing variety of oil products: 174 refined distillates, 29 grades of naphthas, 833 kinds of lubricating oils, 21 sorts of asphalt, and 8 types of macadam binder. By 1890 the annual yield of the Standard Oil Trust was $19.131 million with dividends of $11.2 million.

It was as the Standard was about to give definitive form to its trust that it came under truly effective scrutiny for the first time. Social critic Henry Demarest Lloyd exposed Standard practice in "The Story of a Great Monopoly" for *Atlantic Monthly* in March 1881. Lloyd's most damaging indictment was that "The Standard has done everything with the Pennsylvania legislature except refine it." Rockefeller had created a whole set of values. Henry Demarest Lloyd recognized his insidious and pervasive influence in the general movement of business and industry towards monopoly control. In a second article for *Atlantic* of July 1882, "The Political Economy of Seventy-three Million Dollars," he declared: "Rings and bosses are rising to the top in the evolution of industry as in that of politics . . . A few individuals are becoming rich enough to control all the great markets, including the legislatures." Thus, big business brought supreme weight to bear down on the economy and invalidated its traditional tenets. The economy supposedly worked in such a way as to give freely competing individuals an even chance of success but was actually run for the benefit of the big business at the expense of the small. When the Cullom committee of the Senate reported on the oil trust as a ruthless monopoly in 1886, it did not mince its words:

It is well understood in commercial circles that the Standard Oil Company brooks no competition; that its settled policy and firm determination is to crush out all who may be rash enough to enter the field against it; that it hesitates at nothing in the accomplishment of this purpose, in which it has been remarkably successful, and that it fitly represents the acme and perfection of corporate greed in its fullest development.

As time went on, Rockefeller's stratagems to win monopoly control became more devious. He lost any scruples he had once had about criminal activities. They were now standard business practice. Under Lewis Emery, Jr., an association of independent companies was formed as the Producers' Oil Company at Warren, Pennsylvania, in January 1891. The new association succeeded in laying its own pipeline for refined oil to Hancock, New York. In January 1895 Emery extended the pipeline farther, from Wilkes-Barre to Bayonne. When it came to crossing the tracks of the Delaware, Lackawanna and Western Railroad at Washington, New Jersey, a battle royal ensued between 50 of Emery's men and 250 men of the railroad, and of Standard Oil who were determined to prevent it. A truce was called, and both sides agreed to settle the matter in court. But the Standard men broke the truce and resumed the offensive. Emery described what happened next to the Industrial Commission of 1899. When he came to the torture inflicted on his men, he broke down.

I found the traitors who had promised me that they would put this thing into court there with two locomotives standing on top of the track and they were running hot water and hot steam down into this pit on my men. And they went to the fire box and threw hot coals down on them. I ordered every man out of the pit. We barricaded ourselves and the G.A.R. gave us 48 muskets and I sent to New York and got 18 Springfield rifles . . . and we stayed there for seven months holding possession until the courts decided we had a right to stay there.

By various ruses Standard delayed completion of the pipeline until 1901.

Before the turn of the century public opinion was aroused by such stories. It turned on the monopolies or "trusts" in general and on Rockefeller in particular. He was vilified as the obvious symbol of the most hated trust. What incensed the public was the monopolies' ability to secure discriminatory rates among the railroads. Big business eliminated competition and subverted politics. The bone of contention was not mass production; it was social and political manipulation. Kansas was the first state to pass an antitrust law, in 1889. Within two years fifteen others, led by North Carolina, Tennessee, and Michigan, had followed suit. The tide had turned against Standard Oil.

In 1889 David K. Watson, attorney general of Ohio running for reelection, discovered that Standard Oil had violated the state corporation laws, not because it had formed a trust, but because it had placed the direction of the company in the hands of non-resident trustees. In May 1890 he advised the Ohio State Supreme Court that the company had acted *ultra vires* and should be dissolved. On March 2, 1892, the Ohio State Supreme Court ruled that the Standard Oil Company must withdraw from the trust. The trust requested and received a period of grace to wind up its affairs. Standard Oil was at the height of its capacity. It rewarded its stockholders with dividends of 12 percent up till 1894. In 1895 it paid them 17 percent. Thereafter it paid between 30 and 43 percent for the next ten years. Yet its actual profits were still greater. They amounted to between 15 and 20 percent on investment to 1894. In the following ten years they were more than 50 percent three times, more than 60 percent twice, and more than 80 percent twice.

Henry Demarest Lloyd's full-length attack, *Wealth Against Commonwealth*, which was first published in 1894, showed its author's mastery of facts, opinions, and rhetoric. Although Standard and Rockefeller were not mentioned by name but given the allusive titles "combination" and "head of the combination," fear of libel deterred four publishers from producing the book before Harpers and Brothers did so. A seminal work with all its salient facts carefully documented, *Wealth Against Commonwealth* showed that the essence of monopoly was control of transportation. Lloyd's selective synopsis of Rockefeller's career exposed chicanery at every opportunity and was expressed in a plangent style. Lloyd distinguished a paradox. Americans opposed anarchy in politics, yet they accepted it in business. The book's impact on intellectuals was profound. Edward Everett Hale compared it to *Uncle Tom's Cabin*. Novelist William Dean Howells said the "monstrous iniquity" of Standard Oil was "so astounding, so infuriating that I have to stop from chapter to chapter to take breath." Social Gospel minister Washington Gladden was only astonished "that it does not cause an insurrection."

At the instigation of David K. Watson, the new attorney general of Ohio, Frank Monnett, advised the state courts there in November 1897 that the Standard had not obeyed the ruling on dissolution of 1892. Hearings were held in October 1898 and March 1899 in various places at which Monnett intended to show that the trust still existed. But crucial evidence was missing. Books, journals, and documents were all burned in November 1898. The Ohio Supreme Court could not decide on the charge of contempt, and it was therefore abandoned. The antitrust suits against companies in Ohio were eventually dismissed.

Rockefeller and his associates had learned their lesson, however. The trust would no longer do, so they found an alternative. In 1889 New Jersey had passed a law authorizing holding companies. In 1896 it went further in an amendment by which "Any corporation may purchase . . . the shares or any bonds . . . of any corporation or corporations of this or any other state." Moreover, only one member of the board of directors had to reside in New Jersey. There was no limit on the capital stock. Annual reports were not required. This law led to the establishment of Standard Oil of New Jersey as a holding corporation in 1899. Capitalization was increased from $10 million to $110 million. Trust certificates were exchanged for shares. Once again Standard Oil had set a precedent but, as we shall see, Rockefeller was not the only robber baron to take advantage of the new law.

CARNEGIE AND STEEL

The steel tycoon Andrew Carnegie was driving along the same road to the same destination as Rockefeller—monopoly control. Yet he consistently opposed the formation of pools and trusts, which he likened to the ephemeral procession of Banquo's ghosts

Andrew Carnegie's route to monopoly in steel making was vertical integration, the control of all processes from extraction of ore to the manufacture of finished products. His public persona of generous benefactor was sustained by his numerous charities but did not conceal a ruthless determination to thwart his rivals by fair means or foul. (Library of Congress).

in *Macbeth*. His preferred solution to the problems of consolidation was vertical integration. Because he achieved it, he did not have the same sort of problems of organizing disparate companies that Rockefeller experienced.

Andrew Carnegie was born in Scotland in 1835. His family emigrated from Dunfermline, Fife, in 1848 when his father, a master weaver, lost his job. He rose from telegraph operator to become, at eighteen, personal assistant to Thomas A. Scott at the time Scott was general superintendent of the Pennsy. He took full advantage of Scott's advice and inside knowledge when it came to investing his money. In a letter to his cousin George ("Dod") Lauder of June 21, 1863, he expressed his boundless ambition to acquire and enjoy great wealth in the style of a British gentleman. At that time his income was $49,300, although his actual salary was only $2,400. In 1864 at the relatively advanced age of twenty-nine Carnegie became a stockholder in the Iron Forge Company and later its owner. Thereafter his career was indissoluble from the development of the iron-and-steel industry, which had reached a crucial stage in the United States.

During the 1840s enormous deposits of iron ore were discovered in Michigan in the northern peninsula, the land between Lakes Superior and Michigan. The Marquette range contained a mountain of solid iron ore, 150 feet high, from which shipments were first made in 1855. Other ranges soon yielded their natural treasuries: the Menominee (1877), the Gogebic (1884), the Vermilion (1884), and the Missabe (1892). This iron range, later known as the Mesabi, turned out to be the world's greatest field of iron ore. By 1900 it was yielding a third of all the ore mined in the United States, a sixth of the world's supply, and half of all the raw materials required to make steel. In the 1880s the iron-and-coal-fields of the Appalachians were also developed. Both Pittsburgh to the east and Birmingham to the south became centers of the iron, coal, and steel industries.

Natural iron is impure, containing molecules of carbon, manganese, oxygen, phosphorous, silicon, and sulfur. The removal of these other elements produced successively cast iron, wrought iron, and steel. Until steel was perfected, wrought iron was used for rails and bridge parts, but for a long time it was produced more easily in Britain than the United States. Successive methods of manufacturing better steel were devised in England by Henry Bessemer, Wilhelm and Friedrich Siemens, and Pierre Martin, and were developed in the United States. The extent of the Industrial Revolution in the American iron-and-steel industry is illustrated by the following comparative figures. In 1860, 2.8 million long tons of iron ore were extracted; in 1900, 27.3 million long tons. In 1860, 821,000 short tons of pig iron were produced; in 1900, 13.7 million short tons.

Carnegie achieved almost total control of the steel industry in three stages: the establishment of his own companies by 1872; his diversification into all related industries in the 1870s and 1880s; and his war with John Pierpont Morgan at the close of the century. Like Rockefeller, he was ready to consolidate by almost continuous reorganization and did so again and again—in 1872, 1874, 1881, 1886, 1892, and 1900. His route to wealth was speculation for accumulation. He used his investments to finance iron companies supplying either railroads or war contracts. In the brief period of railroad expansion between 1865 and the collapse of 1873 Carnegie concentrated on iron railroad bridges. They could carry the new, heavier trains for which the old wooden bridges were inadequate. In December 1868 the states of Iowa and Illinois awarded him a contract for the Keokuk and Hamilton Bridge across the Mississippi. For Illinois and Missouri his Keystone Bridge Company built the famous Illinois and St. Louis Bridge.

Fritz Redlich describes Carnegie as "the new type of entrepreneur, the captain of business in contrast to the older captain of industry." He knew the whole market past, present, and future. He was always alert to the possibilities of change. His lack of formal schooling beyond childhood spurred him on to self-improvement. By cultivating his artistic taste he sharpened his wits until he could live by them. In 1890 he argued in an article, "How to Make a Fortune," that he preferred the "scientifically educated youth" to the "trained mechanic of the past" because he "has no prejudices, and goes on for the latest invention or newest method, no matter if another has discovered it."

For an initial investment of $250,000 Carnegie was able to launch his own steel company in 1872, Carnegie, McCandless and

Company. It built a steel plant at Braddock, Pennsylvania, at the junction of the Pennsylvania Railroad, the Baltimore and Ohio Railroad, and the Ohio River. In 1874 Carnegie changed the company's name to the Edgar Thomson Company Ltd., and had it capitalized at $700,000, of which his shares were worth $250,000. His associates included William Coleman, Tom Carnegie (his brother), Henry Phipps (a boyhood friend), and Andrew Kloman. Carnegie always emphasized that his company was a ministry of all the talents. He maintained that the personnel of its organization were worth more than all the property of the company. Carnegie could deploy clever men. Captain ("Bill") Jones, Alexander Lyman Holley, Charles Schwab, and others all had particular talents greater than his. He liked to think his epitaph would be, "Here lies the man who was able to surround himself with men far cleverer than himself." He thought the possibility of promotion from the ranks ensured the loyalty of his employees.

During the depression of the mid-1870s Carnegie disposed of all his other assets in order to extend the Braddock plant. He was backing his conviction in the country's recovery and the future of railroads and steel rails. When the Edgar Thomson Works at Braddock went into production in September 1875, Carnegie cut his market price for steel rails by $5 a ton. This tactic ensured his company's survival in the depression. In April 1881 Carnegie combined Edgar Thomson with other companies, the Union Iron Mills, and the Lucy Furnaces. The new consolidation, Carnegie Brothers and Company Ltd. was capitalized at $5 million, of which Carnegie owned shares worth $2.7 million. In 1883 he acquired both the Homestead Mills, and the majority shares of the H. C. Frick Coke Company. Homestead and Frick were to cast long shadows over the rest of Carnegie's career.

Henry Clay Frick was, like Carnegie, a self-made man. In 1870, when he was twenty-one, he was working as a bookkeeper in his grandfather's distillery in western Pennsylvania. While Carnegie recognized the significance of steel, Frick realized the importance of bituminous coal for use as coke in making steel. He borrowed $10,000 and built fifty coke ovens. Within two years he had established his own company, Frick and Company. By the end of the depression he had extended his activities and owned 1,000 coke

Henry Clay Frick, the coke baron who became first Carnegie's ally in the quest for vertical integration, then his evil genius in the Homestead strike of 1892, and finally his adversary in the war of attrition between Carnegie and Morgan at the turn of the century. (Library of Congress).

ovens and more than four fifths of coal mines around Connellsville near Pittsburgh. On January 1, 1882, the H. C. Frick Coke Company was formally established. This was the company that Carnegie first infiltrated and then came to control. The injection of Carnegie's funds into the coke company funded its expansion. By 1887 the Frick Company owned 5,000 acres of mines and was producing 6,000 tons of coke a day. In 1887 Frick was made a partner in the Carnegie firm and awarded $100,000 worth of stock to be paid for out of earnings. Capitalization was now $20 million. In two years Frick rose to chairman and, as second partner, was allowed 11 percent of the shares. It was Frick who saw the need and found the means for vertical integration. He had, after all, linked coal mines and coke ovens. He now wanted the Carnegie Company to control its own iron ore mines around Lake Superior and to link them with the complex of industrial plants, ships, and railroads around Pittsburgh. Thus, Carnegie and Frick bought up or established steamship companies to carry the ore and also acquired the Mesabi oil fields to have direct access to it in the first place.

The American steel industry offers a classic illustration of how technological improvement, increased use of energy, superior plant design, and accountable management stimulated and maintained greater and faster production. These various innovations paid handsome dividends. Carnegie's prices were the lowest and his profits the highest in the industry. Carnegie owed much to the skill of Alexander Lyman Holley, who designed eleven of his steelworks. Holley was equal to the task of coordinating within one location a series of processes previously carried out in different places. As he explained in an article for the *Metallurgical Review* in 1877, it was just as important to have expert management and efficient design as the most modern machinery if the object was to produce steel as quickly as possible. At the Edgar Thomson Works (which he considered his finest achievement) and elsewhere, he designed buildings to fit the transportation instead of the other way around. Thus, railroads had easy access to mills, elevators, and stores. Time was money and Holley knew this just as well as Carnegie. The increased velocity of production that Holley achieved demanded highly centralized and most efficient management.

The railroads were Carnegie's biggest customers, and his experience with Tom Scott was invaluable in letting him see what exactly they required and how it could be best achieved. In fact, he adapted the sort of structure he knew from the Pennsylvania Railroad to his steel company. A most significant appointment was that of William P. Shinn as general manager, for Shinn's specialty was the collection and interpretation of statistics. Each department was obliged to account for its costs in material and labor on every order it completed. These vouchers or cost sheets were Carnegie's principal means of control. While his employees knew that Carnegie would check their accounts, they felt his eyes were always on them and acted accordingly. Yet Carnegie—again reflecting his experience with railroads—was obsessed only with prime costs. He had little interest in overhead and depreciation. Because he included repairs and maintenance with operating costs, he could not be exactly sure how much his plants and equipment were really worth.

Carnegie took great pride in his achievement. He could certainly present his career as a rise from rags to riches on account of virtue and thrift. But he went further. What created a public sensation was his presentation of the case for monopoly in an article, "Wealth," published in the *North American Review* of June 1889. He justified social inequality. The poor now enjoyed what the rich could not have afforded previously. He ascribed these benefits to "the law of competition" in modern industrial society. It was this that had made possible better and cheaper goods. "We accept and welcome, therefore, as conditions to which we must accommodate ourselves, great inequality of environment; the concentration of business industrial and commercial, in the hands of a few; and the law of competition between these, as being not only beneficial, but essential to the future of the race." Nevertheless, he advocated social responsibility among millionaires. He said that the career of a rich man should be divided in two: the first part for accumulation of wealth; the second for its distribution to society. Moreover, by his gifts of municipal libraries, his creation of Carnegie Hall in New York for concerts, and his Endowment for International Peace, Carnegie was as good as his word. When his first article and its sequel were printed together in England a striking phrase, "The Gospel of Wealth," was used as title.

STEEL AMALGAMATION AND MORGAN

For a long time Carnegie refused to transform his company into a corporation, preferring to maintain it as a limited partnership, in which he retained a majority of the shares. But the industrial trend of the Gilded Age was toward consolidation by combination. The steel industry could not remain immune. Pools began to appear in the steel industry in the late 1880s and were common in the 1890s, although they were illegal. The proliferation of combinations and holding companies disrupted the steel market. Pools had short lives—a few years at most. A steel-rail pool, formed in August 1887, was disestablished in 1893 and then revived, to die finally in February 1897. A wire-nail pool was formed in 1895 and fell apart in 1896. A steel-billet pool, formed in April 1896, did not last even a year.

The Carnegie Company continuously used its superiority to reduce prices and embarrass its rivals. Carnegie increased his annual production from 322,000 tons in 1890 to 3 million tons in 1900. During the depression of 1893–97 he expanded his production by 75 percent. In that time his profits increased from $5.4 million to $40 million per year, of which his own share was $25 million.

The Carnegie Steel Company Ltd. was organized on July 1, 1892, with a capitalization of first $25 million and later $50 million put up by twenty-eight partners. The stage was set for the final consolidation of the steel industry brought about by a war of attrition between the company of Carnegie and the House of Morgan. Carnegie's main competitor in the 1890s was the Illinois Steel Company. It owned thousands of acres of coal lands in Pennsylvania and West Virginia and had forests in Michigan and iron mines in Wisconsin besides its main plants in Chicago, Joliet, and Milwaukee. Its general counsel was Elbert H. Gary, a Chicago lawyer who cooperated with J. P. Morgan in the absorption of Illinois Steel in the new Federal Steel Company, organized in 1898 at a capitalization of $200 million. The physical reaction was instantaneous. Federal Steel was a giant magnet to other steel firms.

Morgan then moved to merge the mergers, to create a vast national corporation by combining the combinations. In his way

John Pierpont Morgan the financier who drew together the various threads of transportation and communication into his own banking empire and succeeded in unravelling the knots in each. (Library of Congress).

stood Carnegie with his known prejudice against bankers controlling what was his industry. Morgan persuaded his allies to free themselves from Carnegie by going into production of raw steel themselves. Carnegie, in his new baronial home at Skibo Castle, Scotland, remained obdurate. He proposed to go into production of finished steel and to force his competitors out of business. War was the last thing Morgan wanted. Therefore, he resolved to buy Carnegie out. Morgan represented new forces coming into operation. The reasons financiers such as Morgan rather than industrialists sought monopoly combinations were due partly to greed for the kinds of profits to be obtained from the act of merging itself and partly to their constitutional aversion to the sort of cutthroat competition that unsettled the financial market. Unlike Rockefeller and Carnegie, Morgan was more interested in integration than accumulation.

When Carnegie heard in June 1900 that his competitors were cutting their purchases of steel billets and canceling their contracts with his company, he determined to compete with them in their own market, finished steel products. He ordered the building of extra mills at Duquesne, Pennsylvania, for the manufacture of hoops, roads, wire, and nails. He wrote to his managers on July 11, "Briefly, if I were czar, I would make no dividends upon the common stock: save all surplus and spend it for a hoop and cotton-tie mill, for wire and nail mills, for tube mills, for lines of boats upon the Lakes." The new tube mill at Conneau on Lake Erie was itself to cost $12 million. No economy was too small, no expense too great in his war of attrition against his rivals' hastily assembled and overcapitalized companies.

The House of Morgan was not the only threat to Carnegie. He had to fight a war within his own company against the Henries, Frick and Phipps, who both wanted to sell out and retire. This would weaken Carnegie's empire. The bone of contention was the "Iron-Clad" agreement of 1887, a device by which Carnegie planned to protect his company in the event of his death. According to this arrangement, after one of the partners died his stock interest was to be bought from his heirs at book value over an extended period. In addition, the partners could, by a vote of two thirds of the stock (later, three quarters), buy out one of their number. Phipps and Frick were in league with Carnegie's rivals, and when Carnegie discovered this he resolved to take revenge. They could retire only on disadvantageous terms. Using the terms of the "Iron-Clad," he offered Frick the derisory sum of $4.9 million. Both Phipps and Frick retaliated by filing a suit in the Pennsylvania courts in early 1900 charging fraud by the company. Their most substantive complaint was that the company was undercapitalized.

Frick was not, of course, more interested in principle than principal. He explained to the court how Carnegie intended to recompense him in installments, a little at a time. Thus, there would be no real surrender of capital (even the low estimate of $4.9 million) but rather out of interest accruing to Carnegie's total assets. This was not only sharp practice but also fraud. Frick thus formally requested the court to reinstate him in the company and to establish a receivership to liquidate its property. After the suit had been filed the case was public knowledge and open to press comment. Carnegie's critics suggested that his only possible defense would be to deny the true value of his company and thus discredit his achievement and the reputation of which he was so proud.

His associates prevailed on him to minimize the scandal and settle out of court and then to reorganize the company. On March 28, 1900, the Carnegie Steel Company Ltd. and the H. C. Frick Coke Company in a joint statement, the "Atlantic City Agreement," declared they had resolved their differences. Frick had won. The "Iron-Clad" was in the melting pot. On April 2 a new holding company, the Carnegie Company, was chartered in New Jersey and was capitalized at $320 million, of which half was in stocks and half in mortgage bonds at 5 percent interest. It would comprise two unequal parts, Carnegie Steel capitalized at $250 million and Frick Coke at $70 million. It would issue $160 million in common stock and another $160 million in 5 percent first-mortgage bonds. The securities were not offered to the public, and the owners were those who had built the two companies. Because the new corporation was public, the owners could now legally and theoretically dispose of their holdings. Five million dollars of the new stock were set aside for new partners. Schwab became chief officer. This was not the end of the story but the denouement leading to the final climax. The internal crisis had taught Carnegie that the days of his empire were numbered.

At the invitation of J. P. Morgan, Carnegie's executive Charles Schwab addressed the financial elite of the city at a dinner at the New York University Club on December 12, 1900. His remedy for present ills in the steel industry was a national amalgamation that alone could accomplish economies and specialization. At Morgan's instigation he persuaded Carnegie to sell out to Morgan. Negotiations were completed in January 1901, and Morgan paid $492 million for the Carnegie Company. Carnegie and his family received $225.63 million in the new United States Steel Corporation first-mortgage 5 percent gold bonds. The United States Steel Corporation, a holding company, was chartered in New Jersey and launched on April 1, 1901. It was capitalized at $1.41 billion. Principal corporations entering the holding companies were three manufacturers of heavy steel—Carnegie Company, Federal Steel Company, and National Steel Company—and several fabricating companies—National Tube Company, American Steel and Wire Company, American Steel Hoop Company, American Tin Plate Company, American Sheet Steel Company, American Bridge Company, and Shelby Steel Tube Company. The capitalization was probably $400 million more than the corporations were worth. Morgan took a fee of $150 million for arranging things.

Public disquiet at the transaction was expressed in press criticism. Ray Stannard Baker in an article, "What the United States Steel Corporation Really Is and How It Works," for *McClure's* in 1901, gave his interpretation:

It receives and expends more money every year than any but the very greatest of the world's national governments; its debt is larger than that of many of the lesser nations of Europe; it absolutely controls the destinies of a population nearly as large as that of Maryland or Nebraska, and indirectly influences twice that number.

There followed a fever of speculation on Wall Street, and this fueled the fires of resentment among progressive reformers who wanted to curtail the power of the trusts. The rise to absolute economic power of an organizing genius like J. Pierpont Morgan had been predicted thirty years earlier. The brothers Charles Francis, Jr., and Henry Adams, scandalized by the way the railroad

The opulence of the plutocracy was most evident in the splendor and extravagance of their houses such as this neo-classical Vanderbilt mansion in Hyde Park, N.Y., designed by the rising architectural firm of McKim, Mead, and White in 1896. (Library of Congress).

war between the Vanderbilt family and the unholy trio of Gould, Fisk, and Drew had polluted political life in New York State, denounced the corrupt power of the early robber barons in *Chapters of Erie* (1871). They were, however, most perturbed by the realization that this sort of internecine commercial warfare between large corporations would inevitably lead to industrial consolidation on a scale such as to threaten the authority of the central government. By his deal with Carnegie Morgan had achieved an overwhelming monopoly in steel. Later in 1901, as we have already observed, he was also to consolidate his railroad holdings

in the Northern Securities Company. This was economic imperialism with a vengeance. For those who benefited from consolidation by way of handsome dividends, incorporation was a motive of life and growth. To its critics, it became a motive of death
and decay for a whole society.

THE ATTACK ON MONOPOLIES

Captains of industry had lost their heroic image and were roundly
condemned for corrupting politics and exploiting labor. When
Henry Demarest Lloyd argued against the robber barons, he was
speaking for millions who had been disabused of their belief in
progress:

Our industry is a fight of every man for himself. The prize we give the
fittest is monopoly of the necessaries of life, and we leave these winners
of the powers of life and death to wield them over us by the same "self-
interest" with which they took them from us. . . . "There is no hope
for any of us, but the weakest must go first," is the golden rule of
business. There is no other field of human associations in which any such
rule of action is allowed. The man who should apply in his family or in
his citizenship this "survival of the fittest" theory as it is practically pro-
fessed and operated in business would be a monster, and would be spee-
dily made extinct.

Moreover, the clergy, thrown into direct contact with the evils
of industrial slums, were stirred to challenge the dominant plo-
tucracy with the Social Gospel movement led by Washington
Gladden, Lyman Abbott, and Francis Greenwood Peabody. They
detested free competition, which they blamed for keeping the
working class in despair and darkness, poverty, and ignorance,
and wanted to modify it. Washington Gladden even warned of
incipient social revolution.

Protest was not confined to general criticism of corporations
but included specific instances of corporate abuse. One form of
protest, the movement to control railroads, eventually led to an
initial solution to the problem of the trusts. The abuses of the
railroads were so gross that people stirred themselves, and was
the whole issue of railroad regulation raised in several states. By

implication, the arguments used extended to other monopolies. As we have seen, railroad operators saw nothing irregular, let alone wrong, in charging customers low rates where they were in competition with one another and charging high rates where they were not to compensate for the losses. Thus, rates became dependent, not on the length of the journey, but on the interests of the management. On competitive runs, such as from Chicago to New York, the railroads charged much less than on noncompetitive runs. Accordingly, it cost more to ship freight of the same kind from Rochester to New York than from Chicago to New York. Another practice was to favor some customers over others. Because they provided considerable trade, big customers such as Standard Oil were more likely to be favored with bargain rates than small ones. Standard Oil also led the notorious practice by which railroads used to turn over part of the rates paid by the smaller customers to the larger customers in the form of rebates. And, as we have also seen, if they infringed their contracts to big shippers, railroads incurred drawbacks or fines—penalties paid for shipping products of their customers' competitors.

There was, naturally, much opposition to such railroad practices among small customers. The hostility engendered by the railroads in the West is suggested by popular jokes of the period. The monogram of the Houston Eastern and Western Texas Railroad was HEWT and supposedly stood for "Hell Either Way You Take It." In 1877 everything went wrong for a Dakota farmer. There were storms in the spring, drought in the summer, and a plague of locusts in the fall. One day his wife found him in a field shaking his fist at the sky, saying: "Goddam the Great Northern Railroad." The movement to curb the railroads started in the midwestern states but spread widely. It had different aims: to deny roads more state aid—as in the constitutions of California, Kansas, and Missouri; to recover land grants; to prohibit rebates and free passes; to regulate rates and services, as in Massachusetts, which supplied a model for others.

The Illinois constitution of 1870 specifically urged the state legislature to "pass laws to correct abuses and to prevent unjust discrimination and extortion in the rates of freight and passenger tariffs." Thus Illinois came to outlaw such discriminations in 1870.

It fixed a maximum rate for passengers and set up a railway and warehouse commission to supervise railroads, warehouses, and grain elevators. Where Illinois led, California, Georgia, Iowa, Minnesota, and Wisconsin, among others, followed.

Within a few years midwestern and western railroads found themselves regulated and restricted by state legislation. Their protests in lawsuits were, at first, to no avail. The U.S. Supreme Court upheld these laws in the *Granger* cases, of which *Munn* v. *Illinois* (1876) was the most important. Munn's argument was that the Illinois law regulating charges of grain elevators contravened the Fourteenth Amendment of 1868 by which no "State shall deprive any person of life, liberty or property, without due process of law; nor deny to any person within its jurisdiction the equal protection of the laws." According to this argument, the fixing of rates by Illinois was confiscatory. Chief Justice Morrison R. Waite, speaking for the majority of 5 in the *Munn* decision, given in 1877, said otherwise:

Property does become clothed with a public interest when used in a manner to make it of public consequence, and affect the community at large. When, therefore, one devotes his property to a use in which the public has an interest, he, in effect, grants to the public an interest in that use, and must submit to be controlled by the public for the public good.

By its decisions the Court establised three principles: the right of government to regulate any business with a public interest; the right of the legislature to decide what is fair and reasonable; the right of the state to act where Congress has not.

In 1881 New York merchants established a National Anti-Monopoly League to promote a program of railroad reforms that was advertised throughout the country. In 1881 and 1882 Congress was inundated with requests for reform. In its pamphlets the league emphasized that its aims were in the best interests of conservative government. It was

trying to lift the safety valve and prevent an explosion which will surely come, if the great financial free booters of the country are allowed to go on corrupting our elections, controlling legislation, debauching our courts, and riding roughshod over public rights.

Unorthodox journalist and photographer Frances Benjamin Johnston captured the glitter and grandeur of the Gilded Age to perfection in a series of beautifully detailed stills such as this imaginative composition of the ball room in the Larz Anderson House, Washington, D.C. (Library of Congress).

Much more was at stake than the variable cost of railroad rates. What was at issue was the ability of government to supervise capital and industry in the public good. As Henry Demarest Lloyd observed in his exposure of Standard Oil in March 1881: "The movement of the railroad trains of this country is literally the circulation of its blood. Our treatment of the 'railroad problem' will show the quality and calibre of our political sense."

More than thirty bills to regulate railroads were introduced in Congress between 1874 and 1885. The most important were those of Senator Shelby Cullom of Illinois and Representative John Reagan of Texas. In the Cullom bill regulation was to be enforced by an independent commission. In the Reagan bill it was to be enforced by the courts.

But while railroads and reformers were coming together, the Supreme Court was retreating from its liberal position of 1877. When confronted by *Wabash* v. *Illinois* in 1886 the Court took a conservative view. The Wabash Railroad had charged certain shippers 15 cents per 100 pounds for carrying goods from Peoria, Illinois, to New York but 25 cents per 100 pounds for the same type of goods from Gilman, Illinois, to New York, although Peoria was 86 miles farther away. What decided the Court for Wabash and against Illinois was that no state could regulate railroad traffic crossing its boundaries. It could decide for itself but not for interstate commerce. Three quarters of rail traffic crossed state lines. Thus, without federal authority and supervision, railroad legislation was useless.

The Supreme Court's decision in the *Wabash* case, though technically correct, was morally indefensible. Public anger could be resolved only by enabling legislation. Thus, the Cullom and Reagan measures were combined to make the Interstate Commerce Act signed by President Grover Cleveland on February 4, 1887. The act declared that rates had to be "reasonable and just." Rebates and discriminations between places, persons, and commodities were now illegal. It was unlawful for a carrier to charge more for a short haul than a long one under similar conditions. Pooling was forbidden. The act established a regulatory Interstate Commerce Commission (ICC) of five members (not more than three from the same party) with the duty of inquiring into the railroads' affairs and making the required reports. Railroads had to give the commission prior notice of increases in rates.

For a short time railroads were willing to accept the new law. But they did so with bad grace and later used every trick to frustrate the commission. A conservative judiciary composed of lawyers trained by corporations protected management against unions and the public. In the *Maximum Freight Rate* case of 1897 the Supreme Court decided that the ICC did not have the power to fix rates, and in the *Alabama Midlands* case, also of 1897, it practically invalidated the long- and short-haul regulations. The Court discovered it could not get railroad agents to testify about malpractices and could not get other witnesses to give evidence consistent with their earlier declarations to the ICC. By 1897 aggrieved shippers had succeeded in collecting refunds due them in only 5 out of 225 cases decided by the ICC.

In any case, by the 1890s most of the country's railroads were part of six huge systems. Four of these were controlled by Morgan (q.v.) and two by Kuhn, Loeb and Company. These huge monopolies could set their own rates at will. The ICC was an irrelevance. In its annual report of 1898 it admitted its failure. Justice John Harlan of Kentucky described it as a "useless body for all practical purposes."

Nevertheless, after the passing of the Interstate Commerce Act in 1887, it was inevitable that public opinion would demand full reform of the trusts. In exchange for their votes in Congress for the McKinley tariff of 1890 Republicans gave reformers opposed to monopolies their support for John Sherman's bill to make monopoly combinations illegal. The most important provisions of the Sherman Anti-Trust Act of July 2, 1890, were contained in the first two articles:

1. Every contract, combination in the form of trust or otherwise, or conspiracy, in restraint of trade or commerce among the several States, or with foreign nations is hereby declared to be illegal.
2. Every person who shall monopolize, or attempt to monopolize . . . any part of the trade or commerce among the several States, or with foreign nations, shall be deemed guilty of a misdemeanor.

Sherman had intended to give supervision to a federal commission along the lines of the ICC. But in the Senate Judiciary Committee George F. Hoar of Massachusetts and George F. Edmunds of Vermont had this changed, giving jurisdiction to federal courts. No attempt was made to define "trust," "conspiracy," or "monopoly," let alone the allusive phrase, "in the form of trust or otherwise." In other words, the problem was treated before it was analyzed.

The Sherman Anti-Trust Act represented a last opportunity for successful government regulation of monopolies. It failed. Yet it was not the fault of Congress so much as of the Supreme Court.

The dining room of the Anderson house, with its mélange of Flemish tapestries and Oriental ornaments, is representative of upper class taste at the close of the Gilded Age. The house was built between 1901 and 1905 to designs by Little and Brown as the home of diplomat Larz Anderson. In 1938 it became the headquarters of the Society of the Cincinnati, an organization of male descendants of veterans of the Revolutionary War. (Frances Benjamin Johnston, Library of Congress).

President Benjamin Harrison initiated a trial case against the sugar trust that controlled 85 percent of the nation's sugar refining. The appeal, *E. C. Knight and Co.* v. *United States*, did not come before the Court until 1895 when all but one justice found against the government. According to a sophistical distinction, the Sherman Act did not apply to production, only to commerce. Attorney General Richard Olney had not even prepared the case properly. He offered no evidence that sugar was sold and price-controlled across state lines and hence subject to federal laws. He had not bothered to show how different companies in different states were connected with one another in a trust.

Only seven suits under the Sherman Act were instituted by Benjamin Harrison, eight by Grover Cleveland in his second administration, and three by William McKinley. All were ineffective. Yet, in deference to the Sherman Anti-Trust Act, the trust itself was abandoned. To evade the law, robber barons used the new Standard Oil device of the holding company. By establishing nominally independent companies, each with the same board of directors, or a series of interlocking directorships, both of which had a controlling interest rather than owning companies outright, they could outwit the law. Between 1893 and 1904 the number of giant combinations increased from 12 to 318 with an increase in aggregate capital from less than $1 billion to almost $7 billion. These 318 companies controlled about two fifths of the capital invested in manufacturing.

Attempts to curb big business by federal legislation represented a ritual clash between an old-fashioned ideal and modern needs. "In this atmosphere," said Thurman Arnold in his *Folklore of Capitalism* (1937), "the antitrust laws were the answer of a society which unconsciously felt the need of great organizations, and at the same time had to deny them a place in the moral and logical ideology of the social structure." On the surface it seemed that the trusts were to be changed to suit the institution; it was really the other way around, however. What had been accomplished with the rise of the corporation was a revolution in business management. The new tier of executives was now in control, not only of individual businesses, but of the market as well. As Alfred Dupont Chandler, Jr., remarks in his seminal work, *The Visible Hand* (1977):

the visible hand of management replaced what Adam Smith referred to as the invisible hand of market forces. The market remained the generator of demand for goods and services, but modern business enterprise took over the functions of coordinating flows of goods through existing processes of production and distribution, and of allocating funds and personnel for future production and distribution. As modern business enterprise acquired functions hitherto carried out by the market, it became the most powerful institution in the American economy and its managers the most influential group of economic decision makers.

CHAPTER THREE

IMMIGRATION, INTEGRATION, AND IDENTITY

A T THE TURN of the century the most famous magician in the world was Harry Houdini, an American immigrant who specialized in great escapes. He could free himself from handcuffs, iron collars, and straitjackets. With consummate ease he emerged from prison cells and padlocked safes, from river beds and buried coffins. He captivated audiences who saw in his escapes a symbolic reenactment of their own emancipation from the Old World and their flight to the New. By his art Houdini could express their fantasies, needs, and fears. His own experiences of displacement and assimilation had equipped him perfectly.

Born Ehrich Weiss in 1874, Houdini took the name of another, the French conjuror Robert-Houdin. His life story, personal and professional, was a series of escapes. His rabbi father fled Budapest to evade arrest. The son ran away from home in Appleton, Wisconsin, when he was twelve to free himself for his chosen career. In 1894 he eloped with a Catholic girl, Beatrice Rahner, whose widowed mother would not accept him; neither, at first, would the world of American show business. It was only after he held London audiences spellbound that he could make the big time in the United States. When he did so, his stunts and illusions were taken as a celebration of immigration—physical, spiritual, and psychological.

The part played by the United States in the mass migrations of the nineteenth and twentieth centuries is most distinctive—and not for quantity alone. Americans looked to the future, not the past. Where people had come from was less important than where they were going. The very word "immigrant" was invented by Jedidiah Morse in 1789 to describe foreign settlers in New York. By calling them immigrants, rather than the more traditional "emigrants," Americans emphasized the fact that newcomers had entered a new land rather than left an old one.

American immigration was continuous throughout the nineteenth century. Nevertheless, there were three distinct waves, each greater than the one before. According to historian Marcus Lee Hansen they were dominated successively by the Celts, the Germans, and the Slavs and Mediterranean peoples. Of the 5 million people who crossed the Atlantic between 1815 and 1860 and the 10 million who did so between 1860 and 1890 the majority came from Britain and Ireland, Germany and Scandinavia, Switzerland and Holland. However, the 15 million who composed the final wave, from 1890 to 1914, came principally from Italy and Greece, Austria-Hungary and Russia, Rumania and Turkey.

The extent of the change is best illustrated by a comparison of immigration figures at the crest of the second and third waves in, respectively, 1882 and 1907. In 1882, 788, 992 immigrants arrived—a record for the nineteenth century. Of these, 250,630 were from Germany (the highest number ever), 179,423 from Britain and Ireland, and 105,326 from Scandinavia. Only 32,159 were from Italy, 29,150 from the Hapsburg Empire, and 16,918 from Russia and the Baltic. Thus, 87 percent were from north and western Europe and only 13 percent from south and eastern Europe. In 1907, however, when 1,285,349 immigrants arrived, 19.3 percent were from north and western Europe, and 80.7 percent from south and eastern Europe. The "old" immigration was now much smaller than the "new."

It was political, economic, and religious discontent in Europe that stirred both old and new immigrants to leave. Throughout the nineteenth century industrial and agricultural revolutions transformed European society. The additional pressure of increasing population provided the impetus for emigration. Such changes began in western Europe. As the century progressed they spread to the east. The causes and sources of American immigration moved with them.

A whole series of factors stimulated the exodus from Germany. More German immigrants arrived than any other ethnic group in all but three years from 1854 to 1894. Agricultural depression and industrial recession stirred Britons, Norwegians, and Swedes. In Ireland the root cause of unemployment and poverty was agricultural mismanagement by absentee landlords. After 1890 the birthrate began to fall in northwestern Europe. Moreover, increased industrialization afforded new employment for those displaced from agriculture. The old immigration began to decline.

Of all factors stimulating the new immigration the most obvious was an increase in population. At the close of the century the annual rates of increase in eastern Europe were more than 10 in every previous 1,000. Increased population threatened traditional standards of living. There was not enough food to go around. Developments in the three states from which Slavic and Mediterranean emigration flowed (Austria-Hungary, Russia, and Italy) illustrate this. Italian immigration to America rose from 12,000 in 1880 to over 100,000 in 1900; immigration from Austria-Hungary rose from 17,000 in 1880 to 114,000 in 1900. The catchment area of Slavs was especially wide. The term "Slav" covers a western division of Poles, Bohemians (Czechs), and Slovaks, and an eastern division of Russians, Ruthenians (Ukrainians), Bulgarians, Serbs, Croatians, and Slovenians.

The impulse for migration from Russia was as much political and religious as it was economic. The greatest exodus was of Russian Jews, fleeing new persecution. The assassination of Alexander II in 1881 set off anti-Semitic riots in the south and west. Henceforth Jews were confined to the Pale of Settlement, Poland, and the western provinces. Outright persecution followed. The number of Russian immigrants to America rose from 5,000 in 1880 to 90,000 in 1900. Even when Poles made up a quarter of the Russian exodus, and Finns, Germans, and Lithuanians accounted for almost another quarter, Jews constituted the largest single group, 43.8 percent of the whole. Less than 5 percent of immigrants from Russia were Russian in anything but birth. Muslim oppression of

Armenians in the notorious massacres of 1894, 1895, and 1896 compelled Armenians to emigrate.

Not all immigrants came across the Atlantic. Between 1860 and 1900 about 300,000 French-Canadians left the Province of Quebec where neither agriculture nor industry could support the population. By the end of the nineteenth century, French-Canadians constituted one of the major minority groups in New England and rather smaller ones in northern New York, Michigan, Wisconsin, and Illinois. Only when the Canadian frontier reached the prairies at the turn of the century did immigration from Canada begin to decline. A small number of Mexicans immigrated—according to official statistics less than 10,000 before 1900. Some historians believe that the actual numbers were twice that figure. Mexican immigrants usually went first to El Paso, Texas, a city with three railroad lines offering transport to jobs on nearby farms, mines, and smelters, and in railway construction.

A comparatively small but significant number of Orientals crossed the Pacific. Between 1849, when gold was discovered in California, and 1882, when the Chinese Exclusion Act was passed, 300,000 Chinese settled in California. Like many Europeans, their primary motive was economic. The Taiping Rebellion that began in 1848 devastated southeast China. The lure of high wages on the railroads enticed men from the province of Guangdong. Chinese comprised an overwhelming majority of laborers who laid the track of the Central Pacific through the Sierra Nevada in the 1860s. In 1870 Chinese miners accounted for a fifth of all miners in Montana, a quarter in California and Washington, and more than half in Oregon and Idaho. In 1886 nearly 90 percent of all farm laborers in California were Chinese.

In 1885 a Japanese exodus began after the emperor revoked a ban on emigration. Japan's population explosion was greater than that of any Western country. However, only from 1891 onwards did more than 1,000 Japanese come in any one year. In the 1880s and 1890s most immigrants went to Hawaii to work on American sugar plantations as contract laborers. After the annexation of Hawaii in 1898 they could travel to the United States.

What prospective immigrants learned about the United States was not all hearsay. There were many travelers' tales. More important, there were advertisements in guidebooks, pamphlets, and newspapers. For example, the guidebook *Where to Emigrate and Why* was published by "Americus" in 1869. It described journeys by land and sea, calculated the cost, and reported on wages in the United States. It was one of a series of tracts describing the advantages of life in America. The gospel was not only that of wealth and economic opportunity but also of political equality and religious tolerance.

Prospective immigrants were shown why, where, and how to go. Steamships had revolutionized the transatlantic traffic. In 1867, 92.86 percent of passengers arrived in New York by steamship. Of all the benefits the most significant was a shorter journey. The old sailing ships took from one to three months to cross the Atlantic. The crossing by steam lasted, on average, fourteen days in 1867 and only five and a half days forty years later. The journey was much safer, for ships were getting bigger and better. The introduction of steel hulls, improved boilers, and the triple expansion engine made possible ships of 5,000 tons. Each could accommodate about 300 passengers first-class and more than 1,000 in the steerage.

During the American Civil War, British and German steamship lines seized the bulk of the transatlantic traffic from American companies. Lines such as the Inman and Cunard from Liverpool, the Hamburg-Amerika from Hamburg, and the North German Lloyd from Bremen built new fleets of passenger ships and expanded their trade. They were joined by new lines: by 1882 there were 48 steamship companies competing with one another in the Atlantic.

Steamship companies proudly advertised their facilities. It was said in 1890 that the five largest shipping lines had 3,600 agents in the British Isles alone. The French line, Compagnie Générale Transatlantique, employed 55 agents, each with 200 or 300 subagents working part time. Moreover, there were also agencies throughout the United States where Americans could buy tickets for their relatives abroad. In 1890 nearly a third of immigrants arrived on prepaid tickets; in 1900, almost two thirds. Specific funds to assist immigrants were also provided by public organizations and private individuals. Over the years the sums raised

Miss Dakota and Uncle Sam. Dakota campaigns for immigrants and announces the attractions of life in the Far Northwest. She is also trying to persuade Uncle Sam that she is worthy to take her place in the Union as a fully fledged state. A lithograph of the Forbes Lithograph Company, 1887. (Library of Congress).

and distributed were considerable. Between 1847 and 1887 Irish immigrants received £34 million in advance to pay for their journey. Immigrants from Austria-Hungary received $95 million between 1893 and 1903.

During the 1880s the immigration trade became a matter of fierce competition among British and German steamship companies. One result of these rate wars was a temporary reduction in fares from £3 or £4 ($15 or $20) to £2 ($10). Yet steamship lines also entered "pools" in much the same way American railroads did. Thus, in 1886 British lines agreed with Hamburg-Amerika to divide the traffic and retain their profits. At the turn of the century, however, immigration was possible from the whole of Europe and not just the northwest. British and German companies thus agreed to resolve their differences. They formed the North Atlantic, Continental, and Mediterranean Steamship conferences to end rate wars and reduce competition.

States and railroads were even more responsible than steamship companies for stimulating immigration. After 1865 almost all the northwestern states and territories formed separate agencies. They wanted to dispose of unsold land, and they realized that increased population was essential for material growth. In 1870 midwestern governors called a national convention on immigration to Indianapolis. It was attended by delegates from twenty-two states who petitioned Congress to establish a national bureau of immigration.

State bureaus concentrated their efforts on Britain, Germany, and Scandinavia. Their pamphlets and newspaper advertisements emphasized future prospects. In *Minnesota, the Empire State of the North-West* (1878), Minnesota claimed it could support 5 million people. (This was two years before a census that recorded fewer than 800,000). Before it even became a state Colorado had established a board of immigration that circulated reports on railroads and real estate. According to *Colorado, A Statement of Facts* (1872), "The poor should come to Colorado, because here they can by industry and frugality better their condition. The rich should come here because they can more advantageously invest their means than in any other region. The young should come here to get an early start on the road to wealth." In order to entice immigrants the states claimed to be heavens on earth. A popular joke of the period has St. Peter, as gatekeeper to heaven, admitting the dead to the real thing but warning them that after life in an earthly paradise heaven would be a disappointment to them.

Railroads were especially important in dispersing immigrants. The railroads had vast tracts of land to dispose of, and they could offer transport to reach it. The Kansas Pacific, Missouri Pacific, Santa Fe, and Wisconsin Central all distributed booklets. The Santa Fe even appointed a European agent, C. B. Schmidt. In 1875 he visited Russia to arrange passages for Mennonites who settled in Kansas. In California railroad magnates helped found the California Immigrant Union in 1869. The railroads' lavish inducements to immigrants included reduced fares by sea and land, loans at low rates of interest, classes in farming, and the building of churches and schools. In their advertisements to immigrants railroads were not always scrupulously honest about the Golden West. Jay Cooke of the Northern Pacific deliberately misrepresented the climate of the Great Plains. In the 1870s he had fraudulent weather maps distributed on which the isotherm lines were diverted in order to give the impression that the region had warm winters. This led the press to call the Northern Pacific the Banana Belt.

However, it was railroad policy to establish homogeneous communities. In this way the railroads helped to determine the ethnic composition of the West and Midwest. Most active was the Burlington, which installed British, German, and Scandinavian settlements in Iowa and Nebraska. The Northern also induced British, German, and Scandinavian immigrants to settle in Dakota Territory, Minnesota, and the Pacific Northwest. It was credited with doubling their population between 1880 and 1900.

INTEGRATION

The first stage in the integration of immigrants into American society was their reception. In 1855 New York State established a reception center in Manhattan at the old fort down at the Battery, Castle Garden. Immigrants arriving at the Port of New York first went through quarantine at Staten Island, next through customs at a dock on the Hudson or East River, and finally to Castle Garden. It was here that they were registered and could make arrangements for their new life. Castle Garden had its own labor bureau, separate from the reception center, where immigrants met employers. However, few employers were aware of its existence, and not until 1880 did requests for skilled workers exceed the supply. British, German, and Irish immigrants were given the pick of available jobs. Others were left to fend for themselves.

In 1892 the federal government opened a new immigration depot. Ellis Island had once been a picnic resort and was later an arsenal. Now ships docked in the harbor, and immigrants were ferried to the island where all stages—quarantine, customs, and registration—were completed. Registration covered, in turn: name, nationality, last residence, destination, occupation, age, sex, marital status, number in family, literacy, amount of money, whether a former prisoner or pauper, health, vessel, and date. The clerks' methods were rough-and-ready, their knowledge of other languages rudimentary. If immigration statistics are misleading, it is largely due to them. They were quite likely to call Czechs Germans, and Serbs Hungarians. The Jewish Cooperstein became cooper, the Dutch Kok became Cook, and the Greek Kiriacopoulis became Campbell. One German Jew was so confused by the barrage of questions that he forgot his own name. "Ich vergesse," he admitted when asked. The clerk accordingly registered him as Ferguson.

During the Gilded Age 80 percent of immigrants settled in a northeastern quadrilateral between Canada; the Atlantic; Washington, D.C.; and St. Louis, Missouri. Two thirds remained in New England and in New York, New Jersey, and Pennsylvania. In 1890 there were 9 million first-generation immigrants in the United States. Of these 2.75 million were Germans. Half lived in five states: Illinois, Michigan, Missouri, Iowa, and Wisconsin. They constituted the single largest ethnic group in twenty-seven states. The Irish accounted for 2 million, and nearly two thirds lived in New England and the Middle Atlantic states. Almost 1 million were Canadians. Those from the French provinces settled in New England; those from the British areas, in the states bordering the Great Lakes. There were 1 million English, 250,000 Scots, and 100,000 Welsh—all widely scattered. Of the 900,000

Scandinavians, most lived west of the Great Lakes. One fifth lived in Minnesota (which acquired over 400 Swedish place names) and one seventh in Illinois. Finns also settled in Massachusetts and Michigan. The remaining first-generation immigrants included 250,000 people from other parts of northwestern Europe, 750,000 from east and central Europe, and 100,000 Chinese. Immigrants from Austria-Hungary and Russia settled chiefly in Massachusetts, New York, New Jersey, Pennsylvania, and Illinois. The great majority of Italians moved to California and Illinois. The Portuguese settled by the sea, in Massachusetts and Rhode Island on the Atlantic and in California on the Pacific.

It was principally the Industrial Revolution with its splendid promise of opportunity that had attracted immigrants, old and new. Indeed, without massive immigration the United States could not have developed industrially at anything like the rate it did. In 1890, 56 percent of the labor force in manufacturing and mechanical industries was of foreign birth or foreign parentage. Not surprisingly, public opinion held American industry responsible for increased immigration. As Welsh historian Maldwyn Jones explains, it assumed that between 1864, when Congress made contract labor legal in the Act to Encourage Immigration, and 1885, when it forbade it in the Foran Act, that American industrialists imported cheap labor for the express purpose of depressing wages and breaking strikes. The steady flow of immigrants, ready to seize any opportunity, may have had that effect. But it was not part of a capitalist plot. For the 1864 act fell far short of the aims of its Republican sponsors. Congress appropriated $25,000 to establish a Commission of Immigration within the State Department and a United States Immigrant Office in the Port of New York. But the United States never provided immigrants with financial assistance, and the bureau was closed down in 1868. Financial support was left to private enterprise, whether business or union.

Contract labor was a new version of the indenture system of colonial times. Workers agreed to a period of service in return for having their fares to America prepaid. But the system was now used to bring over skilled workers for specialized jobs. It was not used to import masses of unskilled laborers. Mining companies in particular welcomed skilled immigrants. They lent miners their fare and a third of the fares of their familes in return for two years' work at half pay—about $10 a month. According to the census of 1870, half of the miners in America were first-generation immigrants from Britain and Ireland.

Beginning in the 1860s, first in New York and Chicago and then elsewhere, private firms began to supply labor on commission. For a brief period in the 1860s the American Emigrant Company tried to run an international labor agency. It sought assistance for passages for prospective immigrants. But its activities in Europe fell foul of manufacturers and governments alike. It could not make ends meet and in 1867 gave up the attempt to procure contract labor.

There was also a Latin variation on the theme of contract labor. Immigration from the south of Italy was promoted by *padroni*. The *padrone* system passed through two phases. At first the *padrone* was an independent boss who collected children from villages. He trained them as street musicians and acrobats and took them to America to earn a living. The practice was made illegal and died out. The Italian vice consul in New York assured the Ford committee investigating immigration in 1888 that there were no longer any *padroni* in operation. But the system had changed. New *padroni* now acted in association with Italian travel and labor bureaus. They recruited unskilled laborers in Italy and put them under contract at a fixed wage. They advanced money to cover traveling expenses and boarded them in America. Loans were to be repaid at 6 percent interest. The Ford committee discovered that immigrants sometimes ran up debts of $70 in return for passages originally worth only $20. In 1899 there were eighty Italian banks in New York, most of which ran labor bureaus. About two thirds of the Italian work force in the city owed them and the *padroni* their livelihood.

For a long time it was said that immigrants found employment according to their physical and mental abilities. Thus, Poles and Slavs worked in heavy industry because they were supposed to be strong, stupid, and submissive. English workers were noted for their skill and versatility. For example, cutlers from Sheffield, who had had a long and careful training, were in special demand because they could turn their hand to anything in the iron industry. In New York and Chicago, Russian Jews, widely known for their dexterity, made women's clothes their particular specialty.

However, who worked where and when depended on all sorts of social and economic factors. French-Canadians worked in the textile factories of New England because their immigration coincided with increased demand for labor in the cotton mills of states near Quebec. Moreover, the mills of Maine, Massachusetts, and Rhode Island hired women and children as well as men. Thus, whole families could be employed together. The clothing industry was not attractive to Russian Jews because it offered work to women and children. Their women usually stayed at home after marriage. Their children stayed at school until they were in their teens. The principal attraction of the rag trade was an avenue to commerce. Pay was by piece-work; earnings were related to individual effort. Workers could therefore amass capital and invest in their own businesses.

ACCULTURATION

"We call England the mother country," observed humorist Robert Benchley, "because most of us come from Poland or Italy." Indeed, it was only the British with conspicuous advantages of language and literacy who remained indifferent to American citizenship. In 1890 more than half of the first-generation immigrants had already been naturalized and many others had filed for citizenship. The immigrant's key to acculturation in America was his new citizenship. It confirmed a new identity. For a long time, however, immigrants were American only in name. Their language, customs, and religions were quite different from those of many natives. Their lives revolved around their own ethnic group.

Certainly, the culture of ethnic ghettos owed little to English tradition. The facades of city houses and apartment blocks would not have been out of place in continental Europe: New York City's Orchard Street was reminiscent of old Vienna, Hester Street of Warsaw. Taste and smell were as much affected as sight and sound. The new American cuisine included Irish stew, Hungarian goulash, German liverwurst, Russian borscht, Rumanian pastrami, Italian lasagne, Greek moussaka, and Jewish bagels and lox.

In their new and alien environment immigrants required special services: mutual aid societies; foreign language businesses and newspapers; churches and synagogues for culture, ceremony, and consolation. Organizations like the Illinois Immigrants' Protective League and the North American Civic League for Immigrants were primarily concerned with integrating their members into American society.

Of all the different ethnic groups the Jews were most prepared to unite for the sake of their people as a whole. Successive Russian pogroms provided a continuous reminder of cultural obligations to others in distress. Moreover, Jewish religious observance preserved cultural identity and solidarity. As early as 1860 there were 27 synagogues in New York City. With the passing years many German Jews became americanized in their attitudes to teaching and services. Their reform movement was given theological respectability by the arrival of learned rabbis from Europe. The most influential was Isaac Wise, who published the *Israelite* and made Cincinnati the center of Reform Judaism. By 1890 there were more members of Reform than Orthodox synagogues. Yet, without the whip of persecution religion flagged. Many Russian Jews came to prefer socialism to religion.

The influx of Russian and other eastern European Jews prompted the established community to offer help by way of the Hebrew Immigrant Aid Society, the Educational Alliance, and other organizations. The newcomers disliked taking charity from americanized Jews and were quite capable of founding their own Hebrew Sheltering Society in 1890. They also established 300 schools to teach Hebrew. These newcomers brought an intense piety, sustained by strict religious observance, and deep commitment to secular causes—socialism, anarchism, and Zionism.

The Roman Catholic Church was *the* church of immigrants. After the Civil War there were 42 dioceses and 3,000 churches. In 1900 there were 70 dioceses and 10,000 churches. As historian John Higham explains, "Immigration transformed the church into an ethnic fortress." Yet the Roman Catholic Church became a source of controversy among immigrants rather than a means of assimilation. When the Irish first arrived, it was the only institution ready to accept them. But it was ambiguous about the Irish movement for Home Rule. Churchmen were sympathetic to the idea of Irish independence from Protestant England. But they realized that the removal of Irish members from the British Parliament would weaken the representation of Catholics there. They also resented secret societies such as the Fenians. Furthermore, they distrusted the Irish movement as a nationalist rather than religious cause. However, other ethnic groups thought that the Irish were getting more than their fair share of attention from the church. In 1886 the Reverend Peter M. Abbelen, vicar general of the Diocese of Milwaukee, complained to the Vatican that Irish bishops were hostile to German culture. In 1891 the St. Raphaelsverein, a society for the protection of German immigrants, went further. It submitted the Lucerne Memorial to the Vatican. This was a petition asking that each ethnic group should have its own priests and parishes. Officially the church refused. Tacitly it complied.

The foreign language newspaper was a crucial immigrant institution. It nourished group solidarity. Between 1884 and 1920, 3,500 new foreign language papers appeared. In 1890, 800 of the foreign language papers were German, three quarters of the total number. A few were city dailies such as the *New Yorker Staatszeitung*, the *Anzeiger des Westens* of St. Louis, the *Cincinnati Volkesblatt*, and the *Wisconsin Banner*. Most of the others were Scandinavian, French, or Spanish. Later on, more groups were represented. The first paper ever published in Lithuanian was in America, not Europe. Only a fraction survived, and the total number of foreign language papers increased only a little, from 794 to 1,052.

The local political boss gave immigrants employment, protection, and housing. It was he they repaid. As Oscar Handlin puts it, "The machine was the means through which the immigrants sought services no one else performed." First in the field were Irish machines. The heyday of Irish bosses was from 1870 to 1920. The Irish had arrived earlier and, unlike many who followed, spoke English. They also knew how democratic government was supposed to work. As Leonard Dinnerstein and David Reimers acutely observe, "For two centuries they had been oppressed by the English in Ireland and during that period they had learned how Anglo-Saxon law could be manipulated to satisfy the ends of those who governed and work against those who did not." From the Catholic church they learned organization and discipline. Thus, among ethnic groups they alone had the understanding and techniques to dominate politics after the Civil War. "Honest John" Kelly, Richard Croker, and Charles F. Murphy in succession ruled Tammany Hall. Mike McDonald, Johnny Rogers, Michael ("Hinky Dink") Kenna, and "Bathhouse John" Joseph Coughlin dominated Chicago. Col. Ed Butler was the Democratic boss who ruled the Republican city of St. Louis. Hugh O'Brien became first in a long line of Irish mayors of Boston. These men led the first and most enduring ethnic bloc in American politics. On the whole, the Irish remained loyal to the Democrats and resisted Republican attempts to entice them away.

Although the political contribution of new immigrants was, at first, hesitant, their cultural contribution was distinctive from the outset. Through the simultaneous experiences of displacement and assimilation many second-generation immigrants showed a special feeling for the theater. Playing a part and projecting a personality were second nature.

It was in theater that Jewish artistry in particular first achieved its fullest expression. Three Yiddish theaters on New York's Bowery specialized in problem plays. The plots were drawn from comic operas and melodramas, the dialogue from vaudeville patter. They were immensely popular among audiences of all classes. It is estimated that 2 million people attended 1,100 performances each year at the turn of the century. The extraordinary popularity of the Yiddish theater was due to its realism. In the plays of Jacob Gordin audiences could recognize and identify with situations from everyday life. The most influential statement about assimilation was *The Melting Pot* (1908), a play by Israel Zangwill, an English Jew. The subsequent contribution of American Jews to vaudeville, radio, and cinema became a legend of show business. Their contribution to American literature was also outstanding. It began with *Yekl: A Tale of the New York Ghetto* (1896) by Abraham Cahan, the first novel of American immigrants written by a naturalized citizen in English.

The phenomenon of apparently sudden, spontaneous, and exceptional Jewish creativity in the fields of music, art, and, later, science was so astonishing after centuries of silence that it requires some explanation. Emancipation from one world and reception into another provide only part of the answer. English political scientist Bryan Magee has defined and analyzed the phenomenon. He calls his article "Of Jews—Not Least in Music" (1968) because it is in music that he finds the Jewish achievement so striking. His argument, by extension, accounts for newfound creativity among other immigrants. He dismisses an obvious explanation, that the cultural achievement of Jews at the turn of the century arose from their unique religious tradition. Because Judaism is by and large authoritarian it does not allow its basic values to be questioned. Originality is inimical to closed religious and political systems, but it is essential to truly creative art, which expresses the artist's conscious ideas and needs and his subconscious conflicts and desires. Throughout central and eastern Europe, Jews had been obliged to live in a closed religious culture of their own. They had no opportunity either within or outside their ghettos and shtetls for free expression. But in the course of the nineteenth century these closed communities were broken up and their people scattered in the wake of European nationalism.

The first emancipated Jews spoke the Gentile languages of the new society around them with foreign accents. However talented they were, Jewish artists and philosophers in Europe could, at first, make no more of their art than a self-conscious synthesis of form and idea. But this was not a permanent state of affairs. Two things were happening. As generations passed, Jews became more integrated with the culture around them. In the United States they helped to create it. At the same time, Western culture itself was disintegrating. The skein of nineteenth-century history is woven from national struggles for liberation, imperialist wars, mass migrations, and the dispersal of refugees. They are its very warp and woof. The fragmentation of society and the alienation of the individual from society and himself became major themes of modern culture. Because of their experiences, new immigrants, particularly Jews, were far more involved in, and identified with, each of these things than other immigrants. They could articulate their responses both consciously and subconsciously. Many benefited from the dubious distinction of double alienation. They rejected Orthodox Judaism, yet remained victims of anti-Semitism. The Yiddish theater, with its special themes of expatriation and assimilation, was an ideal forum for the first flowering of Jewish expression and creativity in a Gentile world. It served as a focal point of acculturation and also helped reshape the developing culture of the New World.

More than anything else fluency and facility in English liberated immigrants from the past. Once children had mastered the language they were beyond their parents' control. It was they who led. They could reject the traditions of the Old World. Perhaps this partly explains the Italian hostility to education. It weakened ethnic ties. When in 1889 and 1890 the states of Illinois and Wisconsin decided that English was to be the medium of instruction in schools, there was a great outcry from Germans and Scandinavians. Catholics and Lutherans alike believed that it would destroy their ethnic culture. Eight midwestern states agreed to retain German as the medium wherever there was a demand. However, it was particularly important to Jews that towns afforded free secular education. Their fascination with the new language in part explains their cultural renaissance.

NATIVISM

Throughout the 1860s, 1870s, and early 1880s no effort was spared to encourage immigration. Immigrants themselves chose as a symbol of welcome and promise the Statue of Liberty in New York Harbor. But this was not an official view. The gigantic statue, unveiled before President Grover Cleveland on October 28, 1886, was a gift from the people of France. Created by sculptor Frédéric Auguste Bartholdi, it was conceived, not as a symbol of welcome, but rather of republican solidarity. Intended for the Centennial Exhibition of 1876, it was not ready until ten years later. This was just as well. It took nine years for a committee of New York socialites and businessmen to raise the necessary funds to pay for the pedestal on which Liberty would rest. In 1883 they organized an art exhibition. New York poet Emma Lazarus, moved by the plight of bedraggled Jewish refugees fleeing the Russian pogroms of 1881, submitted a sonnet. In *The New Colossus* the Statue of Liberty was "Mother of Exiles," her torch a beacon for newcomers:

> Give me your tired, your poor,
> Your huddled masses yearning to breathe free,
> The wretched refuse of your teeming shore.
> Send these, the homeless, tempest-tost to me,
> I lift my lamp beside the golden door!

However, economic fear bred ethnic intolerance. Immigrants came to be regarded, not as a source of strength, but as a drain on American resources. This was especially true of the East, where most immigrants arrived and where the social system was already hard and fast. Even the English did not escape censure. The *New York Herald Tribune* charged on November 7, 1879, that English workmen "must change their habits if they are to make good in the United States. No longer can they give the worst work for the highest wages." The complaint was to become traditional. In the 1880s and 1890s magazines such as *Harper's, Atlantic Monthly, Puck,* and *Life* contained an astonishing share of ethnic jokes, all prejudiced against newcomers. Scots retained in the New World the reputation for meanness they had first acquired in the Old. The day a funeral parlor in Camden, South Carolina, advertised "Bargains in Coffins" there were supposed to have been fourteen suicides among Scottish immigrants. A Scottish boy killed his parents rather than pay to go to the annual picnic of a local orphans' society. His friends commiserated with a Scot scalped by the Sioux because only two days earlier he had paid for a haircut. And so on.

Cartoonist Thomas Nast expressed the attitude of many Americans when he showed the Irish as ugly, brawling drunkards. Norwegians and Swedes brought from Scandinavia their mutual hostility. When a Norwegian immigrant in Minnesota reported a sleighing accident in which he had run down and killed a Swedish farmer, the local Norwegian constable brushed aside his protestations of innocence: "Aw, forget it. But you'll have to go to the county seat to collect your bounty." Contrary to statistical evidence, Italian men were not considered regular churchgoers. They attend only their baptism, wedding, and funeral. Each time they had to be carried in.

Far more insidious was the charge that Italians were deeply involved in syndicated crime. The Hennessy case of 1890 led to widespread speculation about the existence of a transplanted Mafia in the United States. The original Sicilian Mafia was a prototype of illegal protective societies based on theft and extortion throughout Italy. A feud between two rival gangs of dock racketeers in New Orleans reached its climax in the trial of Joe and Pete Provanzano for the attempted massacre of the Matranga gang. When David Hennessy, the superintendent of police, disclosed that he had evidence about the Mafia, he was assassinated by five armed men on the streets of New Orleans. In the public outcry following Hennessy's murder nineteen Sicilians were indicted for conspiracy or murder. Eight escaped and evaded prosecution. When the trial of the others ended inconclusively, a lynch mob of loyal Americans stormed the jail and seized the eleven defendants. They mowed down nine with guns and hanged the other two from lampposts. A grand jury investigating the murder of David Hennessy confirmed "the existence of the secret organization styled Mafia." The press went further and began using the term as a generic name for any crimes involving Italians.

However, no group received as much abuse as the Jews. Anti-Semitism was of course not new to America. Still, Jews were barred from voting until the mid-nineteenth century, and social ostracism continued. The exclusion of banker Joseph Seligman from the Grand Union Hotel in Saratoga, New York, in 1877 was widely publicized. Hotels, clubs, and colleges then began to turn Jews away. Some even displayed signs such as "No Jews or Dogs Admitted Here." A Jewish parvenu dressed like a dandy was the object of ridicule and contempt. He was a "Jew de Spree." The more established Jewish community responded by making scapegoats of the new immigrants from eastern Europe. A German-American Jew, W. M. Rosenblatt, wrote an article for *Galaxy* in 1872 in which he implored the public not to judge Jews by the "ignorant . . . . bigoted, and vicious Poles and Russians arriving on the scene."

Chinese immigrants to California were also subject to a barrage of abuse. Three fifths of them had come from one small area, the district of Taishan in the province of Guangdong, a province that had ninety-eight districts. Thus, in the words of ethnic historian Thomas Sowell, they were "highly cohesive in culture, dialect and family network." This cohesiveness sustained them in American society against seemingly impossible odds. They developed their own welfare institutions. Through the Chinese Benevolent Association, or "Six Companies," they took care of the poor and imposed order and honor in Chinatown. But the secrecy of the Six Companies was held against them. So was the fact that the Chinese were willing to take menial jobs. They awakened white fears of a new slavery in a nation that had just fought a war to remove the old.

To labor they were "coolies," a subversive and servile class that threatened the existence of white workers. In 1875 the Union Pacific imported 125 Chinese laborers to Rock Springs, Wyoming, to break a miners' strike. Labor determined to fight back. In 1877 Dennis Kearney, a naturalized Irish immigrant, used the new Workingmen's party as a pulpit to denounce them. His oratory resulted in hostile demonstrations in San Franscisco, mob violence, and general public demand for an exclusion law. Rather than face industrial and agricultural anarchy from hostile artisans and laborers, conservatives were ready to give in to radical demands. The new state constitution of 1879 was permeated with racial intolerance. Article 19 gave the state legislature power to regulate immigration of paupers, criminals, diseased persons, and aliens. Corporations could not engage Mongolians, nor could they be employed on any public works. Coolie contracts were declared void. A state law of 1849 prohibiting Indians and blacks from testifying against whites was construed to bar Chinese testimony as well. Occupational licensing laws and special taxes were also used against them. Thus, Chinese immigrants could no longer work in the very businesses they had created. Two occupations were left to them, the laundry and the restaurant.

President Rutherford B. Hayes could hardly repudiate the Burlingame Treaty of 1868 that granted the Chinese the right to immigrate. However, party politics compelled him to persuade

China to accept a different form of limitation. In 1880 China gave the United States the right "to regulate, limit or suspend," though not to prohibit, the immigration of laborers. There followed the Chinese Exclusion Act of May, 1882, which suspended Chinese immigration for ten years. It also forbade the naturalization of Chinese residents and imposed further restrictions on them. Many returned to China. In 1892 the Chinese Exclusion Act was renewed for another ten years, and in 1902 it was extended indefinitely. The Chinese–American population declined from about 100,000 in 1890 to 60,000 in 1920. Traditional Chinese culture was oriented toward family life. But in America Chinese men outnumbered women by a ratio of 20 to 1. It was no wonder that Chinatowns acquired the problems of prostitution, drug abuse, and high suicide rates.

Chinese exclusion set a precedent. Congress eventually responded to the clamor for reform by passing an act in August 1882 that imposed a head tax of 50 cents on every foreigner arriving by sea and that excluded convicts and lunatics.

Immigration was now beginning to divide American society. A great gulf was opening between a predominantly native plutocracy and a predominantly foreign working class. The United States was becoming two nations separated by language and religion, residence and occupation alike. Not only was the new tide of immigration depressing wages, but also the closing of the frontier and settlement of available land in the West had sealed off the traditional escape route for discontented easterners. Thus, Americans began to lose confidence in the process of assimilation. The outcome was nativism, what John Higham calls "a defensive type of nationalism." Nativist agitation was the work of three groups: unions that regarded unskilled immigrants as a threat to organized labor, social reformers who believed the influx of immigrants exacerbated the problems of the cities, and Protestant conservatives who dreaded the supposed threat to Nordic supremacy.

Skilled workers had most to fear from the importation of contract labor. After skilled Belgian and British glassworkers were brought under contract to work for lower wages in Baltimore and in Kent, Ohio, the two unions of American glassworkers amalgamated. The new union, Local Assembly 300, was pledged from its inception in February 1882 to oppose contract labor. Union leader James Campbell pressed for federal legislation on this point. Congressman Martin Foran of Ohio, himself a former president of the Cooper's International Union, had already introduced a bill against contract labor in the House in January 1884. In 1885 the bill was revived by Senator Blair of New Hampshire, and it passed the Senate on February 18 by a vote of 50 to 9. The new ban on contract labor did not extend to skilled workers needed for new industries nor to actors and singers, lecturers and domestics.

The acts of 1882 and 1885 thus contradicted' one another. The first obliged immigrants to show that they were not likely to become public charges. The second excluded them if they had taken precautions by obtaining work in advance. The craft unions were disappointed. They had wanted a bill to exclude skilled contract labor on economic grounds. Congress had passed an act against unskilled labor on racist grounds. The comparatively new American industries such as tin, silk, hosiery, and lace received skilled immigrants on contract. In a test case, the *United States* v. *Gay* (1897), the Supreme Court upheld the principle that skilled labor could be imported on contract.

The most widespread hostility was directed at Roman Catholics or, more precisely, at their church and its increasing strength. In 1890 Catholics claimed that 600,000 children were enrolled in their schools. They renewed demands for a share of public school funds, which enraged staunch Protestants. A bizarre pun managed to attack the Church of Rome and two ethnic groups at once. It was said that Italians had exchanged the old Roman religion of Jupiter for the new Roman Catholicism of Jew-Peter and were no better for the swop. Protestant extremists joined secret societies pledged to defend the school system and to oppose Catholic influence in politics. The most powerful was the American Protective Association, founded in Clinton, Iowa, in 1887 by a lawyer, Henry F. Bowers. Bowers, whose family name had been anglicized from its original Bauer, was a leading Freemason who abhorred Catholicism. The APA spread first through the Upper Mississippi Valley and from there through the entire Midwest. But, although the APA claimed a total of 2.5 million members, it declined after 1894. It was faction-ridden and unequal to the task of persuading government to restrict immigration.

The distinction between old and new immigrants was first put forward by New England academics who resented the intrusion of outsiders in politics. They provided the nativist movement with plenty of social cachet but with very little intellectual respectability. Social scientist Richard Mayo Smith doubted the economic value of immigration. The whole process of assimilation, he believed, was being jeopardized by the sheer size and changing composition of the new immigration. "It is scarcely probable that by taking the dregs of Europe," he wrote in 1890, "we shall produce a people of high social intelligence and morality." In 1894 a group of Bostonians, Charles Warren, Robert DeCourcy Ward, and Prescott F. Hall, founded the Immigration Restriction League. Bostonians were notorious for their egocentricity and ignorance. When introduced to visitors from Iowa and Idaho, the Beacon Hill set thought these names were simply funny ways of saying Ohio. They did not believe that travel broadened the mind. "Travel?" they asked when the suggestion was put to them. "Why should I? I live here." A maiden aunt from Boston visiting relatives nearby noted a slab of granite beside the railway track by their home. It read, "I–m [mile] from Boston." She thought it was a tombstone that declared, "I'm from Boston," and said to herself, "how very simple and yet how sufficient." Boston was thus a natural center for a nativist movement.

In 1896, for the first time, the volume of new immigration exceeded that of the old. That year the crucial victory of white over black was won in the notorious decision of *Plessy* v. *Ferguson*: "separate but equal" (q.v.). Racists transferred this educational principle to their fight against new immigrants. Rather than restrict immigration on an openly racist basis, the IRL preferred the more devious device of a literacy test as a means of excluding undesirable southern and eastern Europeans. Senator Henry Cabot Lodge of Massachusetts sponsored a bill that would have excluded any adult immigrant unable to read forty words in any language. Of course, as was pointed out at the time, a literacy test examined not natural intelligence but social opportunity. but it was not a sure means of separating the northwestern sheep from the south-eastern goats. For example, Armenian immigrants surpassed all others in this respect. They had a literacy rate of 76 percent. The bill passed Congress, but President Cleveland vetoed it as unworthy of the United States.

It was precisely the fusion of old and new cultures that gave the politics and philosophy, the literature and art of the United States their distinctive character and universal appeal. Some immigrants had known this all along. In the fall of 1892 Czech composer Anton Dvořák became director of the National Conservatory of Music in New York. He was expected to stimulate the development of an original American music that would express the landscape, folklore, and ideals of the New World. He tried to show Americans the possibilities of their own folk music and told the *New York Herald* of May 21, 1893, how Indian melodies and black spirituals should be the foundation of music in the United States. He integrated them into his new symphony, *From the New World*, given its premiere at Carnegie Hall on December 15, 1893. Yet Dvořák's recollections of Bohemia were also an important source of inspiration; his musical personality remained Slavic. For what was new about the New World if not its people and their culture?

CHAPTER FOUR

TALL STORIES AND
TALES OF TWO CITIES

WHETHER CELEBRATED by artists as some sort of precious flower or cursed by social critics as a kind of cancer, the American city stood at the center of civilization in the Gilded Age. It was the glass of fashion and the mold of form. As sociologist Philip Slater explained a century later, "'Civilized' means, literally, 'citified', and the state of the city is an accurate index of the condition of the culture as a whole." In the late nineteenth century, American cities were unsurpassed for the scope of their activities, the scale of their skyscrapers, and their general spectacle and sound. Their rate of growth was astonishing. Whereas in 1860 only 1 American in 6 lived in a community of at least 8,000 people, by 1900, 1 in 3 did so. Between 1860 and 1900 the urban population rose four times, whereas the rural population only doubled. For every town dweller who went to live on the farm, there were twenty countryfolk who moved to the city.

The new urban civilization was not spread evenly among the states. In the South, the Mountain states, and the plains cities were few and far between. The huge developing cities flourished with industry mainly in the Northeast, by the Great Lakes, and along the Pacific coast.

During the Gilded Age the railroad revolution in transportation and the telegraph revolution in communication both served to

The most striking characteristic of the new American metropolis at the close of the nineteenth century was its profusion of soaring, sepia-colored skyscrapers, giant buildings made possible by new advances in the technologies of construction and communications. This photograph of Randolph Street east from LaSalle Street, Chicago, was taken in 1900 by the Detroit Publishing Company. (Library of Congress).

bring widely distant cities into the same commercial basin. Breweries, refineries, steel mills, and meatpacking plants, previously dispersed, were brought round the major rail terminals. Railroads attracted transcontinental trade to Chicago and St. Louis in the Midwest, and to Denver, Portland, Seattle, and Los Angeles in the Far West. Some cities manufactured regional farm products and prospered in the process: Minneapolis made flour from wheat; Milwaukee made beer from cereals; and Memphis made oil from cotton seed. They attained metropolitan status because of their manufacturing services. Others developed because they used local labor to make or sell goods not produced nearby. This was the job of mill towns in the Northeast and the Midwest. While Albany made shirts, Troy, nearby, made collars. New Bedford and Fall River, Massachusetts, produced cotton textiles. Elizabeth, New Jersey, made electrical machinery, and Dayton made machine tools and cash registers. Bridgeport, Connecticut, combined the worlds of metal and cloth by producing brass, corsets, and machine tools. Such towns were able to benefit from mechanical and industrial technology because it was based on the traditional processes of iron and steam on which they themselves were built.

Cities not only provided markets for agriculture and labor for industry but also stimulated economic growth in their own right. Just as postwar railroad expansion (q.v.) was coming to an end, developing cities provided necessary, new opportunities for industry with their insatiable needs for private housing and public buildings, street construction and lighting, transportation and other services. As architectural historian Richard Guy Wilson puts it: "Upward and outward moved the city. New or vastly enlarged communities came into being: the ghetto for the immigrant, the suburb for the middle and upper classes, and the resort or spa for those who could afford to escape." Thus, city dwellers were diverse in ethnic origins, education, occupation, and style and standard of living.

Given the amazing changes taking place in the United States during the Gilded Age, it is not surprising that after the Civil War the American city was transformed from big city to industrial metropolis by the turn of the century. The paradigm of each was New York circa 1870 and Chicago circa 1890. Other cities came to resemble them in their particular heyday more than they did their former selves. These two cities also provide an architectural prototype and a social archetype of each period: in New York in 1870, the dumbbell tenement and the city boss, William Marcy Tweed; in Chicago in 1890, the skyscraper and the urban reformer, Jane Addams.

THE BIG CITY AND THE INDUSTRIAL METROPOLIS

In 1870 New York City comprised Manhattan and the small islands in the East River. Its population was 942,292. Brooklyn was a separate town. Its population of 419,921 made it the third largest in the country. Until the Brooklyn Bridge was opened in 1883 Brooklyn (and Long Island) were linked to Manhattan only by ferry. In 1868, nine boats carried more than 48 million passengers across the East River. In turn, Manhattan was also linked to the mainland by ferry and by the lines of one railroad, the New York Central.

In 1870 big cities might have looked a muddle to casual visitors. But they all had a clearly defined internal structure obvious to the discerning eye. Because intracity transport was expensive, businesses with a large volume of goods huddled by the shipping wharves or railroad stations. Commerce was conducted in St. Louis by the banks of the Mississippi, in Philadelphia by the Delaware, and in New York by the East and Hudson rivers. Service areas and housing radiated outward from these centers in a large fan. Those who wanted the convenience of a central address paid dearly to live on Beacon Hill in Boston, Nob Hill in San Francisco, Chestnut Street in Philadelphia, and Washington Square in New York, from which they set the standards of fashion. Between fashionable blocks and shantytown slums were mixed commercial, industrial, and residential neighborhoods offering a genuine association of classes and ethnic groups.

In 1867 the *Evening Post* described New York as the "most inconveniently arranged commercial city in the world." The major indictment was the inadequacy and inconvenience of public transportation. A wit once defined martyrdom as a journey through New York on an omnibus or streetcar. Twelve separate companies ran twenty-one routes through New York at average speeds of four to six miles an hour. Like railroads across the country, they clung to profitable routes and ignored certain districts, which were left isolated.

Because public transportation was so limited, city limits were restricted to manageable walking distances. Eighty-five percent of the population lived within two miles of the city center, Union Square at Fourteenth Street. The major downtown institutions were places for businessmen to meet and make transactions, such as the Stock Exchange and Merchants' Exchange. The tallest buildings were still churches with spires. Even a great daily newspaper like the *New York Tribune* could contain office and plant in one modest five-story building. City factories were two-story buildings, something like backyard barns. City lots for commercial and domestic building were rectangular plots of 25 by 100 feet. Such was the value of land and the pressure for accommodation that space was at a premium. Architects had a solution for compressing the maximum number of people into the minimum amount of space, the dumbbell tenement.

In December 1878 Henry C. Meyer, proprietor of the *Sanitary Engineer*, offered prizes of $500 in a competition for the best tenement designs. The first prize was awarded to James E. Ware for his double-decker dumbbell tenement, so called because the middle part of the ground plan tapered in. The idea was to allow light and air to the central portions of the building without reducing the width of front and back. The dumbbell tenement usually had four apartments to each of its six or seven floors, two on either side of the separating corridor. Only one of the three or four rooms received light and air from the street at the front or from the yard at the back. The air shaft separating the tenements at the sides was no more than 5 feet wide along its 50- or 60-foot length.

Although Ware's design became the prototype for tenement buildings until the end of the century, it was widely criticized. The *New York Times* in its editorial of March 16, 1879, took account of the restrictions placed on the competing architects by considerations of size and cost but condemned the whole experiment. The most common criticism was of *lack* of light and air and of inadequate sanitary facilities.

City streets also had their share of problems. They were littered with merchants' wares; peddlers' carts blocked access to roads and houses. Street and market were one and the same. Neither was cleaned except by private contract. In the area south of Fourteenth Street ancient sewers got clogged with accumulated filth; sometimes they burst open, and their contents rose to suffuse the streets with refuse and slime. Their narrow pipes could not even contain rainwater, and after a shower a major avenue like Broadway was awash with mud.

Lower Manhattan was notorious for crime. The common joke was that some of the neighborhoods were so rough that if you saw a dog with a tail it was a visitor from out of town. Maintenance of law and order was the task of the city police. In 1844 the state legislature had created a professional city police force of 800 men. It was the first organized police force in the United States. The chief of police was appointed by the mayor, the others by ward councilmen. Thus, the police force was subject to political control.

The common complaint was that it was the best police force money could buy. An investigation in 1894 disclosed that jobs were sold to the highest bidder and those who bought their way into the force made money out of it by bribery and the blackmail of prostitutes and of gambling and liquor interests. There were at least 12,000 prostitutes working in New York in the late 1860s. During an investigation of 1875 one police captain, Alexander ("Clubber") Williams, was asked why he did not close down the brothels in his precinct. He answered, "Because they were kind of fashionable at the time." In 1868, 5,423 crimes were reported but never came to court. The same year 10,000 indictments were dropped. The captains' unofficial slogan was "Hear, see, and say nothin'. Eat, drink, and pay nothin'."

In time, the industrial metropolis superseded the big city as the typical American city of the Gilded Age. Urban historian Sam Bass Warner, Jr., describes the industrial metropolis as "the city of the mechanized factory, the business corporation, the downtown office, and the segregated neighborhood." The special industrial structure of New York, based as it was on small shops and subject to constant social upheaval caused by the continuous influx of immigrants, precluded the kind of industrial concentration that gave rise to the industrial metropolis. It was Chicago rather than New York that was the model of this new form of city in 1890. It had then a population of 1,099,850 people.

Chicago, like New York and other major cities, owed its importance to its situation. After the completion of the Illinois and Michigan Canal in 1848 and of ten trunk-line railroads by 1856 Chicago was ready for its role as a major regional center. It rose to service the Midwest when railroad construction made western expansion profitable as well as possible. It developed first as a market for livestock and grain; an industrial base for railroad and town, home and farm; and a bank for all these. Its future destiny as a metropolis was assured by its part in the most rapidly rising sectors of the national economy—mechanized manufacturing, transportation, and commerce.

Then the city encountered a major disaster. The Chicago fire of October 8, 1871, swept across 1,688 acres in the city center and consumed buildings valued at 192 million dollars. Most buildings were made of wood and burned easily. The heat was such that in those few structures that incorporated metal beams the iron and steel became a molten river spreading the fire ever farther. However, Chicago was too important commercially for business and industry to allow this disaster to impede, let alone halt, the city's inevitable growth. Within eighteen months the city had risen like a phoenix from the ashes.

The rapid growth of all its component parts—factories, machine shops, railroad yards, warehouses, offices, stores, and banks—had, by 1890, produced a clearly discernible and closely defined spatial structure that was entirely new. This was the radial city with a single center. It was based on the so-called sector-and-ring pattern, in which a ground plan of the city resembled a wagon wheel. The pivot of this wheel was the meeting of land and lake traffic at the mouth of the Chicago River. The first spokes of the wheel were the north and south tributaries of the river. In between were the first sectors. The chief difference between the traditional big city and the new industrial metropolis was this: no longer did any one neighborhood accommodate industry, commerce, and the homes of all classes as it had in New York about 1870; industrial, commercial, and residential land was segregated. Radiating outward from the center, specific economic activities were concentrated in central wedges, narrow slices of commercial and industrial property—the spokes of the wheel.

Between these commercial and industrial corridors lay unoccupied land. Into its empty tracts came the new population. It settled in three segregated rings. The truly poor lived in an inner ring of shanties and old apartments. The working class inhabited a second ring of cottages, tenements, and decaying houses. The middle class dwelt in an outer ring of new and better apartments and houses. Thus, an inner core of poverty was surrounded by outer rings of rising affluence. In addition, the truly rich occupied yet another corridor, the attractive and affluent north shore of Lake Michigan and Michigan Avenue. Its fashionable blocks of shops and hotels, mansions and apartments cut across all the other city sectors.

Railroads from the South and the West attracted new industries. Most successful were the Stock Yards and meatpacking plants to the south at the junction of Thirty-ninth and Halsted streets. First opened in 1865, they were developed to comprise 100 acres of cattle pens and 275 of slaughterhouses and packinghouses. This mammoth enterprise depended on a ready supply of cattle and refrigerator cars and relied on regular railroad services for its survival. There followed steel mills and plants making electrical machinery and an entire industrial complex by the Calumet River. These were, in effect, industrial satellites, mill towns within a metropolis, linked to the core city by centripetal rail lines and to one another by new centrifugal belt lines.

The middle class, inspired by Central Park in New York (designed by Frederick Law Olmsted in 1857) and by Georges Haussmann's boulevards in Paris, aspired to an exclusive life-style. They had parks and avenues laid in imitation. In doing so they helped to determine the rings of class settlement. By 1894 the mold was set.

The street railway carried millions of people in and out of the city center to work, shop, and play. The cult of conspicuous consumption in city center stores was a focal point in the lives of women of all classes. Thus, as Warner suggests, downtown Chicago, the Loop, was "the place of work for tens of thousands, a market for hundreds of thousands, a theater for thousands more." Yet the population remained fragmented along economic lines. In the residential districts they were further divided by race, religion, and ethnicity. Only at work, whether mill or sweatshop, store or clerical pool, did they have a common identity.

The symbol of this new urban civilization was the skyscraper, a tall structure built of metal as well as stone that consumed less ground space and yet accommodated more people on its several floors than the largest stone buildings of the mid-nineteenth century. In New York, St. Louis, and Chicago progressive architects, enthusiastic about the invention of a safe passenger elevator, began experimenting with iron-and-steel frame construction beyond ten stories. They were devising skyscrapers in New York and Chicago by the end of the 1870s that would come to depend on telephone, typewriter, and electric light.

Taking advantage of the elevator, architect Richard Morris Hunt designed the ten-story New York Tribune Building in 1874. Such height, however, required massive walls that covered more ground area than smaller, more conventional buildings. It was only after 1884 when William LeBaron Jenney experimented with a steel skeleton for the construction of the Home Insurance Building in Chicago that structures of more than ten stories became practical for conventional commercial use.

The Home Life Building had an internal skeleton of wrought- and cast-iron for the first six stories and Bessemer steel beams for the next four. Although this building was accredited the first skyscraper, it did not look like one. Jenney disguised the frame to make it look like a conventional building. However, two of his junior staff, William Holabird and Martin Roche, went on to design the Tacoma Building in 1886—the first skyscraper that looked the part. It stood twelve stories high, and there was no attempt to make the light brick and terra-cotta walls seem anything more than a mere facade or sheath for the metal frame behind. They were without ornament and carried an almost continuous range of bay windows. Here was the forerunner of the curtain wall in American city architecture. The honeycomb interior spread the maximum possible amount of light and air.

More than anyone else, Chicago architect Louis Sullivan gave form and substance to the modern skyscraper. "It must be every inch a proud and soaring thing, rising in sheer exultation that from bottom to top it is a unit without a single dissenting line," he said. His early inspiration came from various suspension bridges. His partnership with engineer Dankmar Adler was a perfect complement of mind and method. The most famous of their early commissions was the Auditorium Building (1886–89), which comprised an opera house, a hotel, and offices designed in Romanesque style within a structure at first no higher than ten stories and no wider than half a block.

Sullivan exploited steel-frame construction to the fullest. With his Wainright Building (1891) in St. Louis he set the style of American skyscrapers for half a century. The structure was entirely of steel encased in fireproof tiles and carried the walls on shelves at each of its ten stories. What was remarkable was Sullivan's determination to make no concessions to fashion by minimizing its height. Instead of disguising the long upward flow of the building with some kind of ornate embellishments around the windows, he broke with convention and emphasized its height and essential lines. His governing principle was that the form of a building should demonstrate its function. The basic tenet of the Chicago school of architecture was that a building should express a total cultural purpose. Besides Sullivan the other exponents were John Wellborn Root, Daniel Burnham, Dankmar Adler, and Frank Lloyd Wright. Skyscrapers suggested American obsession with individual achievement. The man-made vertical canyons they made of city streets in New York, Chicago, and elsewhere complemented the natural horizontal canyons of the American West. As they reached ever higher into the heavens skyscrapers separated even further the nouveaux riches above from the huddled masses below.

SOCIAL PROBLEMS

The most distinctive feature of American cities in the Gilded Age was their cultural composition of widely different ethnic groups. In 1890 the number of immigrant adults exceeded the number of

In *How the Other Half Lives* (1890) Danish immigrant reporter Jacob Riis exposed the stark horrors of poverty in the Lower East Side of New York with a series of telling photographs such as this one of the courtyard of 24 Baxter Street. (Library of Congress).

native adults in eighteen of the twenty cities with a population of more than 100,000. In two cities, New York and San Francisco, as much as 42.2 percent of the population were first-generation immigrants. Danish immigrant and reporter Jacob Riis provides a most picturesque analysis of the geographic distribution of immigrant ghettos in New York about 1890:

A map of the city, colored to designate nationalities, would show more stripes than the skin of a zebra, and more colors than any rainbow. The city on such a map would fall into two great halves, green for the Irish prevailing in the West Side tenement districts, and blue for the Germans on the East Side. But intermingled with these ground colors would be an odd variety of tints that would give the whole the appearance of an extraordinary crazy-quilt.

Almost as obvious as the cultural nature of cities was their social character. They were overcrowded. In 1890, 1 million people, two thirds of the population, were packed like sardines in 32,000 dumbbell tenement buildings in New York. Conditions were particularly bad in the Lower East Side, that section of Manhattan east of Third Avenue and south of Fourteenth Street. In blocks like Poverty Gap, Misery Row, Penitentiary Row, and Murderers' Alley the rooms were pokey and airless, the halls dark and dank, the lavatories primitive. Charles Loring Brace in *The Dangerous Classes of New York* (1872) reports the comments of a visitor from the Children's Aid Society:

In a dark cellar filled with smoke, there sleep, all in one room, with no kind of partition dividing them, two men with their wives, a girl of thirteen or fourteen, two men and a large boy of about seventeen years of age, a mother with two more boys, one about ten years old and one large boy of fifteen; another women with two boys, nine and eleven years of age—in all, fourteen persons.

When Jacob Riis became a police reporter for the *New York Tribune* in 1877 he learned all about the Lower East Side from the Mulberry Street precinct at the Bend, "the foul core of New York's slums." Riis's exposure of slum conditions pointed to the venality of unscrupulous landlords. It led to the appointment of the tenement house commission, which, at the insistence of mem-

Hell was the brutal title Jacob Riis gave to his flashlight photograph of a basement dive in the Lower East Side in 1896. (Library of Congress).

bers Felix Adler and Alfred T. White, recommended the abolition of rear tenements and the opening of playgrounds. When Riis published the first of his series of books about the tenements, *How the Other Half Lives* in 1890, he offered various suggestions for easing the poverty and degradation of slum dwellers. He had begun to document his study with photographs at a time when news photography was in its infancy. Here was irrefutable proof of the plight of the poor—factual, graphic, stark. Riis's pictures were among the first to demonstrate the power of photography in journalism. Unfortunately the half-tone technique of photo reproduction was still imperfect. Thus the first edition of the book carried only line sketches of thirty-eight of his original pictures. The drawings minimized the squalor of the Lower East Side and softened the pain of his subjects. Nevertheless, when Riis referred to the "sea of a mighty population, held in galling fetters" heaving "uneasily in the tenements," the middle class took it as a portent of incipient class war. One he influenced was a young police commissioner, Theodore Roosevelt, who abolished the police lodging houses which Riis had exposed as breeders of vice and crime. Moreover, in 1901 New York passed a law whereby all tenement buildings had to have windows at least twelve feet away from the building opposite, inside staircases, and running water and toilets in each apartment.

The problem, however, was not confined to New York. Some parts of Chicago had three times as many people as the most crowded parts of Tokyo and Calcutta. In one Polish ghetto there was an average of 340 people to every acre in 1901. In one sector of only three blocks there lived 7,300 children. This Polish district was described as "nothing more than an infested wall-to-wall carpet of rotted wood and crumbling concrete." Whole neighborhoods were congested, filthy, and foul. Offal and manure littered the street along with trash and garbage. It was hardly surprising that, in the large cities, consumption and pneumonia, bronchitis and diarrhea were endemic. Immigrant communities were prone to outbreaks of cholera, typhus, and typhoid. Indeed, Pittsburgh had the highest mortality rate for typhoid in the world, 1.30 per 1,000.

The disposal of human sewage and industrial waste was a most pressing problem. The easy solution was to use local rivers and bays, and despite the hazard to health, this was where garbage, sewage, and waste were commonly deposited. The census of 1880 reported how the soil of New Orleans was saturated "very largely with the oozings of foul privy vaults." Baltimore had very porous soil; its 80,000 cesspools were a menace to wells for drinking water. A large proportion of the population of Philadelphia drank water from the Delaware River, into which 13 million gallons of sewage were emptied every day.

In 1866 New York established the metropolitan board of health, which took prompt action against a cholera epidemic, inspiring other cities to strengthen their boards and to staff them with doctors rather than politicians. The duties of these boards included inspecting sanitation facilities, meat and milk, and recording births and deaths.

The risk of fire was as great as the risk of fever. Successive fires in the 1870s took enormous tolls of life and property in New York, Boston, and Pittsburgh, as well as Chicago. After the Chicago fire sixty-four insurance companies could not meet the claims for damages and went bankrupt. Popular jokes of the period are full of insinuations about the incendiary motives of men who profited from fire insurance. It was commonly said that the cause of a fire was the insurance. The favorite poet of a beneficiary of arson was Burns. A fortune teller at Coney Island was called a fake when she told a client he would suffer a *loss* by fire. A collector who asked a passerby to contribute something to the disabled firemen's fund was advised, "With pleasure. But how are you going to disable them?" The most popular tableau at the Burnupsky Social Club was "Nero Fiddling While Rome Burns."

After a serious fire in Portland, Maine, in 1866 the New York City board of fire underwriters led the movement to organize the national board of fire underwriters. Its policy of reviewing local regulations, inspecting local fire-fighting equipment, and examining fire hazards before determining appropriate rates of insurance provided a powerful incentive for local authorities to insist on improved standards from business and industry. City councils began to insist that construction companies use masonry or brickwork instead of wood for new buildings.

By 1876 most large cities had adopted the Cincinnati plan of a municipal fire department in preference to the discredited volunteer system of private companies each competing for business and quarreling openly with their rivals—sometimes while fires were actually raging. Moreover, the new steam fire engines with their automatic water pumpers, such as those produced by the Silsby Manufacturing Company of Seneca Falls, New York, were more efficient than the traditional manual pumper. The steam engine never tired while the fuel held out. It could also throw a longer stream of water: Clapp and Jones of Hudson, New York, claimed that one of their engines could pump a horizontal stream a distance of 215 feet. Such technological advances allowed firemen to keep a safer distance from a blaze and to fight fires in ever taller buildings.

In the 1870s cities began to provide secondary education for the masses for the first time. By 1891 the typical elementary school year in cities lasted between 180 and 200 days compared with anything from 70 to 150 days in the countryside. Progressive educators, however, realized that it was not enough to teach children the three Rs. Edward A. Sheldon in Oswego, William T. Harris in St. Louis, and Francis W. Parker in Chicago were convinced that immigrant children needed courses in elementary science, handicrafts, and mechanics as well and devised new techniques of object teaching. Boston and St. Louis were the first cities to open kindergartens.

THE TWEED RING

The sheer momentum of economic and industrial, social and political change generated municipal problems of housing and welfare, sanitation and health, employment, transportation, and law enforcement that overwhelmed obsolete city governments and set the stage for the rise of the boss and the city machine. As Alexander B. Callow explains in *The City Boss in America* (1976), "The boss exploited the inability of government to supply the demands of the emerging city. He created a mechanism—the machine—for coping with the complex political, economic, and social adaptations entailed in the transformation of American society."

The city machine was an alternative to formal government. It responded to the needs of three groups. To immigrants and the urban poor it offered patronage and a chance of economic improvement and social opportunity. To legitimate business it offered contracts for industry, construction, and commerce. To illegitimate business, syndicated crime, and commercial vice, it offered profitable order instead of the unlicensed chaos of internecine competition. Despite their corruption and profligacy, city bosses and their organizations performed crucial social and economic functions. The secret of the bosses' success was their sure personal touch. Martin Lomansey, a ward leader in Boston, told

reformer Lincoln Steffens, "There's got to be in every ward some-
body that any bloke can come to—no matter what he's done—
and get help. Help, you understand; none of your law and justice,
but help." Patronage included favor as well as labor—such things
as welfare and relief, legal aid and bail. Ward bosses were pivotal
figures in local clubs and might well own a saloon. A story of the
period tells how a wit hired a newsboy to run into a council meeting crying, "Mister, your liquor store is on fire!" All the aldermen
jumped to their feet and rushed out of the door in disorder.

The neighborhood, with its wards, districts, and precincts, provided the city boss with political power. Control of municipal
services provided him with sources of patronage and profit. The
stakes soared as the cities grew.

The model of the city machine in the Gilded Age was the Tweed
Ring. Between 1866 and 1871 it dominated politics in the city and
state of New York. Although later rings were more ruthless and
rapacious, the Tweed Ring retained the reputation of being the
most notorious and audacious of them all. It comprised only four
men—Chamberlain Peter Barr Sweeny; City Controller Richard
Connolly; Mayor Abraham Oakey Hall; and the ringleader, William Marcy Tweed. Not for nothing were they known, respectively, as "the Brains," "Slippery Dick," "the Elegant," and "the
Boss."

William Marcy Tweed came from a middle-class, Protestant
family of Scots-Americans. In 1851, at the age of twenty-eight,
he was elected alderman for the Seventh Ward. The post carried
considerable responsibilities in the matter of making appointments
and granting franchises; and along with other corrupt alderman,
known as the Forty Thieves, he used his largess to build up a
personal following. He was a jovial, bulky man whose boisterous
manner made him popular in barrooms and back streets across the
length and breadth of the city. Tweed also had boundless energy
and enterprise, and his executive ability was extraordinary.

In 1857 Tweed became a member of the board of supervisors,
hitherto a minor office, but transformed that year by the state
legislature which made the board into a bipartisan council of
twelve with increased powers. He remained in office until 1870
and used his authority to form a supervisors' ring, a profitable

operation specializing in frauds at elections, raising money, and spending it on city improvements.

As controller, Richard Connolly raised revenue from taxes and rents and the sale of stocks and bonds. He spent some of it legitimately but siphoned much more into the coffers of the ring. The money was embezzled by means of fraudulent contracts, padded payrolls, excessive rents, and fictitious accounts. In turn, Connolly was served well by the county auditor, former convict James Watson, who "cooked" the books and covered the tracks. The ring's principal accomplices were the governor, John Hoffman, and three corrupt judges, John McCunn, George Barnard, and Albert Cardozo. Cardozo, a Portuguese-American Jew, had a deserved reputation as an oily master of intrigue. It was said he had the eyes of a serpent and the face of a corpse. The judges' task was to find sophisticated arguments to excuse criminal acts. Truly it was better to know the judge than to know the law.

In the Tweed years covert crime (theft, burglary, and confidence tricks) increased greatly while crimes of violence did not. As contemporary observer Edward Crapsey explains in *The Nether Side of New York* (1872), "The thugs of the city found employment in politics equally congenial and more remunerative." Sometimes Tweed's men went too far and were arrested. They were rescued from the toils of the law by crooked lawyers named, after the city prison, or "Tombs," "Tombs Shysters" or "Tombs Harpies." Most prominent was the firm of Howe and Hummel. William Howe's prose was as purple as his clothes. He once convinced a jury that defendant Ella Nelson had accidentally pressed the trigger not once but half a dozen times.

At no time did the Tweed Ring command a true majority of voters. Its power base was control of the New York quadrilateral—City Hall, the Hall of Justice, the State Capitol at Albany, and Tammany Hall, headquarters of the Democratic party. The original Tammany Society had been founded as a charitable organization by Irish-American William Mooney in 1789 and took its name from an Indian chief, Tammanend. Governed by thirteen senior executives or sachems, it was heterogeneous in character but came to be dominated by an Irish oligarchy after the Civil War. The first Tammany dynasty was the Tweed Ring. Tweed consolidated the Hall's hold on New York politics. Through various forms of patronage, he claimed that at least 12,000 electors in the twenty-one wards were obligated to him. These spoilsmen were known as the Shiny Hat Brigade. In 1868 he had the number of qualified voters increased when his pliant justices naturalized about 60,000 recent immigrants, administering the oath to groups of 144, or one gross, at a time.

The techniques used to cheat at the polls were numerous. They included padding the registration lists with phoney names and addresses. In Philadelphia the list of voters once included a boy of four and his dog. One politician there boasted that the men who had first signed the Declaration of Independence back in 1776 still voted in Philadelphia. Machines employed gangs of men whose motto was "vote early and often," repeaters to vote for the fraudulent names several times over. In several precincts there were more votes cast than there were residents. One repeater who claimed to be an Episcopal bishop, William Croswell Doane, had an argument at the polls. "Come off," said the official. "You're not Bishop Doane," "The hell I ain't, you bastard!" was the retort.

It is hardly surprising that, instead of appreciating the creative potential of New York City, the state legislature at Albany, dominated by rural interests, preferred to picture it as a cesspool of vice and crime, fit only for the feeble, the foreign, and the fradulent. The city's undoubted problems were treated as proof of its ills rather than as symptoms of a disease that could be cured. In popular parlance, New York was "an underground rapid transit railroad to hell." The reputation of other large cities was just as bad. Pittsburgh was "hell with the lid off" and Philadelphia was "the city of brotherly loot."

In 1868 Tweed was at the height of his power. Elected state senator from the Fourth District, he also held the following public offices: school commissioner, deputy street commissioner, president of the board of supervisors, chairman of the Democratic central committee of New York County, and grand sachem of Tammany Hall. He was also a director of Jay Gould and Jim Fisk's bank, the Tenth National, and of their railroad, the New York Central. In addition, he was president of the Guardian Savings Bank and was a director of the Harlem Gas Light Company,

The Monadnock block, West Jackson Boulevard, Chicago by Burnham and Root (1891), an early skyscraper with a basement and seventeen stories conceived by John Wellborn Root along the spare, tapering lines of an Egyptian pylon to please the client, Owen F. Aldis, who persuaded him to "throw the thing up without a single ornament." (Photographed by Cervin Robinson for the Historic American Buildings Survey in August, 1963. Library of Congress).

the Brooklyn Bridge Company, and the Third Avenue Railway Company. Moreover, he was the third largest owner of real estate in New York and occupied a splendid mansion on Fifth Avenue at Forty-third Street. He was rarely with his family, however, preferring the company of a charmed circle of cronies at the Americus Club where they wore tigers' heads whose eyes were set with rubies.

Because he wanted to be well liked Tweed also gave freely to charities and churches, hospitals and schools. Only the Tweed Ring, it seemed, cared for the needs of the underprivileged. In the seventeen years between 1852 and 1869, the state distributed $2 million to private charities. But in the three years from 1869 to 1871, when the Tweed Ring was at the height of its power; it used its influence with the state legislature to increase the appropriations to $2.22 million. There was method in this magnaminity. State aid to hospitals, orphanages, and Catholic parochial schools ensured support from immigrants and the poor at the polls. It was especially galling to reformers to see Tweed gain in public esteem from charity that was paltry compared with the plunder he kept for himself. Moreover, he did nothing to ameliorate the conditions that contributed to disease, poverty, and crime.

The most notorious single act of the Tweed Ring was its embezzlement of public funds appropriated fraudulently in the first instance for a new city courthouse. The design by architect John Kellum was completed in 1858, but not until Tweed became president of the board of supervisors in 1862 did the work of construction commence in earnest. Arguing that the original appropriation of $250,000 was unworthy of New York, Tweed secured additional monies: $1 million in 1862, $800,000 in 1864, $300,000 in 1865, and $800,000 in 1866. By 1871 he had spent $13 million altogether on a building that, after thirteen years, was still incomplete.

Where had the money gone? James Watson, county auditor and bookkeeper of the ring, divided the money raised with 35 percent going to the various contractors and a cool 65 percent going in commission to the ring. The abuse was so flagrant that in 1870 reformers had a board of courthouse commissioners appointed to oversee warrants and contracts. Tweed and the mayor, Oakey

Hall, packed the board with Tammy hacks, and Watson produced fraudulent vouchers to demonstrate that current expenses were genuine. The ring relished its work. It made out checks to "T. C. Cash," signed them "Philip F. Dummey," and even charged for the actual printing of contractors' bills by Tweed's own printing company.

Robert Roosevelt, one of the reformers, said that the bills were "not merely monstrous, they are manifestly fabulous." For instance, for three tables and forty chairs, the city paid out $179,729.60. Carpets, shades, and furniture supplied by the James Ingersoll Company cost the somewhat startling sum of $5.69 million. In short, the courthouse cost four times as much as the Houses of Parliament and twice as much as Alaska.

In the fall of 1870 the ring's control apparently was as assured as ever. It seemed they could survive indefinitely as a self-perpetuating oligarchy once Hall had succeeded Hoffman as governor. But it had antagonized the middle classes, who dreaded displacement among the mounting tides of immigrants. And it had made deadly enemies of its political rivals. James O'Brien, whom Tweed had once made sheriff, joined forces with State Senator Henry ("Prince Hal") Genet and Congressman John Morrisey to lead opposition to the ring within the Democratic party. This faction, usually called the Young Democracy, was directed from the sidelines by Samuel Tilden, chairman of the Democratic state committee of New York. Tilden wanted to become president and had to overthrow Tweed and his supposed candidate, Hoffman, to do so. By the spring of 1870, more than half the general committee of Tammany Hall was taking part with the Young Democracy.

The first conflict between Tweed and his enemies was over a new city charter. It had to pass the state assembly at Albany, and so gross were the bribes offered senators and assemblymen—perhaps over $1 million altogether—that it did so despite bitter controversy. In some important respects, the Tweed charter was a reform measure. It tended to give the city control of its own affairs, to simplify its complex administration, and to place administrative business in only a few hands. Unfortunately, as English political scientist James Bryce observed, "These hands were at the moment unclean and grasping hands." Real power was vested in a new board of audit composed of Hall, Sweeny, and Tweed.

A new publisher of the *New York Times*, George Jones, and his managing editor, the Englishman Louis John Jennings, set out to expose the theft of the city to its people. On September 20, 1870 the *Times* began with innuendo and for a year continued its attacks with smear and sarcasm. Fate unexpectedly took a hand and dealt the reformers the ace of spades. The ring's trusty auditor, James Watson, was killed in a sleighing accident on January 21, 1871. There was no one to prevent new appointees to the auditor's offices from getting at the true facts. Two of them, William Copeland and Matthew O'Rourke, uncovered evidence of gross fraud. Previously, Jennings and Jones had not a scintilla of proof for their accusations. But now Copeland and O'Rourke had saved the situation by feeding them precise facts and figures. The *Times* opened its series of explicit attacks on July 8, 1871. It began with accounts of armory frauds and then exposed the extravagance of the new courthouse. On July 22 it carried the sensational headline, "The Secret Accounts: Proofs of Undoubted Frauds Brought to Light."

The ring realized that it was trapped. It offered George Jones, publisher of the *Times*, and Thomas Nast, its cartoonist, bribes of $500,000 in useless attempts to buy their silence. Tweed himself recognized the mastery of Nast's caricatures. "I don't care a straw for your newspaper articles, my constituents don't know how to read, but they can't help seeing them damned pictures," he exclaimed. Tweed was depicted as gross, vicious, and lowborn. Sweeny was the evil genius. Connolly was the oily intriguer. Oakey Hall was the buffoon.

The public was outraged. At a meeting held in Cooper Union on September 4, 1871, former mayor William F. Havemeyer reported Controller Connolly's confession. During the thirty-month period when the revenue of city and county was $72.54 million, the ring had paid out $139.00 million and stolen at least $45.00 million. The audience called for the appointment of an executive committee of seventy to recover the lost money and reform the city government. Tilden persuaded Connolly to yield his place as controller to Andrew Green of the committee of seventy. Judge George Barnard was obliged to grant an injunction barring the ring from raising or paying money. All government was brought to a stop. There was no money with which to pay city employees their wages.

The Tammany Hall machine was defeated in the city and state elections on November 7, 1871. The new assemblymen included Samuel Tilden. In all, the reformers took 75,000 regular Democratic votes away from the ring. They owed their success to the defection of the ring's repeater gangs and to the despised immigrants and native poor. However, Tweed survived the November elections and was reelected to the state senate. His defiance of his critics passed into a proverb, "What are you going to do about it?" He soon discovered. A grand jury indicted Tweed in December, and he was arrested. Released on bail of $2 million put up by Jay Gould, he was a broken man already; he looked more like sixty than his true age of forty-eight. He was not tried until January 7, 1873, when he appeared before Judge Noah Davis. The jury could not agree on a verdict, and Tweed was tried again on November 5, 1873. During his lawyer's final summary he hid his face in his hands and wept convulsively. This time he was convicted on 204 of 220 counts in the indictment. He was sentenced to twelve years' imprisonment and fined $12,750.

The court of appeals had ruled that, although an indictment might contain any number of counts, a convicted defendant's actual punishment could not exceed that prescribed for one offense even if he were found guilty for all of them. Tweed was, therefore, released on January 15, 1875. However, public opinion was not stilled. The former boss was arrested again on a civil action for recovery of $6 million in loot. He was committed to Ludlow Street Jail. But, on December 4, 1875, he escaped. In August 1876 he was recaptured in Vigo, Spain, after someone recognized him there from the Nast cartoons. After his enforced return to Ludlow Street he offered to turn state's evidence. The new governor, Samuel Tilden, would not let him. Tilden wanted punishment to be restricted to the scapegoat. Tweed died of pneumonia on April 12, 1878, and was buried in Brooklyn.

REFORM IN THE CITIES

The resounding moral victory of reformers against the Tweed Ring was, as Alexander Callow explains, actually an ironic political defeat. Reformers, blinded by their commitment to expose and rout the ring, were oblivious both to the limitations of civic institutions and to the kinds of changing urban conditions in which corrupt political machines could thrive with new people. Members of this middle-class group with patrician ideals were obsessed with the idea of "honest, efficient, and economical government." In 1872 they succeeded in electing a reform candidate as mayor of New York.

The new mayor, William F. Havemeyer, having retired from the sugar refining business at the age of forty to devote himself to public service, was now a sixty-eight-year-old reformer who championed clean government and economy to the interests of business. He proposed structural reform without social improvement. He cut wages on public works, insisted on elaborate scrutiny of public expenditures, and sacrificed public services. In 1874 he vetoed more than 250 bills relating to the maintenance and extension of streets, schools, and charities. In doing so he retarded downtown development and damaged relations between immigrants and natives. Despite his stringent economies, his fiscal policy as a whole was a failure. In 1871 the civic debt had been $88 million. At the end of 1874 it stood at $115 million. Havemeyer's death that year was a merciful relief to the city as a whole. Nevertheless, he was the prototype of other structural reformers such as Grover Cleveland in Buffalo, Seth Low in Brooklyn, and James D. Phelan in San Francisco, all of whom were committed to low taxes and rigid economies.

Across the country what reformers really wanted was a better and more impartial administration of essential urban services. In time they became convinced that only the public ownership of utilities could free American cities from a major source of corruption. Public opinion was hostile both to the power of utility monopolies and to any "socialistic" attempts at their public ownership.

Reformers in Philadelphia, disappointed at their inability to

Frances Benjamin Johnston photographed the World's Columbian Exposition of 1893 in Chicago. The 150 buildings were called the "White City" because the principal buildings, such as the Administration Building here, were finished with white staff, a compound of plaster of paris and jute fiber. For many visitors the White City afforded them their first sight of electric lights and the white buildings and reflective pools enhanced the effect. (Library of Congress).

drive a wedge between Boss James B. McManes and the local gas and transit monopolies, decided to call a national conference of other aggrieved civic reformers in 1893. It was attended by delegates from 29 organizations in 21 cities who founded the National Municipal League, which soon included 180 affiliated societies. At its Columbus conference in 1900 it adopted a model program of advice and directives for reform groups across the country.

New candidates, more representative of the common people

than either spoilsmen or reformers, came to the fore of politics in the 1890s. Samuel M. Jones became the "Golden Rule" mayor of Toledo, and Tom Johnson became mayor of Cleveland. In Detroit Hazen S. Pingree was the Republican nominee of business leaders who wanted an independent mayor to fight against a corrupt Irish ring.

Reformers' well-intentioned attempts to improve the lot of the urban poor were deeply resented by immigrants because they were condescending and high-handed. Yet each side needed the other's support. The link between the two was forged by Jane Addams. Her solution, the settlement house, was also intended to sublimate the private distress of educated women who felt unfulfilled in urban society.

Jane Addams, daughter of an Illinois state senator who was a mill owner and banker by profession, was born in Cedarville in 1860. Her mother died two years later, and in 1867 her father married a widow, Anne Haldeman, who had two sons. From 1877 to 1881 Jane attended Rockford Female Seminary, and during her last year there her father died. The 1880s were years of personal frustration for Jane Addams. She spent them partly in visits to Europe in 1883 and 1887, partly in an abortive attempt at medical study, and partly in an equally useless effort to please her step-mother and become part of Baltimore society. But she also worked for charities. Moreover, these were years of painful physical illness. As a child she had suffered from spinal tuberculosis, and it had left her spine slightly curved. In 1882 her stepbrother, Harry Haldeman, performed an operation on her back that left her unable to bear children. She was confined to bed for a year, and this precipitated gnawing feelings of social and sexual insecurity. Living in mental isolation, she was unsure of her future role, torn by a desire to escape from her family and from society and a plunge into some vocation. She was trying to escape from herself.

During her stay in England in 1887 Jane Addams visited Toynbee Hall, a settlement house organized by Samuel A. Barnett. With her was her closest friend from Rockford, Ellen Gates Starr. Together they decided to devote themselves to social work. On their return to Chicago they produced a carefully considered proposal for a settlement house, part residence, part club, part school. They persuaded churchmen, charity workers, and women's groups to join them. The settlement could thus offer the urban ghetto the sort of essential social services that the city council was unwilling to provide—entertainment, welfare, and relief.

The idea was not new to America. New York already had a Neighborhood Guild, and a group of Smith College graduates were planning to open a college settlement in the Lower East Side. What Jane Addams wanted, however, was an informal organization, something different in kind from the relief agencies of religious or temperance societies. Jane Addams's family opposed the plan. Without Ellen Starr she would not have had the courage to break with them. "Let's love each other through thick and thin and work out a salvation," she wrote to Ellen on January 24, 1889.

For the center of their proposed settlement Jane Addams and Ellen Starr chose Hull House, the dilapidated mansion of Charles J. Hull on the corner of Halsted and Polk streets. A Victorian suburban house that had survived the fire of 1871 and subsequently been surrounded by tenements of the growing metropolis, it was situated between a saloon on one side and a funeral parlor on the other. After delicate negotiations with the present owner, Helen Culver, they leased part of the building. Preceded by a barrage of favorable press publicity, they moved in on September 18, 1889. The *Chicago Tribune* of March 8 described it as "A Project to Bring the Rich and Poor Together."

Even before Hull House was opened the press was imposing on Jane Addams the image with which she was to become identified, that of Saint Jane. It was easier for reporters to explain that two young women who went to live in the slums and care for the needy were motivated by spirituality and self-sacrifice than to ascribe their move to the sort of determined break with convention that Jane Addams and Ellen Starr were actually making. The press might suggest that Jane Addams was a genius in the day and Ellen Starr a beauty by night, but there was no hint that this Adam and Eve were able to raise Cain in the community.

Jane Addams's life's work against the concentrated power of capital would not have been possible without the values of hard work, ambition, and thrift upon which the wealth of her father and other entrepreneurs were based. Her unyielding confidence in the virtues of self-help could be both callous and condescending. She once told a shipping clerk who came to Hull House asking for relief that he should work outdoors on a construction gang cutting a local canal. Although he was used to working indoors, he did so. After two days he contracted pneumonia and died a week later. Jane Addams cared for his two orphaned children but could not quiet her conscience.

Jane Addams did not just want to help the poor, she wanted to find a new role for educated women in society. At Hull House many talented women gained experience and confidence as administrators. It provided a practical training ground for the first generation of professional women such as Florence Kelley, who became head of the National Consumers' League, and Alice Hamilton, an industrial chemist, who became the first woman professor at Harvard Medical School.

Within a year of the opening of Hull House Helen Culver waived the initial rent of $60 a month. By 1895 she had turned over the adjacent property to Hull House, and that year gave both land and buildings to the University of Chicago. Hull House was made a corporation with a board of trustees, of which Jane Addams was president. She expanded the original activities, adapting and extending the various houses. The complex was completed in 1907 and comprised thirteen buildings including lodgings, kindergarten, childrens' clubs, gymnasium, art gallery, coffee house, and theater.

Hull House also contributed to the growing academic discipline of sociology. The Illinois Factory Act of 1893, passed in part because of the Hull House lobby, did not meet the expectations of Florence Kelley. She turned her attention to a project to study the neighborhood block by block. The resulting publication, *Hull-House Maps and Papers* (1895), described ethnic groups, wages, sweatshops, child labor, and union activity. It was favorably reviewed by a few critics, sold poorly, and soon went out of print. But it stimulated similar research in other cities and convinced Jane Addams that the future of Hull House lay in providing a special arena for social work and social research. It was not coincidence that Hull House figured prominently in the essays of the first volume of the new *American Journal of Sociology*, launched in 1895.

Nothing concerned residents of the Nineteenth Ward more than the stench and filth of their streets, which were littered with refuse. In 1895, tired of submitting pleas to the city council that fell on deaf ears, Jane Addams put in a bid for garbage removal in the ward. It was refused. But the publicity she earned was worth a fortune. The story of an upper-class lady who wanted to become a scavenger was sensational copy across the country, and this more than any other action turned her into a national celebrity.

Critic Frederika Randall has observed, "Garbage has always been with us, but it took the zealous generation of turn-of-the-century progressives to define it as a menace to civic harmony and social order." In New York, Civil War veteran Col. George E. Waring, Jr., used his knowledge of military strategy to devise means of collecting and disposing of garbage when he became commissioner of street cleaning. His enthusiasm and ingenuity almost succeeded in giving the grammar of garbage collection an unexpected glamor of its own.

Because of the publicity surrounding Jane Addams, Mayor Carter Henry Harrison, Jr., appointed her garbage inspector at a salary of $1,000. She accomplished little. She realized that the real villain was the powerful and corrupt local boss, Johnny ("DePow") Powers, chairman of the council's finance committee, who had much to gain by keeping his electorate in conditions of squalor and ignorance. Jane Addams determined to unseat him and launched two unsuccessful but widely publicized campaigns against him in 1896 and 1898. She discovered she could not compete with his reputation for generosity. He boasted that 2,600 ward residents owed their city jobs to him. He distributed railroad passes, Christmas dinners, and free coal. Ordinary people could appreciate such minuscule largess without realizing that they usually paid for it in the extortionate street railway fares Powers secured for his allies, the railway companies. Ironically, they preferred his top hat and opulent life-style to the cloth caps and austere behavior of Jane Addams's candidates. She conceded defeat, and she expressed her grudging admiration for someone who was at least "engaged in the great moral effort of getting the mass to express itself and of adding this mass energy and wisdom to the community as a whole."

Hull House provided the model for other settlement houses,

including South End House in Boston, Henry Street and University Settlement in New York, and Chicago Commons. From only 6 houses in 1891 the movement spread quickly. In 1897 there were 74 settlements and over a 100 by 1900.

Progressive reformers made the middle classes well aware of urban problems. Whatever the positive contribution of individuals to social reform, the part played by the class as a whole was a negative one. It took flight to the suburbs. Between 1887 and 1894 a series of technological improvements in intracity transportation—cable lines, electric surface lines, and elevated transit—allowed the middle class its flight to the suburbs. Men of affairs and women of fashion could have the best of both worlds, the city by day, the suburbs by night.

Idealists wanted this for all classes. Commissioner of Labor Carrol D. Wright, in an article for *Popular Science Monthly* for April 1892, reviewed the findings of the census of 1890 and concluded that adequate urban transportation was "something more than a question of economics or business convenience; it is a social and an ethical question as well." For only suburbs could supply the "sanitary localities, [the] moral and well-regulated communities, where children can have all the advantages of church and school, of light and air," which were necessary for "the improvement of the condition of the masses." His views were echoed by other writers on urban affairs, including Adna Weber in his seminal work, *The Growth of Cities in the Nineteenth Century* (1899). Progressive authorities in the larger cities understood these arguments and encouraged the development of efficient intracity transport. Moreover, the laying of additional railroad lines provided opportunities for lucrative construction contracts. On January 16, 1900, contractor John B. McDonald and banker August Belmont were awarded the contract for the first subway in New York to be constructed at an estimated cost of $35 million.

Rather than just accept the drift to the suburbs as an inevitable fact of city life, town planners began to consider more seriously ways of improving urban conditions to retain their residents. In *Looking Backward* (1888) Edward Bellamy had offered a vision of "miles of broad streets, shaded by trees and lined with fine buildings, . . . large open squares filled with trees, among which statues

The obelisk at the southern end of South Canal at the World's Columbian Exposition, Chicago, 1893. The impact of the ensemble of the design on those who attended it was such that it stimulated a movement for modern city design in the United States. (Frances Benjamin Johnston, Library of Congress).

glistened and fountains flashed . . . [and] Public buildings of a colossal size and an architectural grandeur unparalleled." It seemed that Bellamy's vision had become a reality in 1893 when Chicago acted as host to the World's Columbian Exposition on the shores of Lake Michigan. The impact of its landscape and architecture was considerable, mainly for its general ensemble. Frederick C. Howe in *The Modern City and Its Problems* (1915) wrote: "The World's Fair in Chicago in 1893 marks the beginning of city planning in America. People left it with the inquiry: "Why cannot cities be built like a world's fair; why should we not employ architects and artists in their designing; why should we not live in cities as beautiful as this fugitive play city, that will disappear at the end of the summer?'"

To this end the devastation wrought in Galveston, Texas, by a cyclonic hurricane in September 1900 concentrated citizens' minds wonderfully. The flood deluged the streets with water seventeen feet deep. Six thousand people died and property worth $20 million was destroyed. The disaster prompted citizens to appoint a special commission with dictatorial powers to rebuild the city. The idea came from an emergency commission devised by Memphis after an epidemic of yellow fever in 1878. Within five weeks of the catastrophe the commission had protected the coast with a seawall of granite and concrete and raised the level of the city. The success of the commission was such that in 1901 the Texas legislature gave it permanent form in a new charter. This provided for a mayor-president and four commissioners, two elected by the people and (at first) two appointed by the governor. The system of city government by commission was so successful that by 1917 more than 500 cities had instituted management by commission.

CHAPTER FIVE

SKELETON AT
THE FEAST

THROUGHOUT THE Gilded Age the specters of poverty and oppression waited on the banquet of expansion and opportunity. Economist Henry George compared the want of the huddled masses with the wealth of the dominant plutocracy. In his pioneer work, *Progress and Poverty* (1879), he conceded that the Industrial Revolution had increased wealth and improved and distributed comfort, leisure, and refinement. But he emphasized that the lowest class was excluded from these gains. "There is a vague but general feeling of disappointment; an increased bitterness among the working classes; a widespread feeling of unrest and brooding revolution."

Between 1865 and 1900 more and more workers were drawn into factories, foundries, and mills on the same low terms as common laborers. The total number of people employed in manufacturing increased from 1.3 million to 4.5 million. The number of factories or sweatshops rose from 140,000 to 512,000. In factory, foundry, and mill wages were low, hours of work long, and conditions unhealthy. Millions were denied the basic amenities that their own labor made possible for others. Their impoverished status seemed to contradict the economic prosperity of the business and industry they were creating. Progress and poverty were, apparently, inseparable.

Workers had as much right to their guilds as had industrialists and capitalists of a Gilded Age. No one has put the case for unions better than utopian socialist Edward Bellamy in his influential *Looking Backward* of 1888. Reviewing the drive for industrial monopolies, he argued: "The individual laborer, who had been relatively important to the small employer, was reduced to insignificance and powerlessness against the great corporation, while at the same time the way upward to the grade of employer was closed to him. Self-defense drove him to union with his fellows." However, in the United States the development of trade unions was more hesitant and much slower than in Western Europe. No strong working class movement emerged to complement the increasing concentration of capital and industry. By the end of the nineteenth century, the dominant form of trade unions was craft unions restricted to skilled artisans.

Trade union development was retarded by a number of factors. Labor unions existed to promote the interests of their members by securing better conditions, hours, and wages for workers. But, even without unions, the conditions of artisans were improving. Workers' general indifference to unions was compounded by immigration on a massive scale. Immigrants, glad of any opportunity, proved a plentiful source of cheap labor. The steady stream of immigrants could always replace dissatisfied workers who went on strike or even joined a union. Their presence thus placed native workers at a disadvantage in their fumbling attempts at collective bargaining. The very fact that the work force was so heterogeneous made it difficult to establish class consciousness, let alone working class solidarity.

As the business of a particular industry became nationwide, its costs, wages, and prices rose and fell in accordance with economic conditions across the country. New technology divided labor as surely as it divided and simplified different industrial processes. Unskilled novices could replace skilled mechanics—and at a lower wage. Dramatic oscillations in the business cycle between prosperity and depression hit at unions in two ways. Depression diminished workers' ability to support labor organization; prosperity dampened their enthusiasm. No sooner had unions grown in strength and assurance than both industry and labor were struck by the panic of 1873 and the ensuing depression. Both recovered in the 1880s, only to succumb to a much worse depression in 1893. The determination of new industrial entrepreneurs to outwit labor was complemented by the conservative attitude of courts and public opinion to the new cause. Farmers and agricultural workers were preoccupied with their own sectional interests and were too narrow-minded to appreciate that the cause of labor was, in part, their cause as well.

The growth of national unions was marked by three stages: the National Labor Union (NLU) in 1866; the Noble Order of the Knights of Labor (the Knights) in 1869; the American Federation of Labor (AFL) in 1886. They provided, respectively, the backdrop, procession, and ceremony for the exciting drama of labor disputes that occupied the center stage. Until the Civil War strikes had been short, local, and peaceful. Thereafter the United States had to endure long, widespread, and violent industrial strife. In particular five violent strikes damaged the reputation of unions: the Molly Maguires' in the 1870s, the Great Railroad Strike of 1877, the Haymarket affair of 1886, Homestead in 1892, and Pullman in 1894. These five incidents corresponded to the five acts of a classical tragedy: exposition, development, crisis, denouement, and catastrophe.

NATIONAL LABOR UNION

In the 1860s and 1870s the most durable labor organizations were the traditional local unions and city trade assemblies. It is not coincidence that the movement for national federation was led by men from those factory crafts that had already established national unions: William Sylvis of the molders and Jonathan Finer and Ira Steward of the machinists. By 1873 there were twenty-five national unions with a membership of 170,000. Another 130,000 workers were members of unions that lacked a national association.

Capt. William R. Jones, superintendent of the Edgar Thomson Steelworks, commented on the skill of English workers in mobilizing the labor force. He observed in 1875 that they "are great sticklers for high wages, small production and strikes." In almost every industry it *was* British and Irish immigrants who founded the labor union: in coal mining, John Rae, Robert Watchorn, John Hinchcliffe, David McLaughlin, and John Siney; in textiles, George Gunton and Robert Howard; in iron and steel, John Jarrett.

As wartime prosperity evaporated, labor leaders found it more difficult to gain advantages from collective bargaining. Nor were they ready to risk cooperative ventures. They sought an alternative. The eight-hour day became a popular demand among the rank and file. Indeed, it forms a continuous thematic thread running through labor history in the Gilded Age. The prophet of the eight-hour millenium was a Boston machinist, Ira Steward, "the eight-hour monomaniac." He believed that increased leisure with the same wages would encourage workers to consume more industrial goods and thus lead to an increase in industrial growth. Steward's central argument was propagated in a popular jingle attributed to his wife:

> Whether you work by the piece or work by the day
> Decreasing the hours increases the pay.

Not only did workers believe that a shorter working day would improve their health, welfare, and opportunities for education and advancement, but they also thought that a reduction in hours would spread work more evenly in a recession and thus protect jobs.

Union leaders required some sort of new organization to unify the eight-hour movement. In the summer of 1866 they called a congress of labor organizations at Baltimore for August. There seventy-seven delegates representing 60,000 workers launched the National Labor Union. It had a program of reform including workers' cooperatives managed by producers and consumers alike. It also wanted a federal Department of Labor and the disposal of public lands only to actual settlers.

On the surface, it seemed that the NLU was successful in promoting the eight-hour day. Six states enacted eight-hour laws in 1867: California, Connecticut, Illinois, Missouri, Wisconsin, and New York. However, in the first four the law excepted companies that issued labor contracts stipulating longer hours. In Wisconsin the law applied only to women and children. In New York, Governor Reuben Fenton refused to enforce it. A report to the NLU could well describe the states' eight-hour laws as "frauds on the laboring class." Sylvis's successor as president of the NLU, Richard Trevellick, prevailed upon Senator B. Gratz Brown of Missouri to introduce a bill granting an eight-hour day to laborers and mechanics working for the federal government. It passed Congress in June 1868. But federal departments then reduced wages by 20 percent as well as hours. However, in an executive order of May 1872, President Ulysses S. Grant condemned such reductions in pay, and Congress enacted a law compensating federal employees for their loss in wages since 1868. In addition, the NLU attempted to address its conventions to the special problems of women and black Americans.

During the war industrialists began to employ an ever larger number of women in factories and sweatshops. They were paid less and treated worse than men. The most significant protective society for women was the Working Women's Protective Union, founded at the instigation of Moses Beach, editor of the *New York Sun*. It offered legal advice and ran a placement bureau that trained women for occupations that were underemployed. In 1869 the NLU refused to seat suffragist Susan B. Anthony because she had allowed the Protective Union to be used to break strikes. Thereafter, male support for women's unions declined. Employers could harass women's unions with impunity. Their main weapon was ridicule. In 1869 Kate Mullaney, second vice president of the NLU, led a strike of collar laundresses of Troy, New York. They were protesting about long hours of work in temperatures of 100 degrees for only $2 to $3 per week. The employers produced a new paper collar requiring fewer laundresses, and the strike collapsed. By 1872 most women's unions had disappeared.

The migration of black Americans from South to North intensified racist attitudes among white workers in northern industries. They resented the freedmen's willingness to work for lower wages and their enforced lower standard of living. Black leaders created a National Colored Labor Union in December 1869. Its platform emphasized the problem of racial discrimination. Its proposed remedy was black workers' cooperatives. In 1870 Isaac Myers, a Baltimore calker, tried to recruit and organize black workers throughout the South. He wanted to ensure that they would never be ousted from skilled trades and left as "the sweepers of shavings, the scrapers of pitch and the carriers of mortar."

Individual unions—among them the bakers, carpenters, coopers, hatters, printers, shipwrights, and shoemakers—tried to make a success of workers' cooperatives. All failed. They found it almost impossible to obtain credit. This problem led to the NLU to recognize that labor could never help itself without a reform of the currency. This, in turn, led it into an ill-advised, ill-fated alliance with the Greenback movement (q.v.). After the war, farm joined factory in the demand for an inflationary policy through the retention of wartime greenbacks. But their motives were different. Farmers wanted to return to their wartime prosperity. Factory workers wanted to free the economic system from the gold standard. In 1872 the NLU took an irrevocable decision and transformed itself into the National Labor Reform party. Its avowed program was reform of the currency. But when its presidential nominee, Judge David Davis of Illinois, withdrew from the federal election, he dealt the NLU a mortal blow. It adopted the candidate for dissident Democrats, Charles O'Connor, a Tammany Hall hack. In the election O'Connor disappointed his allies. He took only 29,489 votes. The party was well and truly over. Only seven delegates turned up for the convention of 1872.

YEARS OF UPHEAVAL

The panic of 1873 heralded a prolonged depression. It was estimated that by 1877, 20 percent of the labor force was unemployed, 40 percent worked for only six or seven months a year, and only 20 percent worked regularly. Three million out of work gathered in shantytowns on the fringes of cities. Relief, if it came at all, was irregular, arbitrary, and inadequate. Local unions could not survive. Before the panic there had been thirty national unions. In 1877 the *Labor Standard* listed nine. Total union membership declined from 300,000 to about 50,000.

The most obvious signs of labor discontent during the 1870s and 1880s were demonstrations by the unemployed and strikes by exploited workers on such a scale that some historians refer to these years as a period of great upheaval. Spontaneous protests led to pitched battles with police and militia, to riots and bloodshed. Labor historian Foster Rhea Dulles concludes, "As never before the nation came to realize the explosive force inherent in the great mass of industrial workers that were the product of its changing economy." The most notorious riot was that of Tompkins Square in New York on January 13, 1874. It began when a scheduled meeting between unemployed workers and city authorities was canceled by the police at the last minute. When a crowd did assemble, they were charged by a squad of mounted police armed with billy clubs.

Public opinion was far more disturbed by the strike of the Molly Maguires in eastern Pennsylvania. The Molly Maguires was a secret society, named after a redoutable widow, and formed by tenants in Ireland against their landlords. Its official title was the Ancient Order of Hibernians. The clandestine organization in the anthracite coal fields of Pennsylvania was its natural American successor. It was incorporated as a "humane, charitable, and benevolent organization" in 1871.

The tribulations of the miners were real enough. Miners endured worse conditions than workers in industry. They had no legal protection from industrial accidents. Between 1865 and 1875, 556 men were killed in the anthracite fields and 1,565 were maimed for life. In 1868 they formed a new Pennsylvania coal union, the Workingmen's Benevolent Association of St. Clair, led by John Siney. About 85 percent of the anthracite miners joined. In 1870 its dispute with mine owners was resolved by the "Gowen compromise," proposed by Franklin Benjamin Gowen, president of the Reading Railroad. In the future, miners' wages were to be adjusted on a sliding scale in accordance with the price of coal.

But, when prices and wages fell dramatically that winter, a new strike began in January 1871. A series of terrorist acts followed— arson and sabotage of property, assault and murder of personnel. The exact part played by the Mollies in all this has remained a mystery. Gowen certainly believed that his coal empire was being undermined by the Mollies, and he was determined to destroy them. As early as 1872 he accepted an offer of help from detective Allan Pinkerton. Pinkerton was a Scottish immigrant who had resigned from the Chicago police to found the Pinkerton National Detective Agency in 1850. At first he specialized in cases of railway theft. During the war he served the North as a military intelligence officer. Beginning in 1865 he began to transform the scope of the agency's activities. He now offered intelligence, counter intelligence, and internal security services to both business and government. These services included strikebreaking.

Allan Pinkerton chose James McParland, a twenty-nine-year-old immigrant from Ulster, for the delicate and dangerous task of infiltrating the Mollies. On October 27, 1873, McParland began to move from town to town in the Pennsylvania coal fields posing as a fugitive from a murder charge in Buffalo. A man of easy charm, he had no difficulty in ingratiating himself with the Irish mining community and soon discovered that the Mollies' headquarters was at Pottsville, where he was initiated into the order on April 13, 1874. They were so taken with his ease at reading and writing that they made him secretary of the Shenandoah Lodge. This post afforded a good cover for his secret reports.

In December 1874 mine owners led by Gowen reduced wages below the agreed-on minimum standard. In January 1875 the miners, led by John F. Walsh, retaliated by going on strike. According to sensational press accounts, the Molly Maguires had intimidated miners who wanted to go back to work and prevented them from doing so. They were supposedly terrorizing the coal fields with murder and mayhem. Contemporary historian Francis P. Dewees in *The Molly Maguires* (1876) described the Mollies' activities as "a reign of blood. . . . They held communities terror bound, and wantonly defied the law, destroyed property and sported with human life." It was discovered much later that the managers themselves had instigated various attacks on their own mines as a pretext for crushing all unions. The way the strike was actually suppressed suggests that this really was the case. Whatever crime wave already existed, it was certainly intensifed by the arrival of the Pinkertons. On April 28, 1875, Pinkerton and Gowen agreed to support McParland with a reserve of six Pinkerton detectives and some railroadmen. They would constitute "a flying squadron," a mobile police force, able to assemble anywhere a crime was about to be committed in order to gather evidence to be used later in court.

Miners could continue the strike for several months because, although they were not being paid, they were allowed food on credit by stores friendly to their cause. But by May 1875 the stores were no longer willing to accept the financial risk of an indefinite strike and refused further credit. Union leaders tried to avert disaster by offering the mine operators a deal. They would forego the old sliding scale in exchange for a flat weekly wage of $15 for six eight-hour shifts. The operators had no reason to give in. They said they would reopen the mines and offer work and protection to any miner who returned. Italian strikebreakers were taken to Clearfield County in western Pennsylvania in sealed boxcars like cattle. Strikebreakers were sealed off from strikers, not to protect them from harm, but to prevent them from hearing the strikers' case. Sometimes immigrants were not even told they had been hired as strikebreakers until they arrived on the scene. Their success in bringing the miners to heel contributed to the decline of some unions.

In early 1876 McParland became principal witness for the prosecution in the trial of Mollies accused of the murders of mine boss Thomas Sanger and his boarder, William Uren, on September 1, 1875, at Raven Run. His testimony at subsequent trials was corroborated by other witnesses who turned state's evidence to save their own hides. Much of their evidence was false. As a result, all twenty-four of the Molly Maguires who had been indicted were convicted. Nineteen were hanged for murder. The others were given prison sentences ranging from two to seven years. The "King of the Mollies," Jack Kehoe, was among those found guilty and sentenced to be hanged. After losing a desperate legal battle to save his life, he died a torturous death. The noose on the gallows slipped. He strangled slowly and died in great agony. The plight of the miners remained the same as before. The strikers were routed. The secret society was shattered. The Miners' Benevolent Association was broken. Not until 1890, when the United Mine

Workers was formed, did miners achieve an effective union. And only in 1900 was their formidable leader, Johnny Mitchell, ready to pit miners against mines in well-organized strikes.

Local violence in the winter of 1874–75 was only a prelude to widespread disorder in the summer of 1877. The Great Railroad Strike of 1877 was a dramatic revolt. A difficult situation was compounded by the hostility of railroad entrepreneurs to anything beyond their own immediate gain. Moreover, workers were dismayed by the failure of labor unions to help them. Their strike was a blind gesture of embittered defiance against a capitalistic society willfully insensitive to human needs.

Railroad work sometimes involved shifts of fifteen or even eighteen hours at a stretch. Railroad workers had suffered average wage cuts of 35 percent over the three years to 1877. That year the Pennsylvania Railroad announced a further reduction of 10 percent to take effect on June 1. Other eastern railroads announced similar cuts, effective July 1. This was the straw that broke the camel's back. The workers were thoroughly aroused. On July 16, 1877, forty firemen and brakemen of the Baltimore and Ohio Railroad went on strike at Camden Junction, Maryland. They were dispersed by police. The following day there was a second strike at Martinsburg, West Virginia. This time the strikers took the precaution of seizing the depot to keep trains from moving until their full wages were restored. Their leaders were arrested by police but released by a large crowd. The affair ended only after President Rutherford B. Hayes ordered 200 federal troops to the scene.

At first public opinion sided with the strikers. For one thing, the general public had endured much from the railroads in their selfish policies toward consumers. Everyone knew that the wage cuts were arbitrary and that, despite the recession, high dividends were still being paid on watered stock. But soon the strike was widespread. The action of employees of the Pennsylvania Railroad at Pittsburgh on July 19 led to a terrifying riot. When 650 federal troops arrived from Philadelphia, they fired into the crowd, killing 25 people and wounding more in order to capture the roundhouse and machine shops. It was now the turn of the strikers to besiege the soldiers. They set freight cars afire and sent them into the roundhouse. When it was ablaze, the soldiers fought their way out and beat a quick retreat. The way was clear for wanton destruction of railroad property by the mob, now swelled to 4,000 to 5,000 by hoodlums and vagrants. They broke up the cars and tore up the tracks. What they could not destroy in this way they set on fire. In the conflagration 500 cars, 104 locomotives, and 39 buildings, including the depot, were destroyed. Newspapers across the country sensationalized the uprising with headlines like "Pittsburgh Sacked—the City Completely in the Power of a Howling Mob." To the *New York Times* of July 26, 1877, the strikers were now "hoodlums, rabble, bummers, looters, black-legs, thieves, tramps, ruffians, incendiaries, enemies of society, brigands, rapscallions, riffraff, felons and idiots."

All along the line towns and cities were given over to riots—Altoona, Easton, Harrisburg, Reading, Johnstown, Bethlehem, and Philadelphia—and freight was immobilized. As federal troops entered city after city rioting subsided and strikers returned to work. They were beaten and they knew it. Nothing was done to assuage their grievances. By August 2, 1877, the railroads had had what was left of their property restored to them. Damage to them and other property owners cost more than $10 million to repair.

The crisis had lasted a month, the consequences were felt for several years to come. The conflict involved more people than any other labor dispute in the nineteenth century. It seemed to the upper and middle classes like a slave uprising—for miners in Martinsburg and Scranton, millhands in Pittsburgh, sewermen in Louisville, and stevedores in Cairo, Illinois, as well as small businessmen and farmers across the country had actively assisted the strike. The business community resolved to suppress labor associations by every possible means. In its editorial of August 2, 1877, the *Nation* explained that it was necessary to be cruel in order to be kind:

The kindest thing which can be done for the great multitudes of untaught men . . . is to show them promptly that society as here organized, on individual freedom of thought and action, is impregnable, and can be no more shaken than the order of nature. The most cruel thing is to let them suppose, even for one week, that if they had only chosen their time better, or had been better led or better armed, they would have succeeded in forcing it to capitulate.

In its turn, labor was convinced that the hostility engendered by the strike virtually precluded further strikes for the time being. Therefore, labor must advance its cause by outright political activity.

The contemporaneous history of American socialism provides variations on the theme of the rise of American labor. Indeed, the entire labor movement was discredited in grim accounts about the subversive activities of anarchists and socialists. They rose to a torrent of abuse in reports of the Haymarket affair of 1886.

In 1864 Karl Marx founded the International Workingmen's Association in London. In 1872 the International in Europe foundered on differences between Marx and anarchist Mikhail Bakunin and moved its organization to New York. But it was only through union and unanimity that the socialists could possibly hope to make headway. They held a congress in Philadelphia in July 1876 that founded the Socialist Labor party. During the Great Railroad Strike, Socialists buried their differences and cooperated with the strikers. In St. Louis they succeeded for a time. In *Reign of the Rabble* (1966) David Burbank concludes: "no American city has come so close to being ruled by a workers' soviet, as we would now call it, as St. Louis, Missouri, in the year 1877." But they soon found themselves isolated. Their executive committee was arrested on charges of conspiracy, and four members were sentenced to five years in the state penitentiary and fined $2,000.

From its new headquarters in Cincinnati the Socialist Labor party concentrated its efforts on winning state and municipal elections in New York, Chicago, and St. Louis in 1878 and 1879. Any success was short-lived. By 1883 the Socialist Labor party had no more than 1,500 members divided among rival factions. Yet, they were still capable of rallying to a cause. At a Chicago convention of October 1881 these minuscule sects constituted themselves the Revolutionary Socialist party. The eastern wing was anarchist. Its leader, Johann Möst, prophesied a society in which the state would be replaced by a federation of producers' cooperatives. He advocated propaganda by deed, execution of capitalists, and seizure of their estate. The "Chicago idea" of native American Albert Parsons and German immigrant August Spiess was syndicalism based on existing trade unions. Unions were not to contend for higher wages and shorter hours. These would be superficial gains. they were to work for the overthrow of capitalist society. Socialism was about to face its first major crisis in the United States.

At its Chicago convention on October 7, 1884, the new Federation of Organized Trades and Labor Unions (a politically moderate successor to the defunct NLU) passed a resolution that "eight hours shall constitute a legal day's labor from and after May 1, 1886." Both the Central Labor Union and the Black International committed themselves to the movement. Of course, many employers would not assent to the demand. Across the country some 350,000 workers from 11,562 firms went on strike.

A strike and lockout at the McCormick Harvester Works in Chicago that had continued since February precipitated a tragedy. On May 3 a pitched battle took place between strikers, strikebreakers, and police protecting them in front of the plant. When police fired into the crowd, several people were killed and many were injured.

In protest, the anarchists of the Black International called a meeting in Haymarket Square, center of the lumberyards and packinghouses, for May 4. Mayor Carter H. Harrison gave his permission. August Spiess published an open letter inviting citizens to attend. This was the revenge circular. Its tone was inflammatory and it was distributed widely. At the meeting the crowd started to fade away when it began to rain. The mayor had advised John Bonfield, precinct captain, to discharge his police reserves. Instead, Bonfield dispatched a riot squad to the Haymarket. Someone then threw a bomb that wounded more than 60 policemen. One, Sgt. M. J. Degan, died immediately and 6 others died later. The police retaliated, again firing into the crowd, wounding more than 100 people, some fatally.

Public opinion was quick to blame the anarchists and cite their opinions as proof of guilt. According to Illinois state law, anyone inciting murder was also guilty of murder. In the end, eight anarchists were arrested and indicted. Only three (Spiess, Parsons, and Fielden) had actually been present in the Haymarket on May 4. Nevertheless, press denunciation was particularly vituperative. On May 6, 1886, the *Chicago Tribune* declared, "These serpents have been warmed and nourished in the sunshine of toleration until at last they have been emboldened to strike at society, law, order, and government."

No one could be sure who had thrown the bomb. Rather than making the punishment fit the crime, society wanted to make the criminal do so. It was difficult to credit the sorry-looking group of anarchists with the violence and horror of the Haymarket affair. Most newspapermen had concluded at the time that Louis Lingg had made, and Rudolph Schnaubelt had thrown, the fatal bomb. The fact that Schnaubelt was twice arrested and freed when all other suspected anarchists were detained certainly suggests that the police wanted him out of the way. It is possible they had used him as an agent provocateur. Historian Samuel Yellen's interpretation is that Captain Bonfield planted sure proof of terrorism so that he could take repressive measures. In an interview published in the *Chicago Daily News* on May 10, 1889, Chief of Police Ebersold explained that Bonfield's able lieutenant, Captain Schaack, "wanted to keep things stirring. He wanted bombs to be found here, there, all around, everywhere. . . . After we got the anarchist societies broken up, Schaack wanted to send out men to again organize new societies right away."

The trial of the accused anarchist began on June 21, 1886, at the criminal court of Cook County before Judge Joseph E. Gary. It was to become a notorious reference point for radicals suspicious of judicial integrity, especially in the trial of the "Chicago Seven" after the Chicago riots that accompanied the controversial Democratic National Convention of 1968.

Julius S. Grinnell, state's attorney, ignored the usual custom of having jurors chosen at random from names in a box. Instead, he had a special bailiff select men prejudiced against the defendants. One was actually a relative of one of the bomb victims. The evidence against the defendants began with their literature. August Spiess was a printer and editor of the *Arbeiter-Zeitung*. Articles describing the manufacture of dynamite and bombs and urging comrades to "clean their guns" and have them ready for action were turned against him in court. Moreover, dynamite was found in his office and in the home of another anarchist, George Engel. By means of smear, innuendo, and false testimony, Grinnel convinced the jury that Spiess, Schwab, and the missing Schnaubelt had passed a bomb from one to the other at the meeting. On August 20 the jury returned a verdict of guilty for all the defendants and fixed the penalty at hanging for seven of them and life imprisonment for the eighth, Oscar Neebe.

Michael Schwab and Samuel Fielden pleaded for executive clemency and had their sentences commuted to life imprisonment. Another, Louis Lingg, a carpenter aged twenty-one, took his own life in prison. He blew himself up by exploding a stock of dynamite in his mouth. The remaining four—August Spiess, Albert Parsons, George Engel, and Adolph Fischer—were hanged on November 11, 1887. Twenty-five thousand people took part in their funeral procession. Their monument at Waldheim Cemetry became a workers' shrine.

The case was now a public sensation at home and abroad. In 1889 an amnesty association was founded to campaign for the release of Fielden, Neebe, and Schwab. In 1893 a new progressive governor, John P. Altgeld, pardoned the three survivors. As he explained in *Reasons for Pardoning Fielden, Neebe, and Schwab* (1893), he was also exonerating them. He accused judge, jury, and prosecution of falling victim to mass hysteria that had been deliberately generated by the police and maliciously intensified by the press. In effect, he was charging the whole community with the murder of justice itself.

Largely because of the Haymarket affair the eight-hour movement of 1886 was a substantial failure. Of the many workers who took part in the movement only 15,000 retained their gains at the end of the year. Employers had drawn much of the impetus for the campaign by buying off 150,000 potential strikers before the general strike began. Once again labor had failed.

The Socialist movement was being baptized by fire. In New York Socialists adopted the name Progressive Democracy and nominated intellectual and social reformer Henry George as mayoral candidate. Widely supported, George took an astonishing 68,000 votes against Democrat Abram S. Hewitt, who won with 90,000 votes, and Republican Theodore Roosevelt, who came third with 60,000. The New York legislature responded by enacting a series of labor laws. It created a board of mediation and arbitration; instituted a ten-hour day for men working on streets and elevated railways, for women, and for children under age fourteen; insisted that goods made by convicts be so labeled; prohibited employers from intimidating union members; and established a code governing the safety and sanitation of tenement buildings. Outside New York the new political movement achieved more. The movement reached its zenith the following spring when labor tickets carried nineteen communities in the Midwest and the city of Chicago. Yet the numbers of people actively involved in Socialist organizations remained minute. The weight of the labor movement was now divided between two rival associations, the Knights of Labor and the American Federation of Labor.

THE KNIGHTS OF LABOR

The Noble Order of the Knights of Labor was founded by nine tailors in the hall of the American Hose Company in Philadelphia on December 9, 1869. Their leader was Uriah S. Stephens. He wanted to unify all workers in a single order, regardless of color or creed, sex or nationality. Prospective initiates had to undergo searching investigation and ritual before being admitted. The Knights established eighty craft unions in or around Philadelphia within the next two years, among them carpenters and cutters, masons and machinists, blacksmiths and ironworkers. Membership was open to all wage earners but closed to the professions. Retired workers could join, but their number was restricted to a quota of a quarter.

In January 1878 the Knights established a general assembly at a special convention in Reading, Pennsylvania. They adopted the following "First Principles": direct representation and legislation, the initiative and referendum, establishment of bureaus of labor statistics, taxation of unearned increments in land values, compulsory arbitration of labor disputes, prohibition of child labor, federal ownership of the railroads, the eight-hour day, and free coinage of silver at a ratio of 16 to 1. It was due to pressure from the Knights and their affiliates that Congress established a Bureau of Labor in 1884. But their ultimate goal was the establishment of "co-operative institutions productive and distributive." The

Knights membership fluctuated widely. It rose to 42,000 in 1882 and by 1885 was more than 100,000. Local assemblies mixed skilled and unskilled workers. This was the Knights' greatest strength and greatest weakness.

In 1879 Terence V. Powderly, a machinist and union organizer who had just been elected labor mayor of Scranton, Pennsylvania, became grand master workman. The son of Irish Catholic immigrants to Carbondale, Pennsylvania, he also served as vice president of the Irish Land League, practiced at the bar, and managed a grocery store. Diminutive, dapper, even dainty, Powderly did not look like a determined leader of labor. Yet his political skill was beyond dispute. He was eloquent on platform and paper. By adept manipulation he built up a personal machine that enabled him to dominate the general assembly for fourteen years. Powderly envisioned the skilled defending the unskilled, the strong championing the weak. "An injury to one is the concern for all" was the Knights' slogan. But this was not how skilled workers saw it. Traditional craft unions had concluded they could make nothing of unskilled labor. They were unwilling to take the risk and join forces. Thus, the conventional unions were opposed to the aims of the Knights from the start. Soon they opposed the association itself.

The Knights played a crucial role in various strikes during the winter of 1883–84. In 1885 militant knight Joseph R. Buchanan organized discontented workers on the entire Southwest System into local assemblies. The unscrupulous entrepreneur Jay Gould controlled the Southwest System, which included the Wabash. When the Wabash tried to break the local assemblies by firing railway workers who were knights, the district assembly at Moberley, Missouri, ordered Knights remaining with the Wabash to go on strike. Gould's entire system was brought to a halt. He was forced to come to terms with the Knights. The impact of his surrender was sensational. As Joseph Rayback puts it, "The Gould strikes made the Knights the undisputed leaders of the labor movement." In the next few months more local assemblies were formed than in the previous sixteen years. Total membership increased more than seven times to over 700,000, as unskilled and semiskilled workers from mines, railroads, and heavy industry flocked to the association that had beaten Jay Gould. Powderly claimed later that at least 400,000 people came out of curiosity and caused more harm than good.

People expected too much of the Knights, and too much was what they got. As Oscar Wilde remarked, there is only one thing worse than being denied one's heart's desire and that is attaining it. Carried away by past successes, workers continued to press employers and to rely on the national executive to back them up. Employees of the Missouri Pacific and Missouri, Kansas and Texas railroads, who had supported their colleagues in the Wabash strike of 1885, now expected full support from the union in their own claim for higher wages. When a foreman on the Texas and Pacific was dismissed, Master Workman Martin Irons used the incident as a pretext for calling an unofficial strike.

Extravagant demands convinced Jay Gould and his managers that the Knights should be crushed once and for all. He had retreated in 1885 in order to prepare his forces for 1886. As the strike deteriorated into widespread violence, Powderly was obliged to condone in public actions that he condemned in private. This time there was no chance of negotiation. Gould and his allies were adamant. People interpreted the strike as an attempt to violate the rights of business and were as intransigent in their hostility to the strikers as they had been to Gould the year before.

In the last six months of 1886 about 100,000 workers were involved in labor disputes in other industries. The outcome was much the same everywhere. The Knights were most discredited by an abortive strike in the Chicago Stock Yards over the eight-hour day. Powderly intervened at a critical juncture. The strikers had already convinced the associated meatpackers that it was time to compromise. But Powderly ordered his men back to work, and the Knights lost control of the situation. One by one the other strikes fizzled out.

Although the mid-1880s were years of the dinosaur, there were new mammals ready to take their place at its side. Unions crushed by the depression of 1873 slowly returned to life. In 1880 there were already 2,440 local unions. By 1883 they had around 200,000 members. Some of the new or revived unions became adjuncts to the Knights; others stayed aloof. Their revival followed no particular pattern except competition and conflict among themselves. However, as events unfolded, it became clear that the Knights were failing and that their program was partly to blame. Thus, the revived craft unions contracted their scope to expand their theme—a better deal for their own workers.

Powderly refused to associate the Knights with the reviving trade unions' attempt to call a general strike for the eight-hour day on May 1, 1886. However, the Knights' new members, who numbered hundreds of thousands, seized upon the eight-hour movement as an issue with which they could confront employers and demonstrate the fierce power they attributed to the Knights. Primarily unskilled, certainly oppressed, they were looking for trouble and they got it. Despite Powderly's ban, thousands of knights took part in workers' demonstrations. It was at this crucial juncture that the Haymarket bomb exploded. Despite all their denials, the Knights were tainted by presumed association. Public odium was spread by conviction, contagion, and intimidation.

AMERICAN FEDERATION OF LABOR

The union that now played the central role in the movement for labor federation was the International Cigar Makers. It fell into the hands of three remarkable men, Adolph Strasser, Ferdinand Laurrell, and Samuel Gompers. Gompers became president of the New York union, and in 1877 Strasser was elected president of the International union. For the sake of financial stability they adopted initiation fees and high dues. To ensure loyalty they awarded benefit payments for sickness and death. From British unions they took the principle of equalization of funds: a local union that was financially healthy might be required to transfer funds to another that was financially weak.

Gompers was an English immigrant of Dutch-Jewish ancestry who had left London in 1863 at the age of thirteen. He spent his adolescence in the cigarmaking shops of the Lower East Side and absorbed the political discussions he heard among fellow workers. As a young man of twenty-five Gompers had stood among the crowd during the Tompkins Square riot of 1874. Years later in his autobiography (1925) he explained what this formative experience had taught him:

I saw how professions of radicalism and sensationalism concentrated all the forces of society against a labor movement and nullified in advance normal, necessary activity. I saw that leadership in the labor movement could be safely entrusted only to those into whose hearts and minds had been woven the experience of earning their bread by daily labor.

His prime concern was the status of skilled labor. Under his leadership it attained greater stability than ever before. The cost was borne, not by the middle class, but by the unskilled. Gompers and Powderly were rivals, but there was more to their quarrel than a clash of conflicting personalities. In the field of labor relations Powderly's strategy was political education and his policy law reform. Gompers's strategy was economic opportunism and his policy law observance.

In 1886 the Knights played into the hands of its enemies. When the New York Cigar Manufacturers' Association cut wages in January 1886, both the local cigarmakers' unions protested. The manufacturers ordered a lockout of 10,000 men. One union, Progressive Union No. 1, gave in and settled with the employers. The other, Local 144, felt betrayed. It accused the Knights, who had incorporated the Progressive Union, of raiding, or poaching, its fellow workers. Samuel Gompers was head of Local 144 and persuaded the Cigarmakers' International to institute a boycott of all other cigars. This agitation was the catalyst in the explosion of accumulated grievances felt by craft unions against the Knights.

They sent representatives to a conference in Philadelphia on May 18, 1886. They ensured that the Knights' proposals, designed to raise the rights and status of the unskilled, were rejected by every national trade union. In October 1886 the Knights met at Richmond, Virginia, and ordered all members affiliated with the Cigarmakers' International to resign or forfeit membership in the Noble Order. Craft unions responded to the Knights' moves by meeting a second time, at Columbus, Ohio, on December 8, 1886. There were forty-two representatives of twenty-five groups. Their prime interest was the promotion of their particular crafts. Their vehicle was the new American Federation of Labor which now took definitive form.

The AFL acknowledged the discontent provoked by the Knights and was determined to avoid its mistakes. It recognized the autonomy of each trade within it. The executive council could not interfere in the internal affairs of member unions. It levied a tax on member unions to create a strike fund and maintain a secretariat. To promote labor legislation in the cities and the states it formed city centrals and state federations.

Gompers was elected first president in 1886 and served in that capacity, with the exception of one year, until his death in 1924. For the first five years he was the only full-time officer. In an office measuring eight by ten feet he sat on an upturned crate at a kitchen table and kept his files in tomato boxes. He wrote innumerable letters, edited the *Trade Union Advocate*, issued union charters, collected funds, and organized conventions. Gompers never lost the common touch. It was his personality rather than his politics that inspired popular support for the AFL. Growth was slow. In 1892 the initial membership of 150,000 had increased only to 250,000. Government, courts, and industry were all hostile. But survival alone was no mean feat in a depression.

HOMESTEAD AND PULLMAN

In the 1890s the labor movement was scarred by two great strikes, the Homestead and the Pullman. Homestead, a borough of Pennsylvania seven miles east of Pittsburgh, on the left bank of the Monongahela River, had more than 10,000 inhabitants, of whom 3,431 were employed by the Carnegie Steel Company. The plant produced beams, boiler plates, and structural iron. By an agreement of 1889 wages were paid on a sliding scale according to the market price of standard Bessemer steel billets. Only 800 workers were skilled, and they earned, on average, $2.43 for a twelve-hour shift. Unskilled workers were paid 14 cents an hour. The agreement was due to expire on June 30, 1892. About 780 skilled workers at Homestead were firm members of the Amalgated Association of Iron, Steel and Tin Workers. They wanted better terms and union recognition. Moreover, they were supported by the rest of the work force.

On the surface, it seemed that they had good expectations. Andrew Carnegie was on record in the *Forum* in April 1886 as saying that workers had as good a right to combine as manufacturers. In the *Forum* in August 1886 he went much further and implied that he condoned, or at least understood, strike action and sympathized with strikers who turned violent.

Carnegie was in Scotland. His ruthless lieutenant, Henry Clay Frick, chairman of the board, was in charge. J. H. Bridge, once Carnegie's ghost writer, explained in his *Inside Story of the Carnegie Steel Company* (1903) why Carnegie first encouraged and then destroyed the Amalgamated Association of Iron and Steel Workers. At first, the union was his ally in his campaign for monopoly control of steel. A national trade union served to depress wages throughout the entire industry. Carnegie's competitors, unable to cut labor costs below his, must then wither in the face of his great might. After he had eliminated his rivals, however, he had no need of the union. Also, it represented a challenge to his monopoly.

The union had three principal objections to the company's proposals for the new contract. First, it opposed the reduction in the minimum price of the sliding scale from $25 to $23 per ton of steel billets. In effect, workers would lose between 18 and 26 percent of their pay. Second, the union opposed a change in the date of contract from June 30 to December 31. The men knew they could not bargain as effectively in winter as in summer because severe weather precluded strike action. Third, they resented a reduction in tonnage rates at works where new and better machinery had been installed. Throughout the negotiations and the dispute Frick's attitude was utterly unyielding. The union, led by Hugh O'Donnell and John W. Gates, was equally intractable and called a strike.

On June 30, 1892, Frick ordered a lockout. He intended to import strikebreakers and had three miles of barbed-wire fencing twelve feet high erected around the works. That was not his only precaution. On July 4, 1892, company attorneys Knox and Reed requested Sheriff William H. McCleary of Allegheny County for a hundred deputies to protect the works. But he was unable to assemble a posse. The *New York Sun* of July 9, 1892, explained that the original posse was no better than Falstaff's army. Of twenty-three men, two were lame and needed crutches; nineteen presented doctors' certificates that they were unfit to serve; and two were firebrands dismissed as too dangerous for duty. In fact, citizens of Homestead supported the strike.

Frick had struck a deal with Robert Pinkerton, now head of the Pinkerton National Detective Agency, on June 20. He would hire 300 detectives at $5 a day to act as "watchmen." On July 6 they arrived at Homestead in two barges by a tug up the Monongahela River. The workers had already barricaded themselves inside the plant with steel billets from which they now repulsed the Pinkertons in a battle that lasted from four in the morning to five in the evening. In the Battle of Homestead 7 strikers were killed and 3 Pinkerton men were fatally wounded. Even aboard the barges the detectives were not safe. The strikers fired on them from a small brass cannon and then poured oil onto the Monongahela River, which they then set afire. Deserted by the tug, the Pinkertons had no choice but to surrender. Nothing happened for another six days. However, at Frick's request, Governor Robert E. Pattison of Pennsylvania summoned 8,000 state militia who marched into Homestead on July 12 and placed the works under martial law.

On July 23 tragedy turned into black farce. A Russian immigrant anarchist, Alexander Berkman, tried to kill Frick in his Pittsburgh office, first with a pistol, then by dagger. Frick was wounded in the neck, back, and side. In the melee J. G. A. Leishman, company president, was also injured. Berkman was covered in blood when he was arrested. He had intended to cheat the authorities by blowing himself up with two dynamite cartridges hidden in his mouth. But the officers seized him by the throat, and he spat the cartridges out. According to *Reynolds Weekly* on July 31, 1892, one of the soldiers stationed at Homestead, Private Jams, called out after the attempt on Frick, "Three cheers for the assassin!" His commanding officer, Colonel Streeter, had him hung up by his thumbs for half an hour. After he was cut down his head was shaved on one side and he was drummed out of camp.

Frick's injuries were not serious enough to keep him from work on the day he was attacked. But they were fatal to the strike. On July 27 the Homestead plant reopened with 1,000 new workers under temporary military protection. On September 22, 1892, a grand jury returned 167 bills against Hugh O'Donnell and other union leaders charging murder, aggravated riot, and conspiracy. But no jury would find against company workers. When the company failed to secure O'Donnell's conviction, both sides agreed not to prosecute one another further.

Frick had meant to break the strike and crush the union. He succeeded. The union collapsed at Homestead. In the face of continued hostility from the Carnegie Company it dissolved elsewhere. It would be another forty years before an effective steel union was formed in the United States.

The train of events in the Pullman strike of 1894 struck further at the workers' cause. George M. Pullman, manufacturer of railroad cars, founded the town of Pullman, south of Chicago, in 1880. Its 300 acres accommodated houses, shops, and other amenities as well as mills, factories, and a foundry. Although Pullman workers were not trapped in some urban slum, they were living in a ghetto nonetheless. They had no choice but to rent quarters; buy food, water, and gas; and pay for services from the company. And everything was more expensive than elsewhere.

Pullman himself was certainly not penniless. The Pullman Company was capitalized at $36 million in 1894. At the end of the financial year July 31, 1893, dividends amounted to $2.52 million and wages to $7.22 million. However, in the depression the Pullman Company not only discharged more than 3,000 of its 5,800 employees but also cut the wages of those whom it retained while maintaining its old prices for lodging and services. After deductions, most were left with $6 a week, and one had no more than 2 cents. At the same time, the company continued to pay shareholders their regular dividends. Thus, on July 31, 1894, dividends had risen to $2.88 million, although wages had fallen to $4.47 million.

In May 1894 George Pullman received a grievance committee of employees but refused to consider adjustments to either wages or prices. He maintained that there was no relationship between his dual role as landlord and employer. He then fired three of the delegates in violation of a pledge not to do so. It was this action that led to a strike by Pullman local unions on May 11. The company was later obliged to close its plant.

The first meat train leaves the Chicago Stock-Yards under escort of the United States Cavalry on July 10, 1894, and the secondary strike by the American Railway Union in support of the Pullman strikers is broken. President Grover Cleveland intervened in the affair over the protest of Governor John Altgeld of Illinois. The drawing by G. W. Peters after G. A. Coffin was carried by *Harper's Weekly* on July 28, 1894. (Library of Congress).

What transformed the strike from a conventional, if bitter, labor dispute into a conflict on a national scale was the secondary action of the American Railway Union. The American Railway Union had been formed in 1893 by Eugene V. Debs as an industrial union open to all white employees of the railroads. On June 21, 1894, it intervened in the Pullman dispute. Debs secured a resolution ordering his members not to handle Pullman cars if, after five days, the Pullman Company still refused to go to arbitration. Pullman would not give in, and on June 26 the boycott went into effect.

The General Managers' Association, a group of executives of twenty-four railroads entering Chicago, retaliated on Pullman's behalf. It ordered railroads to fire workers who took part. But the ARU was ready. Every time someone was fired for refusing to handle a Pullman car the entire train crew would go on strike. Within a month the strike was so widespread that almost every railroad in the Midwest was affected, and the nation's entire transportation system was seriously disrupted. In the week ending June 30 the ten trunk lines entering Chicago carried 42,892 tons of freight bound for the East. A week later the total tonnage was only 11,600.

One of the most controversial men in labor history, Eugene Debs was an eloquent speaker, a shrewd orator, and an aggressive leader. He was the son of French-Alsatian immigrants who had settled in Terre Haute, Indiana, where his father ran a grocery store. After brief careers as grocery clerk and railway engineer, he became national secretary-treasurer of the Brotherhood of Locomotive Firemen in 1878 when he was twenty-five. In 1892 he resigned in order to form the separate American Railway Union. His passionate concern was the dispossessed.

Although he had called the strike, he did not want it. He thought the ARU was too new and too weak to take on the giant railroads. But he believed that if he gave in before Pullman both he and his association would lose all credibility. To retain public confidence Debs insisted on peaceful, passive resistance from his men. This was the last thing the railroads wanted. They looked for trouble to win public opinion to their sides. When they could not find it they fomented it.

Three quarters of the railroads entering Chicago had been

stopped in their tracks. The strikers were steadfast but no longer disciplined. Declining morale and deteriorating behavior among them gave the managers an important strategic advantage. They devised new tactics to exploit the situation. They imported Canadian strikebreakers and ordered them to attach Pullman cars to mail cars. Thus, if strikers detached the Pullman cars they could be accused of interfering with the federal mails. The owners also persuaded their ally, Attorney General Richard Olney, to hire 3,400 special deputies, whom they themselves paid, to keep the trains running.

Olney appointed a railroad lawyer, Edwin Walker, as special counsel to District Attorney T. E. Milchrist in Chicago, and together with federal judges Peter J. Grosscup and C. D. Wood they also devised an injunction to trap Debs. If Debs obeyed the injunction and protested to a court, the strike would be broken until the case was actually heard. If he disobeyed the injunction, he would face arrest and punishment and disruption of the strike by the authorities. Under an injunction, moreover, there was no trial by jury. The judge issued the injunction and fixed punishment on those he deemed to have broken it.

On July 2 U.S. Marshal Arnold read out the injunction against the strike to a crowd at Blue Island, outside Chicago. He and his 125 deputies were hooted down and jostled. This incident served as pretext to invite President Cleveland to send in federal troops, which he did on July 4. It was their arrival that led to widespread violence. The worst riots occurred on July 7, 8, and 9 when crowds attacked an Illinois regiment, which retaliated by firing back at point-blank range. Scores of people were wounded, about 30 fatally. Soon there were 14,000 thousand state and federal troops at large in the city.

Debs was desperate and sought a general strike. But the AFL would not back him. Samuel Gompers was opposed to strikes on principle and, in addition, was jealous of the success enjoyed by Debs. Bereft, Debs offered to call off the strike if the Pullman Company agreed to take no reprisals. But there was no reason why it should concede anything. The courts were ready to take revenge. On July 19 a federal grand jury returned twenty-three indictments against seventy-five people, including Debs, his vice president, George W. Howard; his secretary, Sylvester Keliher; and the union director, L. W. Rogers. Deprived of leadership, denied their rights, and totally demoralized, the remaining strikers abandoned the struggle and returned to work.

Debs and defense lawyer Clarence Darrow tried to have the conspiracy indictments brought to trial. But, the government was reluctant. A trial opened on February 9, 1895, before Judge Gros-scup. Darrow was obstructed in almost every way, and when a juror fell ill the case was postponed indefinitely. However, the trial for contempt and subsequent appeal, in *in re Debs*, set a major precedent. Debs justified his actions by telling the court, "It seems to me that if it were not for resistance to degrading conditions, the tendency of our whole civilization would be downward; after a while we would reach the point where there would be no resistance, and slavery would come." It was no use. The circuit court used the Sherman Anti-Trust Act to support conviction. When it came to the appeal, the Supreme Court sustained conviction on other grounds. Previously, injunctions had been used to protect property from damage by arson, trespass, or sabotage. But when legal strikes or boycotts remained peaceful, it was much harder to prove irreparable damage. The only way was to establish conspiracy and argue that to conspire in restraint of trade was a civil as well as a criminal offense. Thus, in a notorious piece of sophistry the Court equated expectations with property. In *in re Lennon* in 1897 the Supreme Court went further, giving approval of the "blanket injunction." It declared that anyone who knew of an injunction was obliged to obey it, whether or not it was specifically directed at him.

By imprisoning Debs for six months in Woodstock, Illinois, the courts turned him into a martyr and made many converts to his cause. After his release he was acclaimed by a throng of 100,000 in Chicago. Journalist Henry Demarest Lloyd could describe him as "the most popular man among the real people today." The collapse of his cause had convinced Debs that the true rights of labor could not be achieved under capitalism.

The working class movement could not survive without justice. The crushing defeats of Homestead and Pullman were bitter reminders of the overwhelming power of capitalism. Moreover, any gains industrial workers had made before the depression had been wiped out. Their average annual income was $406. Apart from some highly skilled trades, the eight-hour day was nowhere in sight. Their working week was usually between fifty-four and sixty-three hours. In certain industries—steel and textiles—the hours were even longer.

The only promise for the future rested with the AFL and its traditional trade unions. In 1901 there were 1.05 million members of trade unions of whom 788,000, or 75 percent, belonged to the 87 affiliated unions of the AFL. Gompers, however, opposed industrial unionism, the inclusion of all workers in an industry in the same union regardless of their specific work. Year after year the AFL defeated convention resolutions in favor of industrial unionism, in part because they were proposed by the Socialists. However, in the Scranton declaration of 1901 the AFL accepted the amalgamation of unions serving similar crafts. Craft unions had expanded and diversified. Their names suggest as much: the International Association of Marble, Slate and Stone Polishers, Rubbers and Sawyers, Tile and Marble Setters Helpers and Terrazo Helpers was a single union.

American Socialists continued their fight against capitalism and, sometimes, one another. Daniel De Leon, an immigrant from Curaçao, assumed control of the SLP in the 1890s and tried unsuccessfully to infiltrate both the waning Knights and the waxing AFL. He also insisted on strict adherence to his own somewhat inconsistent interpretation of Marx among his followers. This authoritarian attitude was too much for Jewish groups, which broke with the SLP in 1897 and 1898. Their leaders, Victor Berger and Morris Hillquit, eventually joined Eugene Debs in founding the Socialist party of America in 1901. In the presidential election of 1900 Debs had taken 87,814 Socialist votes.

The most significant gains of labor at the end of the century were in federal and state legislation. In 1898 Congress passed the Erdman Act. Under section 10 interstate railroads were forbidden to discriminate against union members. Elsewhere there were some striking changes in labor legislation. Even so new laws defined, rather than solved, particular problems. Labor legislation between 1886 and the end of the century devolved on six issues:

industrial arbitration; child labor; women's labor; safety precautions; responsibility for accidents; the eight hour day.

Both New York and Massachusetts provided state boards of arbitration to which either side in a dispute could apply. When both sides accepted the service they were found to abide by its decision. Twenty other states created similar boards before 1900. Child labor was a complex subject involving minimum age, maximum hours, and mode of work. Twenty-six states had passed minimum age laws by 1900. The usual minimum was twelve years. All northern states except Illinois established a maximum day of ten hours and a maximum week of sixty hours in industry for children between twelve and eighteen. Eight states prohibited work at night; most forbade child labor in dangerous industries. In 1874 Massachusetts limited the number of hours women could work in industry. By 1900 so had twelve other states. Four states prohibited night work.

Ten states extended rules governing employer responsibility for industrial accidents. They made employers immediately responsible for accidents caused by defective machinery. Seventeen prohibited industrialists or railroad owners from evading responsibility in workers' contracts. Although by 1886 seventeen states had limited the working day for men their laws were incomplete and allowed longer hours by contract. However, after 1892 ten states established maximum hours for workers on public contract including seven northern states who limited railroad labor to fifteen hours of continuous duty.

Most employers feared to meet union demands lest they be applied unequally and they would be placed at a disadvantage with their competitors. American workers had been educated in schools to believe in social and political democracy. Industrialists were schooled by experience to believe in economic autocracy. Thus they resisted the very formation of unions. Some would have rather closed their plants than accept unionization. President Francis Meisel of the Kidder Press Company told the industrial commission of 1901, "I do not believe that a manufacturer can afford to be dictated by his labor as to what he shall do, and I shall never give in. I would rather go out of business."

CHAPTER SIX

RECONSTRUCTION AND THE NEW SOUTH

No STORY in the Gilded Age is more harrowing than the tragedy of American Reconstruction. It proceeded inevitably from a skein of historical contradictions. The American Revolution was achieved by radicals in the name of liberty but the institution of slavery was preserved. Abraham Lincoln fought the Civil War to free the slaves, but to save the Union he would have freed none. The victory of the Union army over the Confederacy dispossessed the very people it had emancipated. Black leader Frederick Douglass described the plight of freedmen. The black "was free from the individual master but a slave of society. He had neither money, property, nor friends. He was free from the old plantation, but he had nothing but the dusty road under his feet. He was free from the old quarter that once gave him shelter, but a slave to the rains of summer and the frosts of winter. He was turned loose, naked, hungry, and destitute to the open sky." Yet the courage, resilience, and lack of vindictiveness of these new black citizens under extreme provocation somewhat redeems the bitter tragedy that unfolded in the South.

The victory of the North had retied the knot of Union, but the rope itself was in shreds. The South itself was in ruins. Large areas had been devastated. Major cities, such as Charleston and Richmond, had been badly damaged by bombardment and fire. Banking had collapsed; agriculture was stagnant; and the entire region lay prostrated. The South was, however, conquered rather than subdued. Because its army had been defeated in the field did not mean that the former Confederates accepted the politics of the North. They were determined that when the South rose from the ashes of defeat it would be on the basis of southern, not northern ideas. They recognized that the South's lack of industry was one of the prime reasons it had lost the war. They, therefore, sought capital to build a New South with industrial muscle. Northern businessmen began to invest in southern plantations, railroads, and mills. However, they too wanted to shape Reconstruction to their own economic ends.

There were three distinct phases of Reconstruction: presidential restoration in the mid-1860s; radical Reconstruction of the late 1860s and early 1870s; and southern redemption thereafter. Reconstruction engendered in the South a legacy of bitterness greater than the hatred caused by the Civil War. It was perhaps the most controversial event during the Gilded Age and provoked passionate historical disputes for a century afterward. This ensured that though the subject was black the books were read. Yet the final outcome of Reconstruction was a compromise, economic and political on the part of the South, social and racist on the part of the North. The achievements of the war—preservation of the Union and abolition of slavery—were not made the foundation for political and economic progress in the New South.

PRESIDENTIAL RESTORATION

President Abraham Lincoln announced his general plan for restoration in his Proclamation of Amnesty and Reconstruction on December 8, 1863. He offered a pardon to former Confederates who took an oath to support the Union and the Constitution. When the number who did so in any state had reached a tenth of the votes cast in the presidential election of 1860 and when they had established a state government, he would recognize it. He excluded black Americans from taking the oath, voting, and holding office. Lincoln intended to put his plan into practice in successive stages as the army recovered more and more land. The most outspoken critics of presidential restoration were radicals in the Republican party, led by Thaddeus Stevens of Pennsylvania, Benjamin Wade of Ohio, Zachariah Chandler of Michigan, and Charles Sumner of Massachusetts. They were determined to safeguard the rights of freedmen in the South, to ensure the supremacy of Congress in government, and to assert the ascendancy of the Republican party in politics.

They put forward their alternative plan of Reconstruction. Proposed by Senator Benjamin Wade of Ohio and Representative Henry Winter Davis of Maryland, it passed Congress in July 1864. It required a majority of enrolled white citizens to take an oath to support the Constitution before state conventions could be called to reconstitute the state government. Prospective delegates and electors had to swear an "ironclad" test oath that they had never voluntarily borne arms against the United States. However, Lincoln vetoed the bill as impractical and unchristian, whereupon his rivals issued a scathing manifesto complaining that he had exceeded his prerogative. Lincoln was not deterred and went on to recognize reconstituted civil governments in Virginia, Louisiana, and Arkansas in 1864, and in Tennessee in February 1865. He also began to widen the categories of former Confederates who could take the oath. Congress, however, refused to seat representatives from the "Lincoln states" and denounced his policies as too lenient.

Lincoln's successor, Andrew Johnson, was sworn in as president a few hours after Lincoln's assassination on April 15, 1865. Johnson had served Tennessee as assemblyman, governor, and senator. His subsequent success as military governor of Tennessee for the Union and the fact that he was a Democratic southerner of unquestioned loyalty convinced Republican elders that he would make an ideal running mate for Lincoln on a ticket of National Union in the election of 1864. In the great emergency of the war it did not seem important that Johnson's political roots were quite different from those of the Republican party. However, his critics made much of the fact that he was undoubtedly drunk during the inauguration in 1865. He was not used to spirits and had taken whiskey for medicinal purposes after an attack of typhoid fever.

Johnson was now the titular leader of a party of national union that had died with Lincoln. Radicals inferred from his vehement condemnation of Confederates that he agreed with their aims. He told Benjamin Wade, "Treason is a crime and crime must be punished. Treason must be made infamous and traitors must be impoverished." But radicals were soon to be disabused of their misunderstanding. Johnson, like Lincoln, believed that it was his duty to secure the prompt restoration of the South to its proper place in Union affairs. But whereas Lincoln was flexible, Johnson was obstinate. Hypersensitive to criticism, he regarded compromise as a sign of weakness.

On May 9, 1865, Johnson recognized the government of Francis H. Pierpont in Virginia. On May 29, he issued his own proclamation of amnesty. It simply required an oath of allegiance from those seeking pardon but also increased the categories of excluded persons by forbidding people with property valued at more than $20,000 to take the oath. This exclusion was more apparent than actual. Johnson wanted to humiliate rather than punish wealthy planters, who had to seek a special personal pardon from the president. On May 29 Johnson also announced his plan for the reconstruction of North Carolina. He appointed William H. Holden provisional governor, empowered to call a convention of loyal citizens who would frame a new state constitution. No one could serve as elector or delegate unless he had been qualified to vote in 1860 and now took the oath of allegiance, but the convention could prescribe its own qualifications for electors and officeholders. Within six weeks Johnson issued the same proclamation to the six remaining states of the Confederacy.

The South was optimistic about the chances of regaining control of its own destiny. But it had several complaints about northern mismanagement of its affairs. It was especially critical of the Freedmen's Bureau. The Bureau of Refugees, Freedmen, and Abandoned Lands had been established by Congress on March 3, 1865, under a commissioner, Gen. Oliver O. Howard, to provide material assistance to refugees and freedman. It was also to establish schools, supervise labor contracts between employers and freedmen, and manage confiscated or derelict land. By 1869 it had distributed 21 million rations, established 40 hospitals, treated 450,000 patients, and helped settle 30,000 refugees. Most abandoned lands were restored to pardoned rebels. But its greatest

The excitement that a stirring speech could generate in the theater of politics during Reconstruction is captured in this wood engraving of a crowd surging to the public galleries of the Senate on February 24, 1868, to hear Thaddeus Stevens call for the impeachment of President Andrew Johnson. An illustration from the *London Illustrated News*. (Library of Congress).

achievement was in the field of education. By 1870 it had placed 250,000 black children in 4,300 schools. Another hated symbol of northern interference were Treasury agents assigned by Congress to appropriate any abandoned land and collect taxes levied on cotton. In payment they were allowed to retain 25 percent of their returns. The more unscrupulous took advantage of the system to line their own pockets.

The six unrestored states held conventions in late 1865 and accepted Johnson's implicit preconditions for readmission by repudiating slavery, secession, and the Confederate debt. However, southerners were so ready to anticipate any revolution in race relations that they overlooked the political need to satisfy northern scruples about the former slaves. On the eve of the Civil War there were 3,953,760 slaves, most of whom worked as field hands or domestics. Their collective value, estimated at $2 billion, had evaporated with emancipation. Moreover, many of the freedmen were on the move. Several had run away from their former masters to the Union army; others had fled with their masters from the army; some were moving about to test their new freedom. Their migration reawakened traditional white fears of a black insurrection.

Republicans who wanted to penetrate the South and build up their party there planned to give blacks the vote on the assumption that they would cast it for the party that had freed them. But they were less disposed to enfranchise blacks in the North, and they recognized that the Constitution guaranteed the states the right to regulate their own suffrage. Johnson did not think that blacks were equipped for political equality and believed that black suffrage would become yet another instrument in the hands of the aristocratic planters he hated so much.

The congressional elections in the former Confederate states were a victory for the Old South. To the Thirty-ninth Congress, meeting in December 1865, were returned the vice president, four generals, five colonels, six cabinet officers, and fifty-eight congressmen of the defeated Confederacy. The pattern was much the same in the state elections. To add insult to injury, the new assemblymen flaunted their Confederate connections. For example, in Louisiana former officers wore their Confederate uniforms in the legislature. Such behavior turned a difficult situation into an impossible one and denied Johnson's policies any chance of immediate success.

The so-called Black Codes, laws that defined the blacks' new rights and status, were the most widely publicized part of southern Reconstruction. They recognized blacks' rights to own property, to sue and be sued, and to marry and bear legitimate children. But they forbade them to marry whites and allowed them to give evidence only in court cases involving other blacks. More important to the South and more controversial in the North were laws governing labor contracts, such as laws against enticing blacks to leave their employers before their contracts had expired. The Black Codes were most severe in those states where blacks outnumbered whites—in Mississippi, South Carolina, and Louisiana. Mississippi decreed that all persons not lawfully employed on January 1, 1866, were to be arrested as vagrants. If they could not pay a statutory fine of $50, they would be hired out to anyone who paid the fine in exchange for the shortest period of labor.

RADICAL RECONSTRUCTION

Congress disliked Johnson's scheme for Reconstruction. It seemed that his policy was to restore defeated and discredited Confederates to power in the South. What northerners wanted was a harsher policy; what Republicans wanted was to strengthen their party. The infamous Black Codes were taken as proof of southern arrogance and a determination to reverse the result of the Civil War. As abolitionist Wendell Phillips declared, "Now is the critical time. The rebellion has not ceased, it has only changed its weapons. Once it fought; now it intrigues; once it followed Lee in arms, now it follows President Johnson in guile and chicanery."

Outraged by the tide of events, Congress refused to seat the southern representatives. It thus served notice on Johnson that it would not accept presidential restoration. Instead, it established a Joint Committee of Fifteen "to inquire into the conditions of the States which formed the so-called Confederate States of America." The committee was not controlled by radicals, but its most influential member was Thaddeus Stevens, leader of the Republicans in the House. At seventy-four he was an embittered enemy of the old southern aristocracy, which he blamed for the destruction of his Pennsylvania ironworks during the Gettysburg campaign. When it seemed that Johnson was shielding the South, Stevens transferred his implacable hostility to him. Stevens made his position crystal-clear: "I am for Negro suffrage in every rebel State. If it be just it should not be denied; if it be necessary it should be adopted; if it be punishment to traitors, they deserve it."

The committee interviewed 144 witnesses and gave especial attention to the problems of race relations and the Freedmen's Bureau. It set a precedent for, and became the prototype of, wide-ranging congressional investigations in the Gilded Age. Its final report of 700 pages was a disturbing testimony of man's inhumanity to man. The joint committee concluded that the states were intact but that their governments were a shambles. Before the rebel states could be allowed to return to the Union it would be necessary to shape them politically and socially so as to ensure the protection of blacks and the survival of the Republican party in the South. To that end, radicals secured the Civil Rights Act, passed over Johnson's veto on April 10, 1866. It conferred full citizenship on all persons born within the United States whatever their color or race, giving them equal rights in contracts, property, and personal security. Buoyed up with their success, the radicals then persuaded Congress to pass a new Freedmen's Bureau bill and to sustain it over Johnson's veto in July 1866.

To ensure the survival of their policies against presidential veto, congressional repeal, or judicial reversal, the radicals and their allies incorporated their policies straightforwardly into the Fourteenth Amendment. The first section of the Amendment defined citizens as those born or naturalized in the United States and enjoined states from abridging their rights to life, liberty, property, and due process of law. The second section threatened to reduce proportionately the representation in Congress of any state denying the suffrage to adult males. The third excluded from Congress, the electoral college, and federal office anyone who had served the federal government under oath and then taken part in rebellion. The fourth upheld the validity of the federal debt but repudiated the Confederate debt and any claims of compensation for emancipated slaves. When it passed Congress on June 13, 1866, there was an underlying consensus of congressional opinion that the rebel states must ratify the Fourteenth Amendment before they could be readmitted to the Union. Tennessee did so promptly and was readmitted on July 24, 1866.

But the process was far from peaceful. Public resentment in Memphis burst in a terrible riot on April 30 and lasted three days. Forty-six blacks were killed, and more than 80 were wounded. Twelve black schools and four churches were burned. In New Orleans an attempt by radicals to take away the vote from Confederate veterans and give it to freedmen led to another riot on July 30 in which 34 blacks and 4 whites died and more than 200 people were injured. The federal commander, Gen. Philip Sheridan, described it not just as a riot but "an absolute massacre by the police . . . a murder which the mayor and police . . . perpetrated without the shadow of necessity." Northern reaction was instantaneous and unanimous. The *New York Tribune* spoke for half the country in its condemnation, "The hands of the rebel are again red with loyal blood."

Johnson was trying to bring moderate Republicans and Democrats into a new National Union party. But there was no true common interest, and the convention at Philadelphia in 1866 was a fiasco. Northern delegates feared that they would be overwhelmed by the South; and when the huge governor of South Carolina, James Lawrence Orr, walked down the aisle arm in arm with the slight governor of Massachusetts, Darius Couch, they feared it might be both metaphor and portent. Johnson then made a whistle-stop tour of the North indulging in vehement exchanges with hecklers and condemning the radicals and their policies. The radicals made small but significant gains in the November elections. The ten remaining southern states chose to defy them by rejecting the Fourteenth Amendment, and this provoked the northern states—albeit reluctantly in some cases—to ratify it.

Congress was now clearly in the ascendant, and the president's many personal enemies were prepared to destroy both him and his power. They could and did override his veto of Charles Sumner's bill enfranchising blacks in the District of Columbia. More significant was the Reconstruction Act of March 2, 1867. It divided the rebel states into five military districts. Each was to be commanded by a high-ranking officer. His task was to supervise the election of delegates to state conventions. They would then write constitutions and establish new governments. The electorate would comprise all adult males not barred for taking part in the rebellion. After a majority of registered voters had ratified the state constitution, after Congress had approved it, and after the state had ratified the Fourteenth Amendment, the state could then be readmitted to the Union.

The Tenure of Office Act, also passed on March 2, 1867, was devised by Thaddeus Stevens to humiliate Johnson. Congress forbade him from dismissing cabinet members (such as Secretary of War Edward Stanton) who sympathized with congressional Reconstruction. It also reduced his considerable power of patronage. Another limitation imposed on the president was the Command of the Army Act, passed on the same day, which required him to issue all military orders through the general of the army. A Second Reconstruction Act of March 23 explained the details by which military commanders were to reconstruct the recalcitrant states, including a provision whereby prospective voters were to take an "ironclad oath." A third Reconstruction Act of July 19 empowered registration boards to refuse registration to applicants who were not taking the oath in good faith.

Some of the southern states retaliated by trying to get the Supreme Court to repudiate the legislation. The Supreme Court found some of the Reconstruction measures unconstitutional in the *Test Oaths* cases of January 1867; *Cummings* v. *Missouri* and *Ex parte Garland*. However, it would not defy Congress and, in the *McCardle* case of 1869, upheld a recent congressional decision to withdraw appellate jurisdiction over habeas corpus, thus evading its responsibility to give judgment. The justices believed that, despite northern opinion on the need for rigorous Reconstruction, the national interest would be best served by judicial restraint on controversial issues on which the Constitution said little.

Johnson's protracted disagreements with his secretary of war, Edward Stanton, his subsequent dismissal of Stanton, and successive failures to replace him first with Lorenzo Thomas and then with Thomas Ewing, gave the radicals an opportunity to be rid of him once and for all. They accused him of violating the Tenure of Office Act. On February 24, 1868, Thaddeus Stevens requested the House to remove the "great political malefactor" in order to restore democratic government to a "free and untrammeled people." Accordingly, a committee drew up a list of eleven articles of impeachment, nine about the removal of Stanton, one condemning his speeches, and one an omnibus denunciation. Having been impeached by the House, Johnson was tried in the Senate. Had he been found guilty and removed from office, he would have been replaced by the radical president pro tem of the Senate, Benjamin Wade.

Stevens's vindictive indictment set the tone for the impeachment proceedings and produced profound public unease about the whole process. The *New York Herald* said the radical leader had the "boldness of Danton, the bitterness and hatred of Marat, and the unscrupulousness of Robespierre." Stevens was terminally ill, and the case against Johnson was led in the Senate trial by Benjamin Butler of Massachusetts. He was the general who had taken New Orleans for the Union in 1862 and was known as "Spoons" for having looted southern houses of their silverware. He argued that the president was trying to overthrow Congress and establish an absolute dictatorship. Butler's most picturesque gesture was to produce a nightshirt supposedly stained with the blood of an Ohio carpetbagger flogged within an inch of his life by hoodlums in Mississippi. This gesture of outraged patriotism lived on in the politics of the Gilded Age and became known as "waving the bloody shirt." But on this occasion the radicals had gone too far. Johnson's able counsel, including William M. Evarts and Benjamin R. Curtis, demolished the case against him. The Tenure of Office Act merely restrained a president from removing a member of the cabinet he had appointed—but Stanton had been appointed, not by Johnson, but by Lincoln.

The Senate voted first on the final article on May 16, 1868: 35 for conviction and 19 against. This was 1 vote short of the necessary two thirds majority. Seven Republican senators would not permit the process of impeachment to be debased in the interests of party politics and had voted for acquittal. A major crisis had passed.

So great was the popular appeal of General Ulysses Grant, victor of Appomattox, that the Republicans hoped that his campaign for the presidency in 1868 would unite all factions within the party. But his actual term of office was a nadir of presidential probity as his old cronies took advantage of their high office for commercial gain. (Library of Congress).

Party politics was now concentrated on the presidential election of 1868. As their presidential nominee the Republicans chose Gen. Ulysses S. Grant, the victor at Appomattox. He was associated neither with the radicals nor with Johnson, and he appealed to all sections of the party as a symbol of reconciliation. The substance of the Republican campaign was that their party had won the war and saved the Union, and that a Democratic victory would undo the peace. They were supported financially by such bankers as Henry and Jay Cooke, and their propaganda owed much to the inventive cartoons of Thomas Nast in *Harper's*. Determined to repudiate the blame for secession, the Democrats chose as their candidate Horatio Seymour, wartime governor of New York. They condemned congressional Reconstruction as Republican dictatorship and affirmed states' rights on the troublesome question of black suffrage. In the election Grant took 3,013,427 popular votes and twenty-six states: Seymour, 2,706,829 votes and eight states.

The rival processes of Reconstruction continued without pause. During Christmas of 1868 Johnson issued his fourth and final proclamation of amnesty, extending pardon to the very few remaining Confederates not included in the previous two amnesties of September 1867 and July 4, 1868. Congress, meanwhile, determined to protect black suffrage in the South by the Fifteenth Amendment, passed on February 26, 1869. The right to vote was not to be denied "on account of race, color, or previous condition of servitude." It also allowed Congress to tax incomes and was ratified on February 2, 1870. Congressional Reconstruction was a monumental undertaking and had momentous consequences. It gave the vote to 703,400 black citizens in the South, most of whom were illiterate and almost none of whom had voted before. About 660,000 whites were enfranchised, some for the first time, and about 35 percent of them were also illiterate. Perhaps the most singular failure of the federal government during Reconstruction was to withhold the promise of forty acres and a mule from blacks, although the government owned enough public land in the South to provide each and every black family with a farm.

After the inauguration of Grant, American politics became more diverse. There was much less emphasis on Reconstruction than in the previous four years. The North and West became preoccupied with the currency and political corruption. Grant had the most appropriate name of any president of the United States. During his two administrations (1869–77) he gave away more than any president before him or since. Corruption in government reached new heights. In his personal and professional values Grant was a typical representative of the age. He had little understanding of the new industrial and economic forces. Yet it was precisely because he lacked political vision that he came to symbolize the age. He was elected president in 1868 for the same sort of reasons that another successful general, Dwight D. Eisenhower, would be in 1952.

The sort of qualities Eisenhower paraded in public Grant really did have in private. He was modest, kind, and open. But this unassuming man had crippling limitations even as a conservative president. Unlike Eisenhower, he was a poor judge of character and trusted only those who made a show of loyalty to him. Thus, his inner cabinet, led by the vain and daring Col. Orville Babcock, whom he made his private secretary, manipulated his fears and prejudices to their own ends.

His critics attacked him for his general slovenliness and bouts of hard drinking. The most vicious condemnation came from Lord Lytton, viceroy of India, who was host to the Grants after they retired from Washington. He said Julia was so ugly and Grant so drunk that he could not make love to her without being sick. It was true that depression in his first years in the army had first led Grant to drown his sorrows. Abraham Lincoln, however, was not disconcerted by the hard drinking of his best commander. After Grant's successful campaign of 1862 Lincoln was supposed to have offered to send a sample of Grant's favorite whiskey to his other generals.

Grant's choices of cabinet officers were bizarre. In his eight years as president he appointed no fewer than twenty-five men to seven cabinet posts. Six were men of integrity. Yet Grant contrived to dispense with them all except Secretary of State Hamilton Fish. Fish was not retained for his honesty, tact, and intelligence. Grant needed him and his wife for their social cachet.

Like Eisenhower, Grant aspired to an affluent, not to say opulent life-style. This he could enjoy when he accepted the hospitality of wealthy people. They cultivated his friendship and expected him to lend presidential prestige to private projects such as Jay Gould and Jim Fisk's gold corner of 1869 (q.v.). Yet Grant remained quite insensitive to the impact his associates had on his reputation even though he knew full well that Jim Fisk had no morals. Press exposure of corruption did not, at first, harm Grant's reputation with the public. As the historian Allan Nevins explains, "The plain man had not elected Grant; he had elected an indestructible legend, a folk-hero." But politicians were now on their guard. Their doubts about Grant were to grow. Senator James Grimes of Iowa wrote to Senator Lyman Trumbull of Illinois in July 1870 about the decline of the Republican party: "Like all parties that have an undisturbed power for a long time, it has become corrupt, and I believe it is to-day the most corrupt and debauched political party that has ever existed."

It seemed that what was happening in Washington set the tone for Reconstruction in the South. The old aristocracy began to present themselves as the abused victims of carpetbaggers, scalawags, and blacks. The term "carpetbagger" was first used in 1846 to describe any suspicious stranger in town. During Reconstruction, so-called carpetbaggers included all types of people from the North—soldiers, businessmen, lawyers, teachers, and ministers—as well as adventurers. Very few were transient. The success of their business ventures depended on the maintenance of law and order and cooperation between government and industry. They believed that only through a strong Republican party in the South could they achieve their aims. Thus, they regarded black suffrage as an essential political foundation without which nothing could be accomplished. But they were not interested in social equality. They also sought help from loyal southerners. To former Confederates these loyalists were "scalawags." The term probably originated in the district of Scalloway in the Shetland Islands where the cattle were especially small. These southerners who had actively opposed secession were largely from the lower classes who resented the planter aristocracy.

The traditional oligarchy reserved its most bitter censure for black delegates to the state conventions. That of North Carolina contained only 15 blacks amid 118 delegates, yet it was denounced as "Ethiopian minstrelsy, Ham radicalism in all its glory" with "baboons, monkeys, mules, Tourgée [a white northerner], and other jackasses." However, those who took an active political part in southern Reconstruction were not only blacks, carpetbaggers, and scalawags. Native whites dominated the conventions of Alabama, Georgia, and North Carolina, and appeared in force in others.

The interaction of divergent groups shaped Reconstruction in a very different way from that intended by the radicals in Congress. The new state constitutions were a considerable improvement on the old. South Carolina, for example, instituted universal manhood suffrage, abolished property qualifications for officeholders, reapportioned representation in the state assembly, reformed the courts and local government, removed "all distinctions on account of color," ended imprisonment for debt, protected homesteads from mortgage foreclosure, expanded women's rights, and provided a system of universal public education.

Universal public education was, in fact, a crucial corollary to universal suffrage. There was intense interest in education among black freedmen who, as slaves, had been forbidden to learn to read and write. Poor whites also realized that it was an essential preparation for professional and political activity. All the state constitutions resolved on free education for children and young people between the ages of five and twenty-one. Black delegates realized that separate schools would result in inferior education for Negroes. But, despite their arguments, only Louisiana and South Carolina accepted the principle of integrated education and maintained mixed schools until the mid-1870s.

When conservatives tried to defeat the new constitutions in one way or another, Congress retaliated by changing the rules of the game. Alabama voters simply stayed away from the polls. Thus, radicals in Congress passed a Fourth Reconstruction Act requiring, not a majority of registered voters, but a simple majority of votes cast to ratify the constitution. When Mississippi actually defeated the constitution, Congress determined that the state could not be readmitted until it had ratified the constitution and the Fifteenth Amendment as well.

By the summer of 1868 seven states had written constitutions, organized governments, and recognized the Fourteenth Amendment, and they would be readmitted on condition they maintained black suffrage. Three—Virginia, Mississippi, and Texas—delayed but were readmitted on the same terms in 1870. Thereafter, conservatives, under many titles, began to undermine the new governments. In the case of Georgia the attack was openly and blatantly racist. By August 1868 the state assembly had succeeded in expelling all three black senators and twenty-five (of twenty-nine) black representatives and, in September, passed a law declaring all blacks ineligible to serve there. Henry McNeal Turner, a most articulate black member, made a plangent speech in protest, "It is very strange if a white man can occupy on this floor a seat created by colored votes, and a black man cannot do it." The displaced members appealed to Governor Rufus B. Bullock, who applied for redress from Congress. When Georgia rejected the Fifteenth Amendment in March 1869, Congress reimposed military rule, making its ratification a condition of final readmission. On the grounds that they were disfranchised by the Fourteenth Amendment, Gen. Alfred H. Terry expelled twenty-four Democrats from the state assembly and replaced them with Republicans. He also reinstated the black members. Georgia then complied with the requirements of Congress and was readmitted on January 10, 1870.

In the reconstructed states revenues were quite insufficient to meet the additional demands imposed on them by programs of education, public works, and railroad construction. State indebtedness became a serious political problem in the South. Between 1868 and 1872 the deficits of Louisiana and South Carolina almost doubled, and between 1868 and 1874 that of Alabama trebled. The states increased property and poll taxes to meet the costs of education and welfare, and they issued bonds to finance railroad construction. But, in the end, Reconstruction administrations could not raise sufficient funds to discharge their responsibilities. It was all too easy for conservative critics to deplore the extravagance and corruption of public officials that had become part of

American society in the Gilded Age. The most outrageous graft in both the South and the North was in railroad construction. The manager of a Georgia railroad was asked how he could make above $20,000 a year on a salary of $2,000. He replied, "By the exercise of the most rigid economy."

The so-called Negro rule was the most controversial aspect of radical Reconstruction. Only in South Carolina in the very first assembly did blacks have numerical superiority, and that state had the greatest number of prominent black leaders throughout the 1870s. They included two lieutenant governors, Alonzo B. Ransier, and Richard H. Gleaves, and two speakers, Samuel J. Lee and Robert B. Elliott. The longest serving were Francis L. Cardozo, who was secretary of state from 1868 to 1872 and state treasurer from 1872 to 1876, and Jonathan J. Wright, who sat on the state supreme court for seven years.

SOUTHERN "REDEMPTION"

Diehard Confederates had no single strategy for subverting Reconstruction. As John Hope Franklin explains they used political tactics, economic sanctions, and mob violence to undermine it. Time was on their side and they knew it. Tennessee was never subject to radical Reconstruction, and in Alabama, Georgia, and Mississippi the conservatives' delaying tactics over readmission weakened radical Reconstruction almost before it had begun. Moreover, radical Reconstruction was brief, either because the states were readmitted as reconstituted states, or after Democratic or conservative victories at the polls. Thus, it was truly over for Virginia and Tennessee in 1869, North Carolina in 1870, Georgia in 1871, Texas in 1873, Alabama and Arkansas in 1874, and Mississippi in 1875. Only three states were "unredeemed" at the end of 1876 and still had garrisons of federal troops: Florida, Louisiana, and South Carolina.

Violence was endemic throughout the South. White hoodlums had continually attacked black citizens, their women, and institutions since the end of the war. Now they included white radicals among their victims. They were especially vindictive to those who took part in organizations that showed blacks their political and civil rights, such as the Union League. In 1865 a social circle, or kuklos, of young men in Pulaski, Tennessee, organized themselves as the "Invisible Empire of the South." It began terrorizing blacks before they were accounted a political factor of any significance. New chapters of the secret lodge were formed in other states. In 1867 they sent delegates to a convention at Nashville that made Gen. Nathaniel B. Forrest head of the "Ku Klux Klan." Its members donned ghostly white shirts and indulged in ghoulish rituals. The idea was to frighten their victims into thinking they were the avenging ghosts of the Confederate dead. Other subversive organizations were formed elsewhere: in Louisiana, the Knights of the White Camelia; in Texas, the Knights of the Rising Sun; and in Mississippi, the White Line.

The supposed wrongs of radical Reconstruction conferred on the Klan and its associate groups a political dignity they could not otherwise have commanded. It counted blacks voting, holding office, and being insolent as part of black determination to assume political power. It deemed white participation in radical Reconstruction and social association with blacks as equally heinous offenses. It met both with murder and mayhem. It was said that in North Carolina the Klan committed 260 outrages, including 7 murders and the whipping of 72 whites and 141 blacks. A special target was the Freedmen's Bureau. The Klan would persuade officials to leave town and catch and flog those who did not heed its advice. In some communities coffins "were paraded through the streets marked with the names of prominent radicals and labeled 'Dead, damned and delivered.'"

Congress responded to the Klan by passing a law on May 31, 1870, by which any interference with qualified citizens casting their votes was deemed a felony. Even this law was ineffective. Witnesses were afraid to testify against the Klan; juries declined to convict. Emboldened, the Klan continued its activities. During elections of August 1870 in Alabama, Klansmen paraded openly in full costume and regalia. The Senate established a committee of seven to investigate the situation. The five Republicans submitted a majority report that the Klan was perpetrating "a carnival of murders, intimidation, and violence of all kinds." Congress resolved to strengthen its enforcement law. The amended act of

January 28, 1871, provided for the federal jurisdiction of elections. Federal courts were to appoint election supervisors. Interference with their duties became a federal offense. A more stringent measure was the Third Enforcement Act, passed on April 20, 1871, after acrimonious debate. Usually referred to as the Ku Klux Act, it allowed the president to act against "unlawful combinations" by proclaiming martial law and suspending habeas corpus. Accessories to conspiracies who remained silent were deemed responsible for injuries. The act was invoked against Klansmen in the Carolinas and Mississippi in 1871 and 1872, but there were very few convictions.

Congress did not rest content and next established a Joint Committee of Twenty-One under Senator John Scott of Pennsylvania to inquire into "the condition of the late insurrectionary states." Its four subcommittees held hearings in Washington and six states in the South. The final report extended to thirteen volumes in which the Republican majority urged the continued protection of blacks under federal laws. Nevertheless, in the face of white racist violence and intimidation, neither the Fourteenth nor the Fifteenth Amendment provided freedmen with any real civil protection. In the absence of federal action, the Klan ensured the steady decline of the black electorate.

During the twilight of Reconstruction the Supreme Court was more confident about repudiating radical Reconstruction. Each of the three postwar amendments contained a novel provision: "Congress shall have power to enforce this article by appropriate legislation." Yet the very provision intended to ensure the letter of the law was declared unconstitutional by the Court and used to render the amendment null and void. In 1873 it found that the Fourteenth Amendment had been framed to protect freedmen, but since civil rights were a matter of citizenship of the states and not of the nation, the amendment could afford little protection to individuals aggrieved by state laws. In 1876 in *United States* v. *Cruikshank*, a case arising out of riots in Louisiana, it found that the Fifteenth Amendment did not allow "the passage of laws for the supression of ordinary crimes within the states."

With one exception, Congress was now practically inactive as far as Reconstruction was concerned. That was the Civil Rights

Act of 1875, first proposed by the late Senator Charles Sumner. Its most important provision about desegregation of public schools was excised before it was passed. However, the act guaranteed blacks full and equal rights in places of public accommodation, such as theaters and restaurants, and forbade their exclusion from jury service. But it provided for no measures of enforcement. In 1883 the Supreme Court declared it unconstitutional in seven cases known as the *Civil Rights* cases. Only two originated in the South. Justice Joseph P. Bradley declared that the Fourteenth Amendment did not authorize general legislation for civil rights. *United States* v. *Harris* (1882) was a case arising from an incident when a Tennessee mob lynched four black prisoners. The Court repeated that the federal government could protect black citizens only against acts by the state. It could not protect them against violence by individuals. In such cases, the victim should seek redress from the state authorities. Reconstruction had fallen apart. In eight states there was no longer any pretense of it.

REPUBLICANS AND LIBERALS

Opposition to Grant and what he represented was mounting in the Republican party both inside and outside Congress. The midterm elections of 1870 suggested widespread dissatisfaction among the rank and file. Although the Democrats gained only six seats in the Senate, they took forty-one in the House. In the Missouri contests the success of the dissidents was spectacular. With the aid of Democratic votes they succeeded in electing B. Gratz Brown as governor and Carl Schurz as senator. Schurz, a German immigrant of 1848, was to become more completely identified with reform movements in the 1870s and 1880s than any other politician.

By 1872 there was open division in the Republican party. The rebels, who called themselves Liberal Republicans, organized a mass meeting at the Cooper Institute in New York on April 12, 1872. Four powerful newspaper editors committed themselves on the side of the Liberal Republicans and were soon known as the Quadrilateral: Samuel Bowles of Massachusetts, editor of the *Springfield Republican*; Murat Halstead of the *Cincinnati Commer-*

cial; Horace White of the *Chicago Tribune*; and Col. Henry ("Marse") Watterson of the *Louisville Courier-Journal*. The support of the Quadrilateral gave the Liberals sufficient confidence to plan an independent national campaign. They were now a splinter group adrift from their party.

At a national convention held in Cincinnati in May 1872 they chose as their presidential candidate Horace Greeley, historian and editor of the *New York Tribune*. Greeley was lukewarm about one of the Liberals' two main platforms (civil service reform) and actually hostile to another (lower tariff). He was better known for his personal idiosyncrasies than for his political opinions. In crumpled white coat, its pockets stuffed with newspapers, he was a familiar figure on the sidewalks of New York. His whiskered face was crowned with a white stovepipe hat. He reminded passersby of Mr. Pickwick or the Mad Hatter.

Democrats realized that they could only profit from the dissatisfaction of Liberal Republicans with Grant if they refrained from dividing them. At their convention in Baltimore on July 9 the Democrats reluctantly nominated Greeley and accepted the Liberals' platform. Thus, Greeley stood as a Democratic Liberal. But Greeley had spent thirty years as an editor in opposition to the Democrats. His opinion that, although not every Democrat was a horse thief, every horse thief *was* a Democrat was widely reported by his enemies.

Greeley campaigned for a "New Departure." His administration would provide equal rights for black and white, offer universal amnesty to Confederate officers, and establish thrift and honesty in government. It was only too easy for Republicans to vilify "Old Chappaquack," as Greeley was known. His proposed withdrawal of troops from the South was misrepresented as a sort of complaisance to old Confederate values. Frederick Douglass in the *New National Era*, the leading black newspaper, even said that Greeley had never been genuinely opposed to slavery. Cartoonist Thomas Nast showed Greeley as both tool and victim of "Liberal conspirators who you all know are honorable men." In one cartoon Nast portrayed Greeley as an assassin, shaking hands with John Wilkes Booth over Lincoln's grave.

In the election Greeley took only six states—Georgia, Ken-

In 1872 Horace Greeley, eccentric editor of the *New York Tribune*, became the presidential candidate of reformers in both parties opposed to Grant. But Greeley was tarred for his generous support of former Confederate leader Jefferson Davis during his trial and accused of never having opposed slavery by his many detractors who ridiculed him as another Mad Hatter or Mr. Pickwick. (Library of Congress).

tucky, Maryland, Missouri, Tennessee, and Texas—and 2,843,446 popular votes to Grant's 3,596,745. Grant had 286 votes in the electoral college, Greeley just 42. Exhausted by the campaign and overwhelmed by his wife's fatal illness, Greeley was in no state to cope with additional financial and professional difficulties. As he said, he hardly knew whether he was running for the presidency or the penitentiary. He died on November 29, 1872, and the Liberals' hopes of routing Grant passed away with him. In spite of their failure, the Liberals' challenge unsettled leading Republicans. The campaign had revealed renewed Democratic strength. In the South the Republicans took only 50.1 percent of the vote. Thus, rather than retain a rigorous form of Reconstruction, Republicans now resolved to attempt some reconciliation with the South. Congress passed a General Amnesty Act in May 1872 that, with some exceptions, made Confederate leaders eligible to vote and to hold public office once again.

No sooner was the election settled than Congress was rocked by the biggest scandal of the decade. It involved the first transcontinental railroad. From California the Central Pacific had moved eastward and from Chicago the Union Pacific had moved westward to meet at Promontory Point, Utah, on May 10, 1869 (q.v.). The Union Pacific Railroad had cost at least $50 million to build. But $23 million of that was not spent on construction. The promoters of the railroad diverted the money to themselves. To cover their tracks they had organized a separate construction company, Crédit Mobilier of America, to which, as directors of Union Pacific, they awarded fantastically profitable contracts. As a result of their duplicity the Union Pacific was forced to the verge of bankruptcy, while Crédit Mobilier paid dividends of 348 percent.

During the election campaign of 1872 no fewer than fifteen leading politicians had been smeared for their association with Crédit Mobilier. The accounts were garbled and easily dismissed as malicious. When Congress convened in December two of the most prominent, James G. Blaine of Maine and James Garfield of Ohio, moved a formal investigation. Both knew full well they could refute the charges against them. The investigating committees discovered that recipients of Union Pacific stock included both Grant's retiring vice president, Schuyler Colfax, and the vice president-elect, Senator Henry Wilson of Massachusetts. James Garfield swore he had received no money, but he was credited in the memorandum book of Union pacific director Oakes Ames as having received $1,376. He appealed to his constituents who continued to support him and he survived the ordeal. Colfax also denied that he had taken money. Ames's book showed otherwise. Not for nothing was he known as "Smiler." The committee also discovered that previously, as chairman of the Post Office Committee in the House, he had accepted a bribe of $4,000 from G. F. Nesbitt of New York. Nesbitt manufactured stationery, and Colfax had made sure that large contracts for government envelopes were awarded to his firm. On March 4, 1873, Colfax left Washington, his career in ruins and, presumably, the smile wiped off his face.

The day before Colfax retired from the political scene, March 3, Congress exposed itself to more charges of venality when it passed the so-called Salary Grab Act. This act raised the president's salary from $25,000 to $50,000. Other public officers, including the vice president, members of the cabinet and Supreme Court, and the speaker of the House, also had their salaries increased. So, too, did senators and representatives, from $5,000 to $7,500. The public was incensed. Congress was, therefore, obliged to repeal all the increases except for those of president and Supreme Court. It was fortunate for Congress that these scandals were dead issues by the time of the panic and depression of 1873.

As we have seen, the root cause of the depression of 1873 was railroad collapse. Not only the railroads but also their supply industries and thus the industrial community at large were hard hit for six years. Whereas conservatives argued that the proper policy in depression was for the government to economize and leave recovery to natural forces, those with special interests at stake argued for a change in fiscal policy.

We have observed that, during the war, the government had increased the money supply with the issue of paper notes. These greenbacks were not based on gold but on faith, hope, and charity. After the war was over there were still $433.16 million in circulation. Their presence was an endless source of confusion. People who had bought government bonds in the war had done so with a depreciated currency. It was in their interest to insist that the bonds should be redeemed in gold. Thus they would make a profit. In addition, greenbacks were not legal tender for all purposes. No one knew if the government would eventually redeem them for gold. They circulated at a discount that varied from month to month. Farmers were also affected by these fluctuations. They had bought land according to the terms of the Homestead Act of 1862 and borrowed money to do so. But in the war paper money was worth only about 40 percent of gold money. If the value of the currency were to be raised by the withdrawal of greenbacks, they would have to repay interest at a higher rate than when they took out the loan.

Most businessmen wanted a stable currency and favored resumption, a return to the gold standard—hard money, as it was called. To confirm business confidence the Republican party agreed with them. However, in 1870 Chief Justice Salmon P. Chase announced that greenbacks were not legal tender for obligations entered into before they were first issued. And in *Hepburn* v. *Griswold*, the first *Legal Tender* decision, also in 1870, he went further. In his opinion they were completely invalid. Ironically enough it was Chase who, as Lincoln's secretary of treasury, had approved the issuing of greenbacks in the first place. The government moved for a rehearing, and in the second *Legal Tender* decision, *Knox* v. *Lee* and *Parker* v. *Davis* of 1871, the Court sustained them.

The controversy over hard and soft money became a burning issue and scorched any politician who tried to handle it. Thus began the conflict between gold and silver that gives the Gilded Age much of its political character. Most politicians did not even understand the issues and deeply resented the fact that the controversy disturbed traditional electoral loyalties. Grant's third secretary of the treasury, Benjamin H. Bristow, was both a westerner and a hard money man. At this prompting Congress passed John Sherman's Resumption of Specie Payment Act on January 7, 1875. Specie payments were to be resumed by January 2, 1879. For every $100 issued in new national bank notes the Treasury would withdraw $80 in greenbacks. Sherman's act did not retire greenbacks. But it represented a moral commitment to a metal currency.

The general public had been indifferent to well-founded criticisms of political corruption when times were good. But in hard times it was different. Public opinion was in no mood to tolerate new scandals. It seemed that no fewer than five cabinet members were guilty of gross malpractice. Secretary of War W. W. Belknap was impeached in the House for the sale of trading posts in Indian Territory to men who made fortunes by selling substandard goods. Secretary of the Treasury William A. Richardson was also obliged to resign before the House could censure him for extortion of tax evaders. Attorney General George H. Williams resigned under suspicion of gross corruption and laxity. Secretary of the Interior Columbus Delano resigned after charges of corruption in Indian affairs were leveled at him. Secretary of the Navy George M. Robeson was suspected of negligence in the matter of contracts for navy supplies.

Worst of all, Grant's private secretary, Orville E. Babcock, was tried with other members of the "St. Louis Whiskey Ring." With the connivance of Treasury officials it had defrauded the Internal Revenue Service of $4 million in taxes to 1874. Babcock and his associates had been paid about $1.5 million in bribes to accept fraudulent returns of the amount of liquor produced by distillers and from which tax assessments were made. On learning about the ring Grant was supposed to have said, "Let no guilty man escape." Nevertheless, he ensured that Babcock did so. At the subsequent trial he swore to Babcock's integrity. The jury accepted the president's word and acquitted his secretary on February 24, 1876. All the other defendants were found guilty.

THE COMPROMISE OF 1876

The election of 1876, the dispute that followed it, and the way both were resolved demonstrated Republican recognition that Reconstruction had to come to an end. Less obviously, but equally important, the election illustrated the insidious influence of big business on high-powered politics.

Grant was coy about running for a third term. By 1876 few Republicans wanted him to. The other preeminent Republican was James G. Blaine of Maine, congressman since 1863, and now acknowledged leader of the group opposed to Reconstruction, the

"Half Breeds." It included John Sherman, James Garfield, George Hoar, William B. Allison, and George Edmunds. Although his followers had three quarters of the necessary votes, Blaine was denied nomination at the Republican National Convention held in Cincinnati from June 14, 1876. Both reactionary and reform Republicans were bound together in their opposition to him. Thus, Rutherford B. Hayes, former Union officer and three times governor of Ohio, was nominated on the seventh ballot.

In early July the Democrats nominated Governor Samuel J. Tilden of New York. A liberal who favored reform of tariff and civil service, he was also a hard money man. Widely known for his part in breaking the Tweed Ring (q.v.) before he became governor and for breaking the Erie Canal Ring during his term of office, he was identified as a fearless foe of political corruption. Yet Tilden had perpetrated a rigging of the stock market years earlier and obtained a court order to confiscate an entire edition of James Parton's exposure of his methods, a *Manual for the Instruction of "Rings," Railroad and Political* (1866). Tilden had also amassed a great forture as a lawyer for railroad corporations. It was for his truck with such manipulators as Jay Gould and Jim Fisk that he won the dubious title of the "Great Forecloser."

The actual campaign was about Grant's administration. The Republicans could make no convincing reply to Democratic accusations. On November 8, after the election, the Democrats claimed, and the Republicans conceded, a victory. According to later tallies, Tilden had taken 4,284,020 popular votes, to Hayes's 4,036,572. But at the time four states—Oregon, South Carolina, Florida, and Louisiana— were still in doubt. Without these states Tilden had 184 electoral votes—1 less than a majority.

In all three southern states the election had been fraudulent. Republicans controlled the returning boards and discounted Democratic votes—at least 1,000 votes in Florida and more than 13,000 in Louisiana. Both parties had been guilty of malpractice, however. On December 6 Republican electors in all four states met and cast their official votes—19 in all—for Hayes. Thus he had 185 votes, a majority of 1. However, in the same states Democratic electors, appointed by Democratic state authorities, also met and cast their 19 votes for Tilden. Both sets of returns were sent to

Congress. The impasse was resolved by a compromise that was to lead to the withdrawal of the last remaining federal troops from the South and the official end of Reconstruction.

On January 29, 1877, Congress set up a Joint Electoral Commission to settle the election by adjudicating on the returns of the four disputed states. It would comprise three Republicans and two Democrats from the Senate, two Republicans and three Democrats from the House, two Republicans and two Democrats from the Supreme Court, and a fifth justice of either party to be chosen by the Court itself. It was assumed in Congress that the fifth justice would be the independent, Judge David Davis. But he was suddenly elected senator for Illinois. He then withdrew from the Court and declared himself ineligible for the commission. The fifth justice chosen by the Court was Joseph P. Bradley, a Republican. By a majority of 1 the commission gave the election to Hayes. The Democrats resolved to retaliate by filibuster. They reckoned without business interests.

A cabal of businessmen was intent on constructing a railroad in the Southwest. It comprised three press barons (William Henry Smith of the Western Associated Press, Murat Halstead of the *Cincinnati Commercial*, and Andrew J. Kellar of the *Memphis Daily Avalanche*) and two railroad enterpreneurs (Tom Scott of the Pennsylvania Railroad and Grenville Dodge, once of the Union Pacific). They elicited support from southern industrialists who were anxious to develop manufacturing and industry in the South and who appreciated the need for a railroad. If Hayes were elected, ran Scott's argument to the South, he would use federal funds to advance social and economic recovery throughout the South. This, of course, would include the construction of the proposed railroad. As pledge of his good intentions Hayes promised to appoint a southern Democrat to the most lucrative spoils office of postmaster general. Most important, federal troops would be recalled from the South.

The Democrats' final acquiescence is usually credited to the "Wormley House Bargain" of February 26, 1877, in Washington. Southern congressmen met with influential Republicans including Sherman, Garfield, Charles Foster, and Stanley Matthews. Owing to their arguments, thirty-two southern Democrats were prevailed upon to abandon the filibuster, and they were also joined by a few influential northern Democrats. The electoral count was concluded at 4:00 A.M. on March 2, 1877, and Hayes was declared president-elect.

It was perfectly clear that the Republican victory had been secured in violation of popular will. Yet subsequent revelations about election malpractice damaged Democrats more than Republicans. When the Potter committee of the House investigated the disputed election, it discovered that the returning boards of South Carolina and Florida would have thrown the election to Tilden if they had been compensated. A wit observed that the Democrats stole the election in the first place and then the Republicans stole it back. There was another factor in this controversial episode. In 1876 the predominantly Democratic House had confidently voted the admission of Colorado to the Union on the expectation that it would give the Democratic party its allegiance. But in elections Colorado proved overwhelmingly Republican. The Democrats' miscalculation cost Tilden the presidency.

By withdrawing troops from the South and bringing Reconstruction to an end, Hayes identified the presidency with public opinion, which wanted to stop punishing the South. But, as Senator Roscoe Conkling pointed out, the removal of federal troops from the crucial states that had accomplished Hayes's election also served to remove the very legal argument that had achieved it. Not until the Little Rock riots of 1957 would federal troops intervene in southern affairs on terms precluded by the compromise of 1877. The history of the New South that now unfolded was the history of a separate region removed from the central issues of national politics.

THE NEW SOUTH

The southern leaders who had emerged by 1877 claimed that they had redeemed the South from carpetbag rule and were generally known as Redeemers. More precisely, they were Democratic Conservatives. They included not only the scions of the old planter class but also the new entrepreneurs in business and industry. This self-perpetuating oligarchy ensured its position by limiting the power of state legislatures. They reacted against the social revolution brought about by Reconstruction with an economic policy of "retrenchment"—reducing public services and cutting taxes. The principal beneficiaries were corporations, especially utilities and railroads; the principal victims were public schools.

Beneath the surface of solidarity southern politics teemed with discontent. Independents, Greenbackers, and Populists stood for office, occasionally won, and unsettled the confidence of the ruling elite. A most divisive issue was the repudiation or "readjustment" of state debts, which in 1877 amounted to something like $275 million for all the reconstructed states. Nine states devised legal means of repudiating their debts. In the process, they outraged otherwise loyal creditors. In Tennessee their protest led to the reelection of the Republicans and in Virginia to victory for a third party, the Readjusters.

Economically the South had still not recovered from the war by the end of the 1870s. Journalist Whitelaw Reid declared in the *New York Tribune* of October 3, 1879, "Fifteen years have gone over the South and she still sits crushed, wretched, busy displaying and bemoaning her wounds." The estimated value of property in the United States in 1880 was $47.64 billion, of which the South had only $5.72 billion. The average per capita wealth of the South was $376, whereas it was $1,086 in the other states. No southern state was within $300 of the national average.

Those who argued that expanded industry would improve material progress in the region described their goal as the New South in which King Coal would succeed Old King Cotton. Henry Grady spoke on the New South to the annual dinner of the New England Society in New York on December 22, 1886. He said nothing new. The ideas had been reiterated by various apologists since Benjamin H. Hill (later senator from Georgia) spoke to the Young Men's Democratic Union of New York in 1868. But Grady was more gracious than his predecessors and his timing was better.

By the 1880s brutal memories of the Civil War had become blurred in American minds. It was at last possible to distinguish between political and personal conviction and pay tribute to the courage and dedication of the fallen in plazas, memorials, and monuments such as those to Adm. David Glasgow Farragut in

Madison Square Park, New York, by Augustus Saint-Gaudens (1881) and Robert E. Lee in Richmond, Virginia, by Jean A. Mercié (1890). Hence, southern investment held no conflicts of loyalty for northern businessmen.

Moreover, the end of the depression in 1879 released northern capital for southern investment. Redeemers promised investors tax exemptions and a plentiful supply of cheap labor if they would only put their money in the South. William H. Harrison, Jr., in *How to Get Rich in the South; Telling What to Do, How to Do it, and the Profits to be Realized* (1888), maintained there was no foreign country "that offers such tempting inducements to the capitalist for profitable investments" as did the New South.

The South's greatest asset was its land. In 1877 five southern states repealed laws reserving federal land for homesteaders in order that they might entice investors to exploit the coal, iron, and timber. They disposed of 5.69 million acres of federal lands between 1877 and 1888. Most were acquired by northern speculators anxious to exploit their investment to the full by devastating forests and laying waste precious natural resources.

Railroad expansion encouraged investors to penetrate the hinterlands. Between 1880 and 1890 railroad tracks increased from 16,605 miles to 39,108 miles. This was a growth of 135.5 percent, 50 percent more than the national average in a period of dramatic expansion. Railroad consolidation was as much a feature of the New South as of the North. The Richmond and West Point Terminal Company determined to combine competing roads and acquired the Richmond and Danville in 1886; the East Tennessee, Virginia and Georgia in 1887; and the Central Railroad and Banking Company of Georgia in 1888. The entire terminal system now comprised 8,558 miles of rail and water lines and became the basis of the railroad empire of John Pierpont Morgan (q.v.) in 1894 when it was reorganized as the Southern Railway.

King Cotton was still alive. The three leading producers of cotton were Georgia and the Carolinas. The number of cotton mills in the South rose from 161 in 1880 to 239 in 1890 and to 400 in 1900. Capital investment in cotton rose from $17.37 million in 1880 to $124.59 million in 1900. In 1880 there were 45 mills in the United States producing 7 million gallons of cottonseed oil for export. In 1890 there were 119 mills; in 1900, 357. All but 4 of them were in the South. The American Cotton Oil Trust, founded in 1884 and modeled on Standard Oil, controlled 88 percent of production of cottonseed oil in the country and dictated the policies and prices of the whole industry.

The New South did acquire new industries. By the late 1880s the South was producing more pig iron than was produced in the entire country before the war. Between 1876 and 1901 the production of pig iron increased seventeen times in the South compared with eight times in the country as a whole. Among southern investors in coal and iron was Henry Fairchild De Bardleben. In 1889 he consolidated his holdings in the De Bardleben Coal and Iron Company, capitalized at $10 million. He controlled 7 blast furnaces, 7 coal mines, 7 ore mines, and 900 coke ovens. "I was the eagle," he boasted, "and I wanted to eat up all the craw-fish I could,—swallow up all the little fellows, and I did it." In time his empire, too, became forfeit to Morgan.

Until the 1880s tobacco was still being produced in four varieties—plug, twist, smoking, and snuff. It was processed by hand according to age-old methods. The crucial breakthrough in the change to almost complete mechanization was the invention of the cigarette machine in 1880 by James Bonsack, a young Virginian still in his teens. In the Bonsack machine a rag of finely shredded and sweetened tobacco was fed onto a continuous strip of paper. The cigarettes were then automatically shaped, pasted, closed, and finally cut to size by a rotary cutting knife. Among the rising entrepreneurs willing to exploit the new invention and promote cigarettes as the poor man's luxury was James ("Buck") Buchanan Duke of Durham, North Carolina. Buck and his brother, Benjamin, entered the tobacco business started by their father, Washington, and in 1890 consolidated their own and their rivals' firms in the American Tobacco Company. Duke transferred his headquarters from North Carolina to New York, and there he ran his corporation, which was registered in New Jersey. Following the precedent set by John D. Rockefeller in oil, he eliminated all his competitors in tobacco. Some historians believe that the American Tobacco Company, which was capitalized at $500 million in 1907, was the most complete and secure of all the trusts.

Despite their well-laid plans to revive the South's fortunes by introducing modern industry, the ruling elite found that old economic habits died hard. In the North people thought the old plantations had been broken up by the war and that, consequently, there was now a more equitable distribution of land in the South than in the old days. The census of 1880 did disclose an astonishing increase in the number of farms compared with that in 1860 and, also, that the new farms were, on average, less than half the size of the old. What had happened was that the land had been subdivided. Planters were short of cash. Instead of paying their workers wages, they devised a system of dividing produce between tenants and landlords according to contracts. Thus the system of sharecropping came into existence. It revived the culture of tobacco and cotton and allowed freedmen to make their own independent family lives. But it also confined poor farmers, first black and soon white, to a life of penury. An Act for Encouraging Agriculture, passed by Mississippi on February 18, 1867, introduced the lien system, which was soon adopted in other states. Merchants advanced supplies for the year ahead in exchange for a lien, a mortgage on the future crop. The plaintive lament of sharecroppers was "It's owed before it's growed." As we shall see in Chapter Nine the injustices of the crop lien system became a most important base of Southern Populism.

The legend that attached itself to this stagnant agrarian economy was that the South was a place forgotten by time, its people marooned by ignorance. Contemporary stories about southern apathy are legion. One tells how a southern farmer, too lazy to gather his cotton crop, excused himself to his wife by pointing up to clouds in the sky that seemed to form the letters *GPC*. He said this meant, "Go Preach Christ." But his wife was quicker than he: "Dose letters don' mean, Go Preach Christ. Dey mean, Go Pick Cotton." It was also charged in the North that southerners were degenerate. In another tale a district attorney in North Carolina was unable to persuade a witness to give evidence in a court case against the defendant. It was well known that the accused was a loafer and a lush, that he had beaten up his wife and his father, that he was a horse thief, and that he had killed farm animals out of malice toward their owners. How, then, could the witness swear that the defendant's reputation was good in the community? "Why, Mister, a man has to do a heap wuss things than that to lose his character in our neighborhood." In a third story the paterfamilias of a landed family in Louisiana persuaded his son to court the daughter of the only other wealthy family in town. At first all went well, but then the son turned on his father—"Shucks, Dad, I can't marry her. She's a virgin." His father agreed. "That's right, son, ain't good enough for her own folk, ain't good enough for us."

RACE RELATIONS

Whatever deals were agreed to by politicians of North and South could not obscure the fact that race relations were a central and potentially explosive problem. When President Rutherford B. Hayes visited Atlanta in the autumn of 1877 he advised freedmen that their rights and interests would be safer in the hands of southern whites if they were "let alone" by the federal government. Whites received this opinion with immense enthusiasm. "Let alone" became as much the government password in race relations as had "laissez-faire" in economics. Blacks still voted after 1877, but in decreasing numbers, and in other respects they ceased to fulfill their duties as citizens. They remained unskilled menials, a ready source of cheap labor, whether as hired hands, sharecroppers, or even convicts. By 1880 there were 6,580,793 of them in the United States, and their expanding numbers increased their problems.

Many migrated from place to place, and some moved permanently to the North and West. Benjamin ("Pap") Singleton was among those farmers who led an exodus of blacks from the South to Kansas in 1879. More than 40,000 sharecroppers left Alabama, Georgia, Mississippi, South Carolina, and Texas for "the freedom lands." At first Kansas welcomed the migrants. The *Topeka Commonwealth* of April 7, 1879, recalling the fight to make Kansas a free state, said that black migration to Kansas was a fitting sequel to it. But when the state realized the scale of the migration and the destitute state of the newcomers, it sent special agents to the South to dissuade more blacks from leaving. The old Freedmen's

The trees bore strange fruit at least once in a generation in many Southern towns in the late nineteenth century. For those who took part lynching was an event to await, to attend, and finally to record as this bizarre photo of a lynch party of 1882 and its unfortunate victim, MacManus, suggests. However, in time the participants felt some shame; the Library of Congress has no record of the supposed crime of the victim or the place of his execution. (Library of Congress).

Relief Association raised $25,000 in cash and clothing and also household goods worth $100,000 to relieve distressed blacks. In time, blacks found work in mines and railroads, and some acquired land.

In the South the gulf between the races was so great that, at first, legal segregation was superfluous. In such diverse public institutions as schools, hospitals, and asylums, custom made it routine. This was, however, better than absolute exclusion. Moreover, in places of public accommodation, such as parks, theaters, and streetcars, race relations were not fixed. By 1890 a new generation of black citizens had grown up who had never experienced slavery. They were less likely to accept white racism. Thus, in the 1890s variety and fluidity were abandoned as state after state adopted rigid segregation in a series of so-called Jim Crow laws. "Jim Crow" was the title of a minstrel song of 1830 that presented blacks as childlike and inferior.

In 1890 Congress considered two bills to revive black suffrage in the South. The Blair Federal Aid to Education bill was intended to improve public schools so as to enable more blacks to qualify in literacy tests. The Lodge Federal Elections bill, supported by President Benjamin Harrison, authorized federal supervision of elections to prevent frauds against black voters. It passed the House by the close vote of 155 to 149. But it was never reported out of committee in the Senate. Senator Don Cameron of Pennsylvania explained why: 'Whatever form it may assume I am opposed to [the bill] in principle and in its details. The South is now resuming a quiet condition. Northern capital has been flowing into the South in great quantities, manufacturing establishments have been created and are in full operation, and a community of commercial interests is fast obliterating sectional lines. . . . The election law would disturb this desirable condition, and produce ill-feeling between the North and the South."

The South reacted against the new tide of black resentment with more repression. Mississippi was the first state to disfranchise black citizens by a constitutional convention in 1890. It was followed by South Carolina in 1895, Louisiana in 1898, North Carolina (by an amendment) in 1900, Alabama in 1901, Virginia in 1901 and 1902, Georgia (by amendment) in 1908, and the new state of Oklahoma in 1910. Four more states achieved the same ends without revising their constitutions: Tennessee, Florida, Arkansas, and Texas. Three pernicious and sophistical arguments were advanced by the proponents of black disfranchisement. The removal of the black vote, they said, would end corruption at elections. It would prevent blacks from holding the balance of power in contests between rival factions of whites. And it would oblige blacks to abandon their false hopes of betterment and, instead, make them accept their true social place. As a result, race relations would steadily improve.

The Mississippi constitution of 1890 set the pattern. It required a poll tax of $2 from prospective voters at registration. Those who intended to vote at elections had to present their receipt at the polls. Anyone who mislaid his receipt forfeited his vote. More insidious was the requirement that in order to register prospective voters had to be "able to read the Constitution, or to understand the Constitution when read." Racist officials used these ordinances to discriminate in favor of poor illiterate whites and against black citizens.

The ruling elites in other states approved of the new Mississippi plan. But they proceeded cautiously. The Lodge bill of 1890 indicated a flickering northern interest in black suffrage that they did not intend to fan into a flame. Moreover, Democrats were now in competition with Populists for votes, and they did not want to excite agrarian radicals into preserving black suffrage by incorporating a specific measure to ensure its survival in a new constitution. The various states borrowed from one another. In doing so they improved on previous attempts to disfranchise blacks. For example, Louisiana believed that the "understanding clause" was so obviously suspect that it could be invalidated in a court case. Therefore it hit on the "grandfather clause" as being more secure legally. Only those who had had a grandfather on the electoral roll of 1867 could vote.

These devices were nothing if not effective. In Louisiana 130,000 black Americans were registered to vote in 1890; in 1900 there were 5,000; in 1904 there were only 1,342. In Alabama there were 181,000 black voters in 1890; in 1900 there were 3,000. In the South as a whole black participation fell by 62 percent. In 1900 Ben

("Pitchfork") Tillman of South Carolina boasted on the floor of the Senate, "We have done our best. We have scratched our heads to find out how we could eliminate the last one of them. We stuffed ballot boxes. We shot them. We are not ashamed of it." Despite concessions to poor whites, white participation in elections also declined—by 26 percent. Thus, while on average 73 percent of men voted in the 1890s, only 30 percent did so in the early 1900s. Opposition parties dwindled away, and the Democrats were left undisputed champions of the South.

Social segregation was also upheld by the Supreme Court. Its most notorious decision came in *Plessy* v. *Ferguson* in 1896. Louisiana state law required "separate but equal" accommodations for black and white on public carriers and provided a penalty for passengers sitting on the wrong car. Homer Plessy was an octoroon so pale that he usually passed for white, but when he sat in a white car he was arrested. He argued that the state law of Louisiana violated the Fourteenth and Fifteenth Amendments. Justice John Marshall Harlan of Kentucky agreed with him, maintaining, "Our constitution is color-blind and neither knows nor tolerates classes among citizens." Moreover, "What can more certainly arouse race hate, what more certainly create and perpetuate a feeling of distrust between these races, than state enactments which in fact proceed on the ground that colored citizens are so inferior and degraded that they cannot be allowed to sit in public coaches occupied by white citizens?" But he was overruled by the other eight justices who approved the doctrine of "separate but equal." Justice Henry B. Brown of Michigan, speaking for the majority of April 13, 1896, ruled with corrosive racist candor, "If one race be inferior to the other socially, the Constitution of the United States cannot put them upon the same plane." Not until 1954 in the celebrated case of *Brown* v. *Board of Education of Topeka* did the Court repudiate the heinous doctrine of "separate but equal." In the meantime, in *Williams* v. *Mississippi* (1898) the Court went further and approved the Mississippi plan for disfranchising blacks.

Not satisfied with depriving blacks of their civil rights, vicious whites also sought their lives. It was said the trees of all southern towns bore strange fruit at least once in a generation. White mobs took the law into their own hands and lynched black scapegoats, especially dissidents, as examples to others. Lynching peaked in popularity between 1889 and 1898 when, on average, there were 187 lynchings a year in the United States, fourfifths of which were in the South. A common charge against black victims of lynch law was that they had raped white women. The research of black journalist Ida Wells showed otherwise. Yet newspapers such as the *Enquirer* emphasized the supposed crime and gave detailed accounts of the atrocious punishment in order to titillate the public and improve circulation. On February 2, 1893, for example, it disclosed how a black accused of raping and murdering a four-year-old girl in Paris, Texas, was burned to death. First his eyes were gouged out with a red hot poker. The *Enquirer* described this atrocity as "unparalleled punishment" for "unparalleled crime."

Blacks were displaced from their traditional trades and confined to menial jobs in the towns. Those who did succeed in entering the worlds of business and the professions were obliged by white society to adopt its attitudes in order to retain their hard-won position. Their undeclared leader was Booker T. Washington, head of the Tuskegee Industrial Institute, Alabama. Washington was invited to speak at the opening of the Cotton States and International Exposition in Atlanta on September 18, 1895, by businessmen who recognized his remarkable powers of expression. His address was one of the most effective political speeches of the age, a model fusion of substance and style.

In what was later called the Atlanta Compromise he abandoned the postwar ideal of racial equality in favor of increased economic opportunity for blacks. He preached patience, proposed submission, and emphasized material progress. Those blacks who rejected the Atlanta Compromise, such as W. E. B. Du Bois, considered it a capitulation to blatant racism. But Washington was in fact telling white society that blacks accepted the Protestant work ethic. His most widely reported remark was a subtle metaphor about racial harmony: "In all things social we can be as separate as the fingers, yet one as the hand in all things essential to mutual progress."

Washington's emphasis on racial pride, economic progress, and industrial education encouraged white politicians and businessmen to subsidize the black institutions he recommended. Through his close connections with business he was able to raise the funds necessary to create the National Negro Business League in 1900. Moreover, he used money, not to advance black acquiescence, but to fight segregation. Others sought a more open insistence on racial pride. In 1890 T. Thomas Fortune, a black journalist of New York, persuaded forty black protection leagues in cities across the country to join in a national body, the Afro-American League. Its aim was to reverse restrictions on black citizens. It was, however, difficult to maintain cohesion among contributing groups, and the league declined to be revived in 1898 as the Afro-American Council.

For those who sought improvement the struggle seemed interminable, as another southern anecdote makes clear. St. Peter would admit good men to heaven only if they could pose him a question he was unable to answer. Thus he refused otherwise eminently well qualified cardinals and rabbis who asked obscure and pedantic theological questions. But when a black Baptist minister wanted to know "When's us black folks gonna get together?" he was stumped for an answer and let him in through the pearly gates.

CHAPTER SEVEN

THE LAST REFUGE OF
A SCOUNDREL

CONTEMPORARY HISTORIAN Henry Adams said of politics in the Gilded Age, "The period was poor in purpose and barren in results." His verdict, "One might search the whole list of Congress, Judiciary, and Executive during the twenty-five years 1870–1895 and find little but damaged reputations," remains a popular one.

That the Gilded Age leaves an impression of political stagnation is largely due to its procession of conservative presidents. By comparison with Gladstone and Disraeli in England and Bismarck in Germany, Lincoln's successors cut poor figures as statesmen. They thought of themselves as administrators rather than as party leaders. What authority they did have was based on political influence, not popular appeal. Ulysses S. Grant (1869–77) was deceived by his associates, who took advantage of high office for financial gain. Rutherford B. Hayes (1877–81) tried to resuscitate the presidency and so fell out with his party. James Garfield (1881) was fatally wounded three months after taking office and dead after six. Chester A. Arthur (1881–85) abandoned the spoils system that had sustained him and was rejected by his party. Grover Cleveland (1885–89 and 1893–97) pursued personal prejudices rather than party principles and lost the election of 1888 by a fluke. Benjamin Harrison's tenure of office (1889–93) was the nadir of presidential authority. Thus, in popular legend as well as in actuality these are the dud presidents: Grant, a president discredited; Hayes, a president defied; Garfield, a president defunct; Arthur, a president dismissed; Cleveland, a president denied; and Harrison, a president derided.

Politicians were dedicated to an American dream of opportunity from the exploitation of fabulous, unrealized natural resources. Yet their parties were imperfect vehicles for coordinating government and popular will. William Hazlitt's description of Whigs and Tories in early-nineteenth-century England is just as apt for Republicans and Democrats in late-nineteenth-century America. According to Hazlitt, the two parties were like rival stagecoaches splashing one another with mud as they raced along the same road to the same destination. Republicans and Democrats were agencies intent on power. They were not parties committed to any philosophy besides the needs of their interest groups. Their task was not to make controversial issues part of political debate. Major problems were brought to the fore of politics by splinter groups, third parties, and nonpartisan organizations.

The Republican party was supposedly in control of government from 1861. It was the party of the respectable North. Launched to supersede the Whigs disgraced for their successive compromises over slavery, it was also the party that had saved the Union. The Republican stronghold was New England and the path of settlement westward: northern New York and the Old Northwest. This was the area which had been most opposed to slavery. At first it was predominantly rural and Protestant. It was also a corn belt, and the new reign of King Corn was even more secure than that of Old King Cotton. From three pivotal states—Indiana, Illinois, and Ohio—the Republicans garnered the winners of nine presidential campaigns: Lincoln, Grant, and McKinley twice; and Hayes, Garfield, and Harrison once.

To the politician the party was an end in itself. To industrialists, businessmen, unionists, and farmers it was a means to an end: their economic interests. The groups that supported the Republicans did not do so for nothing. Farmers gained land by the Homestead Acts (q.v.). Veterans gained pensions. Manufacturers gained tariffs, import duties to protect new domestic industries against cheap foreign goods.

Astute politicians recognized the relationship between the tariff and the value of land and industry. If one rose, then so too would the other. Those who read the signs of the times clearly and interpreted them accurately could gain by promoting increased duties. They were rewarded by protected domestic producers whose prices and profits rose. Thus, John Sherman of Ohio, Justin Morrill of Vermont, James G. Blaine of Maine, and others introduced and supported measures to increase the tariff. They pretended to do so out of patriotism. But their real motives were obvious to all.

But the party of victory had a dent in its armor. The Republicans were beset by a series of factions: first Liberals against "Radicals," then "Half Breeds" against "Stalwarts." The party that had been invincible in war was, apparently, almost invisible in peace. At times there was so much bitterness that Donn Piatt, political commentator, said in the *Cincinnati Commercial* of June 9, 1870: "I am forced to say that there is no more cohesion, beyond mere office holding and public plunder, in the Republican party than there is in a rope of sand. . . . The Republican party in Congress is composed of factions in such deadly antagonisms to each other that the hate among them is more intense than that given the Democrats." This tendency to faction led to the Republicans' losing the presidential elections of 1884 and 1892 and, eventually, to their disruption in 1912.

In this period of Republican ascendancy the Democrats were not weak. They won a plurality or majority of the popular vote in four of the five presidential elections between 1876 and 1892. They succeeded in getting Grover Cleveland elected twice, in 1884 and 1892. They lost the elections of 1876 and 1888 only because they failed to secure a majority in the electoral college. They were powerful not only in the South but also the border states and along the southern path of migration to the West. In addition, they could hold northern cities. In the election of 1880 they achieved a narrow plurality of 24,000 votes in the twelve most populous cities and by 1892 had increased this lead to 145,000. In particular, they captured the allegiance of Irish Catholics. The Irish detested British immigrants, who were natural Republicans.

Nevertheless, the Republicans liked to think that theirs was the natural party of government even when the task was beyond them.

"Why!" said a Republican governor of Illinois. "Why, the Democrats can't run the government! It's all us Republicans can do." Neither party, however, dominated the federal government for any length of time, since neither could sustain working majorities. The Democrats controlled the House of Representatives in eight of the ten Congresses between 1874 and 1894, during which time the Senate was Republican seven times. Thus, only twice did a single party control both the presidency and the Congress: the Republicans from 1889 to 1891 and the Democrats from 1893 to 1895.

Presidents held official power for short periods. On the other hand, the party bosses who nominated them wielded absolute power for as long as a generation. State bosses might be governors or senators. If they were not, they nominated those who were. Their power base was either considerable financial or industrial interests or control of a crucial area of the civil service.

The American civil service was part of a spoils system in which federal patronage was dispensed by party bosses. Officeholders were selected on the basis of party loyalty, not administrative competence. It was standard practice for new administrations to nominate their own appointees. The distribution of spoils after an election victory was called by Matthew Quay of Philadelphia, "shaking the plum tree." The climax came when Lincoln, who had 1,639 places in his gift, removed 1,457 officeholders. By the early 1870s the civil service was made up of incompetent and demoralized party hacks. As A. C. McLaughlin explains in *The Courts, the Constitution, and Parties* (1912), the spoils system "provided a means of financing party management, it furnished the sinews of war to party government."

This was certainly what happened in New York State, which passed along a chain of command of Senators Thurlow Weed, Roscoe Conkling, and Thomas Platt. Each dominated politics by his control of the New York Custom House. New York was the main port, controlling commerce and collecting revenue from imports. Thus, its Custom House afforded unequal opportunities for graft and extortion and was the very center of the spoils system. It employed 1,000 party workers.

One ruse to raise funds was to undervalue imports, then make an official discovery of the mistake. Under the law the entire value of an import that was falsely declared was forfeit. Half of the total then went to the head of the Custom House. Importers thus entangled were willing to settle out of court and bribe the officer in charge. In 1874 the metal importers, Phelps, Dodge and Company, paid a bribe of $50,000 to Conkling's man there, the collector, Chester A. Arthur, his surveyor Alonzo Cornell, and Conkling and Senator Ben Butler of Massachusetts, rather than forfeit a whole shipment worth $1.75 million that had been falsely declared.

It was similar elsewhere. J. S. Clarkson, the newspaper boss, in Iowa; General (and later governor) Russell Alger, the Match King, in Michigan; Governor Joseph Foraker in Ohio; Senator Arthur Gorman of Maryland—all ran state machines or the same sort of lines as Conkling. In Pennsylvania there was a dynasty, Senators Simon and Don Cameron, father and son. The basis of the bosses' authority in the 1870s was federal patronage. But in some states it was business that ran the political machine. The Anaconda Copper Corporation dominated Montana. Collis Huntington, railroad magnate, stood at the center of political life in California.

STALWARTS AND HALF BREEDS

James G. Blaine, who entered Congress as representative for Maine in 1863, led the Republican faction opposed to continuing Reconstruction indefinitely, the Half Breeds. Tall but not handsome, his face conveyed his special character with its dark eyes and flashing smile. He was resourceful, charming, and humorous. His sense of timing was faultless, his memory infallible. Yet Blaine created such intense reactions that wits said men went insane over him in pairs, one for and one against.

At first he kept on good terms with all sections of his party and thus came to be elected speaker of the House in 1869. But Blaine's critics had often suggested that he had obtained his moderate wealth by auctioneering immense land and railroad rights. And in the spring of 1876 he was accused of taking an advance of $64,000 from the Union Pacific Railroad against collateral of worthless bonds in the Little Rock and Fort Smith Railroad. Blaine

James G. Blaine of Maine, the most charismatic and controversial Republican leader between Lincoln and Roosevelt. He helped three lesser men attain the presidency but was denied the prize himself. As secretary of state he had ideas on Latin American policy that were ahead of his time but he aroused deep suspicion on account of his truck with railroad companies to whom he owed his moderate wealth. (Library of Congress).

and the Union Pacific denied the charges publicly on April 24. However, a House committee heard from a bookkeeper, James Mulligan, on May 31 that the story was true. Blaine sought and obtained a private interview with Mulligan, at which he purloined supposedly incriminating letters. From these he read extracts to Congress on June 5 in such a disingenuous way as to convince his audience of his innocence. In fact, he won by throwing sand in the eyes of his accusers.

The term "Stalwart" was first given to his opponents in the party by James Blaine in a letter to the *Boston Herald* of April 10, 1877. His most bitter enemy was their leader, Senator Roscoe Conkling. Their bitter antagonism divided the party and did not ease the problems facing its nominal leaders, the presidents.

Rutherford B. Hayes was only the third Republican to win the presidency. Conkling, who had connived at his election, referred to him as "His Fraudulency the President." This title was taken up by the very Democrats who had also helped to perpetrate the fraud. Critics were even less kind to his wife, the former Lucy Webb. She treated guests at the White House to ice cream in dishes shaped like Indian snowshoes. Because she wanted to raise the reputation of the White House after the alcoholic excesses of the Grant years, she gave them sarsaparilla instead of whiskey. This was too much for some guests, who complained that "the water flowed like wine." To her detractors she was "Lemonade Lucy." She certainly cut no figure in high society. James Blaine's daughter referred to the president's circle as "that nasty Hayes set."

As it happened, though, Hayes's cabinet was the best since Lincoln's. William Evarts of New York, who had defended Andrew Johnson at his trial, became secretary of state, John Sherman of Ohio became secretary of the treasury; Carl Schurz of Missouri became secretary of the interior. A Confederate officer, David McKendree Key of Tennessee, was, as promised, made postmaster general.

Republican senators set out to restrict the power of the president. To some he was no more than a figurehead, like the doge of Venice. They wanted to confine him to ceremonial dignity without real power. Hayes was not skillful at political maneuver and undermined his own position from the start. He said that he

would neither seek nor accept a second term, and he even recommended to Congress a constitutional amendment providing for
a single term of six years.

When it came to matters of currency in the Gilded Age politicians discerned silver threads among the golden. Indeed, the conflict between gold and silver was the very warp and woof of politics between the end of the Civil War and the turn of the century.
As we have seen, postwar administrations tried to restore the currency to hard money, specie based on gold. Between 1865 and
1878 the Treasury reduced the number of dollars in circulation
from $1.08 billion to $773.37 million. Consequently, the per capita
circulation decreased from $31.18 in 1865 to $16.25 in 1878. This
reduction caused slow but grinding discomfort for masses of people, especially in a period when expanding commerce and industry
increased the need for currency. A difficult situation was exacerbated by the fact that there were three kinds of dollars in circulation—gold, silver, and paper. Paper dollars, or greenbacks,
were the principal medium. It was said that they were green because rogue financiers picked them before they were ripe. Their
value fluctuated according to their number and business confidence in them. In general, prices rose with increases in the money
supply and fell with decreases. What cost $1.00 in 1860 cost $2.24
in 1865 (when the money supply was at its greatest) and fell successively as the money supply was reduced to $1.56 in 1870 and
then to 99 cents in 1878.

Because the currency was also composed of gold and silver, its
fate was linked to the different fortunes of these metals. In 1861
American mines had yielded about $43 million in gold but only
$2 million in silver. The traditional ratio between silver and gold
of 15.98 to 1 undervalued silver. Therefore, silver was sold commercially, and only gold was minted for coins. But, after the war,
prospectors discovered new veins of silver in the West (q.v.). Thus
in 1873, for the first time, the value of silver mined was equal to
that of gold at $36 million. In 1874 the value of silver fell below
the legal ratio of 16 to 1. Therefore, investors gained more by
selling their silver to government for coins at the official price than
by selling it commercially at the lower market price. The government was chary of buying overpriced silver. In the Coinage

Act of 1873 Congress eliminated silver currency by omitting any provision for minting silver dollars. Silver interests said that they had been duped and called the act "the crime of '73."

In 1877 the average American had only half as many dollars as he had had at the end of the war. After four years of depression, Congress concluded that the government could restore prosperity by increasing the money supply and encouraging inflation. If people had more money to spend, they would buy manufactured goods. This would stimulate the market, encourage a rise in prices, and increase business confidence. After the comparative failure of the Greenback or Independent National party in 1876, when it took only 81,737 votes, the torch of inflation passed to silver interests. The silverites wanted to expand the medium of currency on the basis that 16 ounces of silver were worth 1 ounce of gold. In fact, this was overvaluing silver, for the commercial price of silver had fallen way below this level. Thus, acceptance of this formula would have weakened the value of gold.

In November 1877 Representative Richard ("Silver Dick") Bland of Missouri introduced a bill for the free and unlimited coinage of silver at 412½ grains per silver dollar. It was passed overwhelmingly with a clause repealing the Resumption Act of 1875. Even if Hayes were to veto the bill in the interests of hard money and national honor, it was clear his veto would be overridden, so sensitive was Congress to labor unrest. Secretary of the Treasury John Sherman worked ceaselessly to effect a compromise and found an ally in William Allison of Iowa, now chairman of the Senate Finance Committee. Sherman and Allison together decided on a strategy of limited silver coinage, with $2 million a month as minimum and $4 million a month as maximum. By restricting the coinage of silver to the lower level the resumption program was saved.

In his efforts to build up American gold reserves Sherman was helped by a bumper crop of wheat in 1878, much of which was sold to Europe, which had had a poor harvest, in exchange for gold. On January 2, 1879, the first day of business, no one claimed gold for government notes. No one doubted the government's ability to pay. The dollar was again on a par with other gold currencies. The apparent success of their policy convinced conservatives that monetarism was the best policy through thick and thin.

CIVIL SERVICE REFORM

Reform of the civil service was one of the few subjects on which both liberals and conservatives could agree. In the wake of new inventions, industry, and technology, it was becoming clear to most people that nothing short of professional expertise would do if the government were ever to govern a nation undergoing momentous industrial and economic transformation. The old spoils system would have to go. Representative Thomas A. Jenckes of Rhode Island had begun to agitate for selection by competitive examination as early as 1865. After Gladstone's reform of the civil service in England in 1870 the movement for reform in America gathered momentum.

Some politicians were genuinely opposed to a civil service selected on the basis of academic attainment rather than practical ability. To James B. Beck of Kentucky and others the existing system represented a natural school of citizenship. As E. L. Godkin, editor of the *Nation*, observed, it was possible that a system of competitive examinations would discriminate against able men from poor backgrounds who could not afford to go to college. Thus, instead of weakening class prejudice it would have the opposite effect. A nonentity like Franklin Pierce could become president while a genius like Lincoln could not.

In 1876 both parties called for reform. Reform of the civil service was one means of reviving presidential power. John Jay of New York investigated the New York Custom House for Hayes and Schurz, and his report of May 24, 1877, substantiated widespread allegations of its bribery and corruption. On the basis of such information Hayes issued an executive order of June 22, 1877, forbidding political intimidation of civil servants by state bosses. The danger of a government without a president had been averted in the spring. The embarrassment of a president without a party in the fall was not. There now followed a contest between the president and spoilsmen led by Roscoe Conkling. On instructions from Conkling, U.S. Navy Officer Alonzo Cornell defied Hayes by calling a New York State Republican Convention in Rochester on September 26, 1877. Their intention was to discredit Republican reformers and have them dropped from the party ticket. Conkling denounced reformers for their hypocrisy: "Their stock in trade is rancid, canting self-righteousness. They are wolves in sheep's clothing. Their real object is office and plunder. When Dr. Johnson defined patriotism as the last refuge of a scoundrel, he was unconscious of the then undeveloped capabilities and uses of the word 'Reform'!" Conkling's candidates were nominated. His denunciation of "Snivel Service Reform" became the new slogan of the Stalwarts.

On October 15, 1877, Hayes sent Congress the names of the men he wanted to succeed Officers Alonzo Cornell and Chester A. Arthur in the New York Custom House. The Senate gave Conkling its support. It was a case of congressional solidarity against presidential authority. However, Hayes bided his time. He waited until the summer of 1878 when Congress was in recess. Then he replaced Arthur and Cornell with his own men. When Congress returned, Conkling was faced with a fait accompli. Conkling had inexhaustible reserves of hate, but the Senate did not and on February 3, 1879, gave way to the president's nominees, Gen. E. A. Meritt and L. B. Prince.

In revenge, Conkling and the Stalwarts proposed retired president Ulysses S. Grant as Republican nominee at the Republican National Convention of 1880 in Chicago. The Half Breeds, however, were prepared to meet the needs of the time and proposed their own leader, James G. Blaine, now senator. Since neither Grant nor Blaine could win, the convention chose a dark horse, congressional veteran James A. Garfield of Ohio. He was nominated on the thirty-sixth ballot with 399 votes against 306 for Grant. Garfield was handsome, large but graceful, with a leonine mane and a deep voice. To balance the ticket he took as his running mate the notorious spoilsman, Chester A. Arthur, formerly of the New York Custom House. Conkling was quite dismayed at Arthur's elevation.

During the campaign the Democratic candidate, Gen. Winfield Scott Hancock, seemed to stir little interest. In the election the popular vote was among the closest ever. In a total of 9 million votes cast only 39,000 separated winner from loser. It was the

"Boss" William Marcy Tweed of New York whose ring swindled the
city of untold millions during the late 1860s. Tweed was made the scape-
goat and imprisoned but many of his partners escaped. Their techniques
were used by other, especially Irish, rings in New York and elsewhere
throughout the Gilded Age but none was as brazen as the Tweed ring.
(Library of Congress).

capture of three doubtful states each with a large electoral vote that gave Garfield a plurality of 214 electoral votes against 155 for Hancock. Garfield had taken Indiana by a tiny plurality of 6,625 votes in a vote of about 500,000. Behind the scenes, oil tycoon John D. Rockefeller had supported him. No fewer than 500 Standard Oil agents were assigned to the Republican campaign. The implication was clear, and Vice President-elect Arthur alluded to poll fraud in Indiana at a banquet at Delmonico's restaurant in New York on February 24, 1881.

Garfield was the last of the seven log cabin presidents beginning with Andrew Jackson. A self-taught scholar who could speak both German and French and write Latin with one hand and Greek with the other at the same time, he nevertheless found presidential duties beyond him. "My god! What is there in this place that a man should ever want to get in it," he exclaimed after a month in office. Garfield and Blaine had been friends since Blaine had protected Garfield from disgrace in the Crédit Mobilier scandals of 1872. Now Garfield needed Blaine more than ever. He had been decisive in making the president; he was stronger in the party. It was inevitable that he would take the leading post in the cabinet, that of secretary of state. Garfield was disposed to conciliate faction by compromise. Blaine wanted his rivals killed off.

The collectorship of the New York Custom House was the most important administrative post outside the cabinet. It now controlled 1,300 apointments. It was there that Garfield and Blaine struck first. Rather than propitiate the Stalwarts, Garfield affronted them by appointing W. H. Robertson as collector. Robertson was not only one of Blaine's allies but also another adversary of Conkling. Conkling and his ally, Senator Tom Platt of New York, retaliated. At first they blocked Senate approval of Robertson and then on May 16, 1881, resigned their seats in protest at Garfield's "perfidy without parallel." Conkling and Platt confidently expected that the New York legislature at Albany would reappoint them. But the Half Breeds discovered Platt in an Albany hotel in the company of "an unspeakable female." He was so embarrassed that he withdrew his candidacy. Conkling was not reelected. The very day on which the public was regaled with newspaper reports of Platt's sex life farce turned to tragedy.

On July 2, 1881, James Garfield had breakfast with the Blaines and left their house for the Baltimore and Potomac Railroad Depot in Washington. He was bound for a college reunion at Williamstown, Massachusetts. But at the depot he was shot and fatally wounded by a disappointed office seeker, Charles Guiteau. As he fired his pistol into the president's back he cried, "I am a Stalwart and Arthur is president now." Contrary to expectations, Garfield did not die immediately. His life hung in the balance, and he lingered for three months. The wound hardly bled and the doctors had great difficulty in locating the bullet, which had lodged in muscle. Among those who tried unsuccessfully to do so was inventor Alexander Graham Bell, who used an electrical device. Ironically, it was not the bullet that killed the president but the efforts to save him. The inexperienced surgeons were clumsy, and their careless probes caused blood poisoning, from which Garfield died on September 19, 1881.

"Martyrdom is the only way a man can become famous without ability" was a cynical observation of George Bernard Shaw's. Indeed, the assassination of Garfield in 1881 brought the agitation for civil service reform to a head in much the same way as the assassination of John F. Kennedy in 1963 gave momentum to the movement for civil rights. While Garfield's life ebbed slowly away people became increasingly aware of the way quarrels over patonage had led to his assassination. They were not even distracted by morbid press accounts of the trial and the hanging of his assassin. On August 11, 1881, the National Civil Service Reform League was founded.

The new president surprised everyone. Chester A. Arthur astonished his admirers and angered his adversaries by abandoning the spoils system that had made him president. He vetoed lavish appropriations of $18.7 millions for a Rivers and Harbors bill in 1882 because it would have provided new opportunities for graft and corruption. And on May 15, 1882, he gave his assent to an act establishing a commission to report on tariff revision.

Arthur's life in the demimonde had made him a good judge of character. His nights spent in smoke-filled rooms had been a political education in themselves. Unlike Grant, Arthur wore the pants in his own home. In fact, he was quite a dude. He had eighty pairs of them. His taste was impeccable. The dude president invited Associated Artists, the company of interior decorators founded by artist and glass designer Louis Comfort Tiffany, to modernize the White House.

Arthur's political resolve was strengthened by public indigation over two new scandals, the Star Route Frauds and Hubbel Hale's campaign letter. In early 1881 Postmaster General Thomas L. James had the postal service investigated by James MacVeagh, who exposed malpractices in the western mail services. In the sparsely populated West, contracts for mail delivery were awarded to private firms that used stagecoaches and horseback riders to carry letters and packets, since train and steamboat were not available. These firms were supposed to deliver mail with "Certainty, Celerity, and Security," the words emphasized on the contracts by three asterisks or stars.

It was the duty of Thomas J. Brady, second assistant postmaster general from 1876, to administer the routes and award the contracts. MacVeagh discovered that Brady had not only given contracts in exchange for bribes but had also accepted outrageous charges from dishonest contractors. The total cost to the government was $4 million. Brady and his confederates were arraigned and tried. A first trial ended inconclusively on September 11, 1882, and a second in a surprising acquittal on June 14, 1883.

The second scandal cut to the heart of the matter of civil service reform, the need for a service independent of party. In May 1882 the chairman of the Republican congressional campaign committee, Jay A. Hubbel Hale, sent to a civil servants the traditional circular letter asking them for "voluntary contributions" to the Republicans' election campaign funds. According to the usual custom, campaign contributions were between 2 and 6 percent of salaries. In the atmosphere following Garfield's death and the unsuccessful prosecution of the Star Route Frauds, the letter inflamed public opinion. Public hostility to the Republicans was registered in the election results of 1882. The Democrats carried both houses. They then promoted legislation to reform the civil service, sponsored by Senator George H. Pendleton of Ohio. Republicans had to prove to the electorate their willingness to support a cause for which a president had died if they wanted to remain in office.

The Pendleton Act, signed by Arthur on January 16, 1883, created a Civil Service Commission of three members appointed by the president with the consent of the Senate. Not more than two were to come from any one party. The commission was to appoint a corps of examiners and provide for competitive examinations for prospective federal employees. The examination regulations were to apply to government departments in Washington and to customhouses and post offices with more than 50 employees. The president could extend the provisions of the act to other offices. The solicitation of campaign contributions was forbidden. By the turn of the century almost 100,000 positions were on the classified list. It was not only fortunate but also essential that the merit principle was adopted and put into effect before the increased role of government in the twentieth century necessitated an expanded civil service. Without it the fundamental reforms of the progressives could not have been attempted.

Agitation for civil service reform had signified much more than public discontent over political spoils It represented a fundamental challenge to government by clique and cabal. In the long battle the public had learned much about political strategy and tactics. The prevailing oligarchy was visibly shaken. But the new plutocracy was not. And when the public turned its attention to trusts and robber barons in the contemporaneous chain of trust and railroad legislation, (q.v.) it was not assured of victory. For reform changed the nature of corruption rather than the nature of politics. During the 1880s it became ever more insidious. The professional politician was to be upstaged by the political businessman.

The Senate was soon known as the Millionaire's Club. Owing to increasingly rigid party control over state legislatures by bosses, it became easy for wealthy men to pay whatever price was demanded and get themselves elected to the upper house. For example, Senator Thomas Collier ("Me, too") Platt, who was New York's "Easy Boss" after Conkling's death, rewarded loyal constituents with favors for services rendered.

The Senate, instead of representing geographical areas, came to represent economic units. Eastern magnates Donald Cameron of Pennsylvania, Nelson Aldrich of Rhode Island, and Stephen Elkins of West Virginia were joined in the late 1880s by Senators

McMillan and Stockbridge who represented lumber rather than Michigan. Calvin Brice represented banks and railroads; H. B. Payne, Standard Oil rather than Ohio. James Fair and John P. Jones represented silver rather than Nevada. George Hearst represented gold and newspaper rather than California; and Philetus Sawyer, appropriately, represented lumber rather than Wisconsin. The reputation of senators for helping themselves to fortunes at others' expense led to a story about President Grover Cleveland being woken in the night by his wife with the news that there were burglars in the house. Cleveland denied it drowsily. "In the Senate maybe, but not in the House." Several senators were corporation lawyers including John Spooner of Wisconsin, Arthur Gorman of Maryland, and Orville Platt of Connecticut. Platt had all the characteristics of a lawyer in politics and was well known for always hedging his bets. One story tells how in 1894 he was visiting his Connecticut constituents including a farmer who commented on a flock of sheep coming along a crossroad, "Them sheep been shorn." Platt, cautious as ever, opined, "'Pears so,— at least on this side."

To the new men party organization was a means to an end, not an end in itself as it has been to the old spoilsmen. English political scientist James Bryce understood how and why political and economic interests came to be mixed together in Congress. In his *American Commonwealth* (1893) he explained the difference between Congress and a European assembly: "Europeans think that the legislature ought to consist of the best men in the country, Americans that it should be a fair average sample of the country. Europeans think that it ought to lead the nation, Americans that it ought to follow the nation."

CLEVELAND

James Blaine's Republican opponents had been routed in the battle over patronage. He intended the Republican party to become the party of business quite openly with protection as its essential doctrine. Since they could no longer win elections by waving the bloody shirt, Republicans responded to Blaine's call and turned to the tariff as a rallying flag. Arthur, who had achieved reform, had satisfied nobody. It was now Blaine's turn to lead. He was duly nominated for president on the fourth ballot at the Republican National Convention in Chicago on June 5, 1884.

Blaine was the most formidable Republican leader between Lincoln and McKinley. Yet it was his candidacy that made possible the first election of a Democratic president in twenty-eight years. This was Grover Cleveland, a former mayor of Buffalo and present governor of New York. A lawyer by profession, Cleveland was considered ugly but honest. He acquired a national reputation not only as an opponent of Tammany Hall but also as a man of principle. He had vetoed a 5-cent fare proposed by the street railway of New York.

The elevated railroads in New York, controlled by Jay Gould, were permitted to charge a fare of 10 cents except in rush hours, when the rate was 5 cents. Public opinion, stirred by Gould for his own ends, wanted the fare to be fixed at 5 cents for all hours. Cleveland vetoed a bill proposing this on the grounds that it violated a contract awarded by state charter. As a result of this action, he became a popular hero of the middle class, which was delighted at Gould's discomfiture. In addition, he gained a reputation for thrift and being able to rise above partisan politics. Historian and journalist Dennis Tilden Lynch has described how skillful was Cleveland's use of the common touch. He would campaign "in saloons with beer barrels and tables for his rostrum. There wasn't a saloon kept by a Democrat, boasting a fair-sized back room, that he did not enter and harangue the thirst-slaking citizens after sharing a drink with them." Reporter William Hudson condensed Cleveland's political philosophy to "Public office is a public trust" and this became the slogan of his campaign. It was generally supposed that Cleveland opposed the power of monopolies and corporations. Yet in his campaign of 1884 Cleveland was supported by big business. He received contributions amounting to a total of $453,000.

The actual campaign was about public morality. Like others on that subject—such as those of 1952 and 1972—it was one of the dirtiest ever. Both sides concentrated on juicy subjects: fornication and fabrication. Cleveland, still a bachelor, had had a mistress in Buffalo, Maria Halpin, who had borne him an illegitimate child.

Another   voice   for   Cleveland.

When promiscuous alcoholic Maria Halpin claimed her illegitimate son, Oscar, was the child of Democratic presidential candidate Grover Cleveland in 1884 the Republican press had a field day as this vicious cartoon by Frank Beard from *Judge* of September 27, 1884 suggests. (Library of Congress).

The Republican press had a field day with insinuations about his indiscriminate son. It was said that as son of a former mayor he knew his oats. Blaine was no luckier. Not only were letters about Blaine's truck with railroads published in unexpurgated form but also a letter of April 18, 1876, which Blaine had written to Warren Fisher explaining his tactics. Blaine had betrayed more than he intended, his character. Thus, the Democratic campaign slogan was:

> Blaine, Blaine, James G. Blaine,
> The continental liar from the State of Maine.

Blaine was unacceptable to several influential Republicans who prized political morality over party loyalty. Celebrated reformer George W. Curtis summed up the choice offered the electorate thus:

We are told that Mr. Blaine has been delinquent in office, but blameless in private life, while Mr. Cleveland has been a model of official integrity, but culpable in his personal relations. We should therefore elect Mr. Cleveland to the public office which he is so well qualified to fill and remand Mr. Blaine to the private station which he is admirably fitted to adorn.

This was also the country's verdict—but only by a small margin. Cleveland took 4,879,507 popular votes to Blaine's 4,850,293 a plurality of only 29,214.

New York, then the most populous state, was pivotal in deciding the outcome. When members of the Prohibition party, founded in 1869, attended the Republican National Convention in Chicago to plead their case they were snubbed, whereas brewers and distillers were welcomed. Their candidate, John P. St. John of Kansas, took 16,000 votes in New York away from Blaine. Cleveland carried New York by only 1,149 votes, and thus the 16,000 Republican votes lost to St. John had given him victory there. Blaine did receive a delegation of Protestant clergymen in New York on October 29, 1884. One, the Reverend Dr. Samuel Burchard, openly disparaged the Democrats as the party of "Rum, romanism, and rebellion." His remark was offensive to Irish Catholics, predominant in machine politics, as was Blaine's attendance at a millionaires' banquet at Delmonico's the same day. Until then Blaine had enjoyed a strong following among Irish-Americans. Now it was entirely dissipated.

The election results were in doubt for several days. Rumors abounded that Jay Gould, Cleveland's adversary over the rail fare, was delaying and falsifying returns by his control of telegraph wires. A mob surrounded the Western Union Building crying,

"We'll hang Jay Gould to a sour apple tree." In fact, he was safe in his yacht on the Hudson River. To show that there were no hard feelings over old scores, Gould cabled his congratulations to Cleveland on November 7, 1884: "the vast business interests of the country will be entirely safe in your hands." His prediction was entirely accurate.

Woodrow Wilson's verdict on Cleveland as president was that he was not a Democrat but a conservative Republican. Despite momentary outbursts of temper, Cleveland had immense stamina and self-control. But he lacked imagination and compassion. He reflected the Democratic party's nineteenth-century distrust of strong centralized government. Nevertheless, it was not party loyalty, still less public opinion, that determined Cleveland's policies. It was his personal prejudices. Cleveland was not ambitious for reform, nor could he have carried a controversial legislative program through Congress. The Republicans controlled the Senate throughout his first term, and the Democrats just barely retained their House majority in the midterm election of 1886. The highlight of Washington's calendar in 1886 was a social, not a political event. In June, Cleveland married at the age of forty-nine. His bride was his ward, Frances Folsom, a girl of twenty-one.

Cleveland was consistent in wanting to cut down on government extravagance and waste. A particular problem was the high cost of veterans' pensions. In 1876 one tenth of the federal expenditure had been spent on pensions. By 1886 it was a quarter. The lists were endless. A particular abuse was the passage of special pensions bills by the House in regular evening sessions. Cleveland refused to sign many of these. One rejected bill was to provide for a man who had never served in the army at all. On his way to enlist he had suffered a fall that had crippled him. Another bill was for the widow of an army captain who had died of apoplexy in 1883, which she attributed to a wartime hernia of 1863. A third was for the family of a man who had deserted and drowned while making his escape. Yet in 1887 Congress passed the Invalid Pension Act, which awarded pensions to all disabled veterans whether their disabilities had been incurred in the service or not. Cleveland vetoed it.

Cleveland, Secretary of the Interior Lucius Lamar, and Land

Commissioner W. A. J. Sparks also restored 81 million acres of public lands to the federal government that had been legally granted to railroads but never used for construction or that had been illegally appropriated by cattle farmers. But his determination to cut federal expenditure was more often turned against those sections of the community who most needed government aid. On February 16, 1887, he vetoed the Texas Seed bill with its modest appropriation of $10,000 for farmers in desperate need of seed grain. His message was pompous if not patronizing: "Though the people support the Government, the Government should not support the people. Federal aid in such cases encourages the expectation of paternal care on the part of the Government and weakens the sturdiness of our national character." But he took a very different attitude to people with money for speculation. To induce investors to turn in their 4 percent federal bonds before they matured Cleveland offered a premium of $28 above the face value of $100 on each.

However, Cleveland did risk his career by questioning the basic assumption of industry, that government would support it through thick and thin. He did so in his annual state of the Union message of December 6, 1887: "Our present tariff laws, the vicious, inequitable and illogical source of unnecessary taxation," he said, "ought to be at once revised and amended."

The Civil War tariffs had been conceived by the government as emergency measures to raise revenue. The most important, the Morrill Tariff of 1861, was also passed at the behest of a bloc representing New England textile and Middle Atlantic iron and steel interests. Thereafter both new and established industries expected the government to protect them against cheap foreign goods. Critics of the tariff system argued that some manufacturers increased prices (and hence profits) in line with the tariff using the difference between cost of production and tariff rate as retail price. Thus prices rose but not wages and exports were harmed as much as imports.

Cleveland was preoccupied with government surplus. Because of the tariff, a "Treasury Octopus" of revenue surplus above and beyond federal expenditure threatened financial stability. By 1888 the accumulated surplus would rise to $140 million—about a third of all the country's circulating capital. In addition, the high tariff encouraged the development of trusts. As Henry Havemeyer, sugar magnate, said, "The Tariff is the mother of Trusts." For every new tariff with increased duties led to increased speculation on combinations. Cleveland believed that the existing system was "a burden upon those with moderate means and the poor, the employed and unemployed, the sick and well, and the young and old." The only proper course of action, he believed, was to reduce the tariff and balance the books. His decision was based on practical considerations rather than on theories about protection and free trade: "It is a condition which confronts us, not a theory." But his words were political dynamite in an election year. They provided the two parties with their first genuine difference in a generation.

In line with Cleveland's recommendation, the new chairman of the House Ways and Means Committee, Roger Mills of Texas, was assigned the task of devising a new tariff. His original bill would have reduced the duty on manufactured goods by 7 percent while making certain raw materials duty free. By June 21, 1888, when it passed from House to Senate, it was already a compromise of different sectional interests. Disinterested philosophy had given way to political expedience. Even so, the Senate Finance Committee, composed of Aldrich, Allison, Morrill, and Sherman, refused to accept it. Neither Democratic House nor Republican Senate would yield. The issue went to the electorate.

What the Republicans needed in the election itself was a presidential nominee who could rally all discontented Democrats to their cause. Blaine declined to run. At the Republican National Convention in Chicago on June 25, 1888, Senator Benjamin Harrison of Indiana was nominated. A frigid Presbyterian deacon, he was no friend of labor. His only qualification for the presidency was his ancestry. His grandfather, William Henry Harrison, had been the ninth president.

Given his limitations, Harrison was lucky to have the astute Senator Matthew P. Quay of Pennsylvania as his campaign manager. Quay began his career as a city boss in Harrisburg and then became state boss of Pennsylvania. Tom Platt called him "the ablest politician this country has ever produced." His aquiline nose, high cheek bones, and sharp chin showed that he was part Indian. As the result of a war wound, one of his eyes drooped, giving him a baleful expression. After a career as a lawyer, newspaper editor, and member of the Pennsylvania legislature, he became secretary of the Commonwealth and recorder of Philadelphia, and in 1879 chairman of the Republican state committee. His particular racket was diverting state funds, deposited in private banks, to private speculators. If these speculations failed, the state lost its money. When $400,000 were discovered to be missing, there was a great uproar. Quay had to retire for a few years. In 1885 he returned to take charge of the state treasury and in 1887 was elected to the U. S. Senate.

Matthew Quay's campaign strategy in 1888 was to obtain considerable contributions from businessmen in exchange for a promise for political favors in future. He secured the cooperation of capitalists William Dudley, John Wanamaker, Mark Hanna, Thomas Dolan, and others. The Republicans admitted raising $1 million altogether in campaign contributions. This was four times the sum acknowledged by the Democrats. The *New York World* of November 25, 1888, reported allegations that the Republicans had raised an additional secret fund of $2 million. In return for this massive financial support from big business the Republicans promised to revise the whole system of internal taxation but to keep the protective system intact. Yet they also declared opposition to "all combinations of capital, organized in trusts or otherwise."

In a close election Cleveland took a plurality of the popular vote, winning 5,537,857 votes to Harrison's 5,447,129. But he lost three key states, Ohio, Indiana, and New York. With these he lost the election. In the electoral college he had only 168 votes to Harrison's 233.

The national contest turned almost entirely on the tariff. In New York it devolved on ballot reform and prohibition. When a naturalized citizen born in England asked the foolish British minister to the United States, Sir Lionel Sackville-West, how he should vote to serve England, West advised him in writing to vote for the Democrats. His reply was published, and his advice was highly offensive to Irish Democrats who deserted Cleveland for Harrison.

Rather than see prohibitionists determine the outcome of the presidential election, as they had boasted of doing in 1884, regular Republicans and Democrats struck a deal with one another in New York State. Harrison was acceptable to the liquor interests. If the wet Democrats would vote for him, then the wet Republicans would vote for the reelection of David B. Hill, Democratic governor. Hill was reelected governor of New York by 19,000 votes, whereas Cleveland lost the state by 9,529. According to reports in the *Nation* of November 29, 1888, and March 7, 1889, the Republicans paid $150,000 for three Democratic political clubs in New York State each having between 10,000 and 30,000 votes.

AN INTERREGNUM

As president, Harrison proved a cipher, and a cold one at that. It was said that he bestowed a favor in such a frigid fashion that he turned a friend into a foe for life. His handshake was compared to a wilted petunia. He was so taciturn when he met people that it was not generally known that his first language was English. Even his political allies derided Harrison's small stature and glacial manners in an anecdote about a visitor to the White House who was refused an audience with the president by a secretary who insisted, "I'm sorry, sir, but the president cannot be seen."

"Can't be seen!" was the retort. "My God! Has he got as small as that?"

Authority drifted from White House to Capitol. In the House there were just 165 Republicans to 154 Democrats. It was now the turn of the Democrats to play fast and loose with the rules. The minority could outmaneuver the majority. The Democrats demanded a quorum call and then refused to answer their names. The lower house would comprise a sizable number and yet remain technically inquorate. However, the new speaker, Thomas B. ("Czar") Reed, was master of the situation. On January 29, 1890, Reed instructed the clerk to record members as present even if they refused to respond to the quorum call. By doing so he precipitated a debate about obstruction in which such tactics were outlawed.

With such a supine president at the helm it was no wonder that

Congress returned to the gross extravagance of the Grant period. The significant difference was that now political venality was perfectly legal. Congress passed a Dependent Veterans' Pension bill in 1890, which was to double the lists of pensioners within four years. Veterans of ninety days' service suffering physical or mental disability (whatever the cause) and their widows were to receive a pension, provided that they had no other source of support. Harrison defended such provisions in 1892. "It was," he said, "no time to be weighing the claims of old soldiers with apothecary's scales."

Since the Republicans had campaigned for increased protection in 1888, they also proposed a new tariff in October 1890. In keeping with Cleveland's pledge, it was officially entitled "An Act to Reduce the Revenue"; but it was generally known by the names of its sponsors, Representative William McKinley of Ohio and Senator Nelson W. Aldrich of Rhode Island. Their intentions were, of course, very different from Cleveland's. McKinley remonstrated against the very idea that poor people needed cheaper goods: "Cheap is not a word of hope; it is not a word of inspiration! It is the badge of poverty; it is the signal of distress." Both this tariff and the Dingley Tariff of 1897 awarded prizes to all allies of the tariff bloc.

The McKinley tariff raised the general levels from 38 to 50 percent. But the increases on textiles and metal goods were so high that people stopped buying these imports. Refined sugar was taxed at 1 cent a pound to the benefit of Henry O. Havemeyer and the Sugar Trust. To gain support of sugar-producing states American growers were to be paid a bounty of 2 cents a pound. Coffee, hides, acorns, and beeswax were put on the free list. The tax on tobacco was lowered, making it possible for the American Tobacco Company to sell more cigarettes. The removal of all duties on raw sugar and molasses alone cut federal income by $50 million a year. Thus, by the time Cleveland returned to office in 1893, the surplus that had so appalled him in 1887 had been turned into a deficit. Even Republicans were dissatisfied. For instance, Secretary of State James G. Blaine was incensed that the McKinley Tariff ran counter to his proposed tariff concessions to Latin America. McKinley took first the acclaim for the decisions and then the blame when he was defeated in the midterm elections of 1890.

The Gilded Age held out promise of gold for all. But there was not enough for everyone, and in 1890 the movement for the coinage of silver revived. In part this was due to a catastrophic fall in the prices of wheat, cotton, and corn, and consequently it brought about renewed calls for inflationary policy from the farmers. But these renewed calls now had extra weight. In 1889 four new states entered the Union, North and South Dakota, Montana, and Washington, in 1890 two more, Idaho and Wyoming. They were western states, part of the silver bloc. As territories they had been just as interested in silver, but as states they each had two senators to press their case and make the silver bloc a sizable minority in the upper house. It now comprised seventeen Republicans and one Democrat who held up passage of the McKinley Tariff until they had forced Congress to accept the Sherman Silver Purchase Act. It required the secretary of the treasury to purchase 4.5 million ounces of silver a month.

Those who put their trust in silver got as much as they deserved. During these years the production of silver increased, and gold became more scarce and more expensive. Inevitably, the gold value of a silver dollar fell to 67 cents. Worse, by 1892 the Treasury had less than the minimum gold reserve, $100 million.

The unpopularity of the McKinley tariff led to numerous Republican defeats in the midterm elections of 1890. Only 88 Republicans were elected to the new House against 235 Democrats and 9 Populists. It was said the Democrats owed their victory to a revolt of consumers from the Republican standard. They wanted to pocket the prizes but not pay the bill. They were sickened not only by higher prices but also by the lavish spending of the retiring Fifty-first Congress. Its appropriations came to the then unprecedented sum of $989 million. When reproached with the extravagance of the "billion-dollar Congress," Speaker Reed remonstrated that it was justified: the United States was a billion-dollar country.

It was inevitable that Cleveland and Harrison would be pitted against one another in the election of 1892. During the interregnum Cleveland had worked as a corporation lawyer in New York

"CZAR" REED IS READY.

THE SPEAKER—I'M READY FOR THE FIFTY-SIXTH CONGRESS. SEE WHAT I DID TO THE FIFTY-FOURTH AND FIFTY-FIRST.

Speaker Thomas B. "Czar" Reed was much criticized in the Democratic press for his dictatorial conduct of House affairs in the 1890s, especially when it seemed congressional business was more than ever subject to the dictates of big business and high finance. (Library of Congress).

City. The action replay ended in decisive victory for Cleveland, who took 5,555,426 votes to Harrison's 5,182,690 and carried a group of pivotal states. He took 277 electoral votes to Harrison's 145. Cleveland had given the Democrats their greatest victory in forty years. But his popular vote was only 3 percent higher than his rival's. A significant feature of the election was the considerable advance made by a new third party, the People's party, or Populists, of the South and West (q.v.).

THE RETURN OF CLEVELAND

No sooner had Cleveland's second term begun than economic disaster struck. As had been the case in 1873, the first signs of industrial crisis came with railroad collapse. The Philadelphia and Reading Railroad failed ten days before Cleveland took office. It was followed by the Erie in July, and then by the Northern Pacific, the Union Pacific, and the Santa Fe in the late summer. The panic of 1893 caused the collapse of a quarter of the railroads representing $2.5 billion of capital and over 40,000 miles of track.

Another factor in the ensuing depression was the weakness of the banking structure. Banking had become increasingly concentrated in New York. Disturbances in Wall Street extended to the rest of the country. The New York Stock Exchange was convulsed in its greatest selling spree. Banks asked for their loans to be paid, and those individuals and firms who could not repay went bankrupt. More than 15,000 businesses failed in 1893. Rural banks collapsed. Of 158 bank failures, 153 were in the West and South. The depression was the worst experienced in America to that time. No one really knew how many people were unemployed. Estimates vary from 2.5 million to 4 million, at least 1 worker in 5 of the labor force.

As conscientious as before, Cleveland was now firmly committed to the capitalist point of view. Ike Hoover, head usher at the White House, attests to the change in the man who once had the common touch, "Of his company he was very choosey and he seemed to prefer moneyed people. Looking over the list one might term it a 'millionaire's crowd.'" He certainly had little sympathy with those who were dispossessed. He once came upon a beggar eating grass on the White House lawn who confessed, "I'm hungry." Cleveland advised him, "The grass is longer in the back-yard." Appropriately, one of the most popular new songs of 1894 was *I Don't Want to Play in Your Yard* ("If you won't be good to me").

Cleveland was out of touch with public opinion and confused by disturbing social trends. But overseas events forced him to take action and try and raise the depression. On June 26, 1893, India joined European countries and abandoned bimetallism. That day the value of the American silver dollar fell from 67 cents to below 60 cents in gold. Attributing the panic to monetary uncertainty, Cleveland believed that there was just one remedy, a drastic one—repeal of the Sherman Silver Purchase Act. On June 30 he summoned a special session of Congress for August 8 to "put beyond all doubt or mistake the intention and the ability of the Government to fulfill its pecuniary obligations in money universally recognized by all civilized countries." America would return to the gold standard. Cleveland recognized that his proposal would split the Democratic party. But he was not deterred. He had immense stamina. The day after he called Congress into special session Cleveland underwent a dangerous operation to remove a cancerous growth in the roof of his mouth. It was performed in the utmost secrecy on a yacht in New York's East River. Part of his jaw was removed and replaced with an artificial jaw made of vulcanized rubber.

By selective manipulation of patronage Cleveland ensured enough Democratic votes to help Republicans repeal the discredited Silver Purchase Act of 1890. Repeal passed the House by 239 votes to 108 on August 18, 1893. Two months later it passed the Senate by 43 votes to 37. Among those who spoke against repeal was Congressman William Jennings Bryan of Nebraska. A most eloquent orator with a sonorous voice, he soon abandoned his written notes and held the House engrossed in his arguments for three hours. The substance of his appeal was faith in the simple people of America. To Bryan the conflict between gold and silver represented a clash of wills between capitalists and ordinary people.

On the one side stand the corporate interests of the United States, the moneyed interests, aggregated wealth and capital, imperious, arrogant, compassionless. On the other hand stand an unnumbered throng, those who gave to the Democratic party a name, and for whom it has assumed to speak. Work-worn and dust-begrimed, they make their mute appeal, and too often their cry for help beats in vain against the outer walls, while others, less deserving, gain access to legislative halls.

This one plangent speech turned an almost unknown politician from an obscure state into a leading candidate for the Democratic presidential nomination in 1896.

The economic results of repeal were not decisive. But politically it was disastrous. Not since slavery and secession had there been such a divisive issue as silver. Moreover, repeal roused public suspicions about the financial probity of the government. Instead of stopping holders of silver certificates from requesting redemption in gold, repeal swelled the tide. It dawned on the president and his cabinet that the government might not be able to meet its legal obligations in gold. Cleveland decided to sell government bonds for gold. But he required the financial assurance of some independent agency in order to convince the public that his strategy was sound. He turned to banker J. P. Morgan, who could assemble a syndicate of financiers to assure the bonds. However, this insurance starved the financial appetite that it was intended to feed. Clients who bought bonds first drew from the Treasury the gold they needed to pay for them. Thus, as soon as one drain was closed another opened. In the winter of 1895 the gold reserve fell to $42 million. Cleveland compounded the problems by seeking two further sales of bonds, again guaranteed by the banks that provided the Treasury with gold to cover withdrawals. They bought bonds at 104½ and sold them at 118. In 1896 the Treasury issued $100 million in bonds supported by public subscription. This fourth measure succeeded in damming the tide and the crisis passed. No single act by the administration aroused as much censure as Cleveland's contract with Morgan. It seemed to ordinary people that this was another tightfisted bargain in which wicked capitalists had profited from a national crisis. Furthermore, the deal had failed to raise the depression, whereas generous public response to the fourth issue of 1896 had saved the situation.

Cleveland also tried to persuade Congress to reduce the tariff, but the Wilson-Gorman Tariff of 1894, passed over his veto, involved 634 changes from the original bill, and most of these were upward. Cleveland denounced it as "party perfidy and party dishonor." However, because Congress recognized the very real financial problems facing the administration, it included a provision for a tax of 2 percent on incomes of $4,000 or more. This was a most controversial measure. Congressman J. H. Walker of Massachusetts stated, "The income tax takes from the wealth of the thrifty and the enterprising and gives to the shifty and the sluggard." Senator John Sherman of Ohio declared, "This attempt to array the rich against the poor . . . is socialism, communism, devilism." And in a widely publicized test case of 1895, *Pollock v. Farmer's Loan and Trust Company*, the Supreme Court decided by 5 votes to 4 that income tax was unconstitutional. The case against the tax was that because it was a direct tax it must be apportioned among the states according to population. However, this would not be practicable. Therefore, the Court decided that the act must fall.

"General" Jacob S. Coxey, a quarry owner of Massillon, Ohio, had a different solution for the depression. He proposed a bill allowing any town or county ready to undertake public improvements such as road building to issue bonds without interest to be held with the secretary of the treasury in exchange for legal tender notes. Public improvements financed in this way would give men employment at a minimum wage of $1.50 for an eight-hour day. Coxey decided to press his claim. Starting on Easter Sunday 1894, Coxey, accompanied by his wife and infant son, Legal Tender Coxey, led a march of unemployed men from Ohio to Washington. This was a "petition on boots" intended to stir the stern countenances of congressmen. Only 500 broken veterans arrived exhausted in Washington on May Day. Coxey was arrested for trespass on Capitol Hill, and his followers were dispersed by the police. In the melee some fifty people were beaten up or trampled upon. In 1894 seventeen industrial armies altogether marched on Washington, scaring the administration into thinking that they represented incipient rebellion across the country.

In the midterm elections of 1894 the Democrats lost the support of urban voters. Two decades of congressional equilibrium between the parties ended as the Republicans recaptured both houses. They were to retain control for the next sixteen years. Silver Democrats had already joined forces with Populists in the West, where it was sometimes difficult to distinguish between them. However, silver interests had not yet given up hope of tying the Democrats to their cause.

When Cleveland left the presidency in 1897 his party was divided, defeated, and demoralized. Cleveland's wife remarried after his death in 1908 and lived until 1947. When she met Gen. Dwight D. Eisenhower, the future thirty-fourth president, she told him how much she missed Washington. "Really," he asked, "where did you live?"

FOREIGN POLICY

During the 1860s and 1870s few Americans were interested in foreign policy. The swelling tide of immigrants seeking refuge confirmed them in their traditional suspicions about Europe. However, it became clear to Secretaries of State William H. Seward (1861–69) and Hamilton Fish (1869–77) that, because of its expanding network of communications, its industry and trade, the United States could not afford to ignore its interests in world affairs. Business and industry put pressure on congressmen to secure or challenge particular policies that did or did not suit their interests. The policies of Seward and Fish reflected these conflicts and confusions. If their policies lacked a sense of grand design, it was also because they had to work without adequate administrative staff. There were only thirty-one clerks in the State Department in 1869.

Seward's policy was expansionist but subject to immense frustration and lost on politicians obsessed with Reconstruction. The collapse of the Spanish attempt to colonize the Dominican Republic, or Santo Domingo, and Spain's subsequent withdrawal from the island in 1865 were attributed to his diplomatic efforts. In 1867 Seward also put military pressure on Napoleon III to withdraw from his attempt to install the emperor Maximilian in Mexico. Seward's most famous act, however, was the purchase of

Alaska from Russia. He signed the treaty in the middle of a game of whist at four o'clock in the morning on March 30, 1867. Hence the purchase was called "a dark deed done in the night." Although the Senate approved the purchase on April 6, Congress did not appropriate the purchase money of $7.5 million until 1870, and then only after the Russian minister, Baron Stoeckel, had spent some of it in advance to bribe influential Republicans in the House. What use, they wondered, was this "Walrussia" or "Seward's Folly" with its frozen wastes? The *Nation* spoke for many when it declared that if the nation was in peril it was not for lack of territory but because of an excess of it.

On July 28, 1868, Seward signed the Seward-Burlingame Treaty of commerce and friendship with China. The Senate, however, rejected his treaty of October 24, 1867, to buy the Virgin Islands, St. Thomas and St. John, from Denmark for $7.5 million. On August 28, 1867, Seward annexed the unoccupied the Midway Islands west of Hawaii, and on June 21, 1867, he acquired American right of transit in Nicaragua for cutting a canal across the Isthmus at a later date.

Most controversial of all were the protracted negotiations with Britain over the *Alabama* claims. On January 14, 1869, the Senate rejected the treaty negotiated by the United States minister to England, Reverdy Johnson, to settle the *Alabama* dispute. It contained not one word of regret for the wartime damage caused by the *Alabama* and the other confederate vessels, the *Shenandoah* and the *Florida*, which had been built or fitted in British ports. Charles Sumner, chairman of the Senate Foreign Relations Committee, charged that Britain should bear half the total cost of the war, $2.12 billion, for having aided the South and prolonged the war. Sumner really wanted the cession of Canada in payment. On May 8, 1871, a joint Anglo-American commission settled the score by establishing a judicial commission of five members to adjudicate the claims of the United States. On September 14, 1872, the new commission reported that Britain had been negligent in allowing the *Alabama* and the other cruisers to participate in the war. It awarded the United States compensation of $15.5 million.

On the advice of his private secretary, Orville Babcock, President Ulysses S. Grant revived one of Seward's schemes for the annexation of Santo Domingo by the United States. In submitting a treaty of annexation for ratification by the Senate, the president was disclosing that he was the tool of predatory businessmen and politicians, including Ben Butler and John A. Rawlins. The Senate rejected the treaty on November 29, 1869. Relations between Spain and the United States deteriorated to a very low ebb over the *Virginius* affair of 1873. The *Virginius* was a ship carrying arms to Cuban rebels against Spain under the American flag. It was seized at sea by a Spanish gunboat, and fifty-three of the crew, including eight Americans, were executed for piracy. The situation was saved by the discovery that the ship was not registered in the United States, and Spain subsequently paid an indemnity for the loss of American lives.

Between the *Virginius* affair of 1873 and the Hawaiian crisis of 1891 foreign relations were comparatively untroubled. However, during Chester A. Arthur's administration politicians showed greater interest in foreign policy and called for an expanded navy to demonstrate American willingness to back it up with force when necessary. A nation without a navy, they argued, could make little headway in world affairs in an age of sea power.

The navy was then not only small but also in poor repair. Representative John D. Long of Massachusetts described it as "an alphabet of floating washtubs." In *The Canterville Ghost* Oscar Wilde has this exchange between the English aristocratic ghost and the pert American girl:

"I don't think I should like America."
"I suppose because we have no ruins and no curiosities," said Virginia satirically.
"No ruins! No curiosities!" answered the Ghost; "you have your navy and your manners."

The most famous advocate of naval expansion was former naval officer Alfred Thayer Mahan. Mahan first propounded his ideas for a larger navy and the acquisition of naval bases in the Pacific and Caribbean in lectures at the new Naval War College in 1886 and then published them as *The Influence of Sea Power upon History* in 1890. He reflected rather than provoked a changing mood in public opinion, but his ideas were most welcome to such advocates of expansion as rising politicians Theodore Roosevelt and Henry Cabot Lodge. Congress set about repairing and improving the navy. In 1883 it commissioned three cruisers and in 1886 two battleships, the *Maine* and the *Texas*. The Naval Act of 1890 authorized the building of three more powerful battleships, the *Indiana*, the *Massachusetts*, and the *Oregon*. Whereas in 1880 the American navy was twelfth in the world, by 1900 it was third with seventeen battleships and six armored cruisers.

A few statesmen and some businessmen favored commercial expansion. On the traditional assumption that the best means of defense is attack, they argued that the United States had to acquire territory to preserve its traditional commercial and strategic rights. They were contemptuous of the European contest for imperial possessions but caught the same mania themselves. They held certain assumptions about America's role in world affairs. They considered the United States to be both a stabilizing and a liberalizing influence on European diplomacy. They liked to think that its own emphasis on material progress and on individual freedom was an inspiration to emerging nations. Thus, politicians confused duty, interests, and power. They could not conceive why in the 1890s movements for national independence in underdeveloped colonies refused to distinguish between conventional European imperialism and American economic expansion.

Emerging nations were not likely to be propitiated by conventional American claims when they were propounded by such advocates of Social Darwinism and Manifest Destiny as Josiah Strong. In *Our Country, Its Possible Future and Its Present Crisis* (1885) he declared:

This race of unequalled energy, with all the majesty of numbers and the might of wealth behind it—the representative, let us hope, of the largest liberty, the purest Christianity, the highest civilization,—having developed peculiarly aggressive traits calculated to impress its institutions upon mankind, will spread itself over the earth. If I read not amiss, this powerful race will move down upon Mexico, down upon Central and South America, out upon the islands of the sea, over upon Africa and beyond. And can anyone doubt that the result of this competition of races will be the survival of the fittest?

From the 1880s American politicians expressed particular interest first in Latin America and then in the Pacific. President James Garfield needed James G. Blaine to conceive foreign policy as well as to make the Republican party more liberal. Blaine's policy was a mixture of capitalist self-interest, bourgeois morality, and liberal faith in economic progress. He believed that if the United States encouraged favorable conditions for political stability and economic growth in Latin America it would gain a double advantage: permission to extract natural resources from developing Latin American economies in need of U.S. investment and the sale of American industrial goods in their markets. To make the New World truly free for the United States he favored a common system of coins, weights, and measures; free trade and unrestricted travel; and a series of hemispheric conferences to educate statesmen and businessmen politically and economically.

Blaine's early initiatives died with Garfield. Chester A. Arthur was reluctant to support such an innovative policy and one, moreover, that was being advanced by a political opponent. Frustrated, Blaine resigned in December 1881.

On his return to power as secretary of state under Benjamin Harrison, Blaine persuaded Congress to incorporate a clause in the McKinley tariff of 1890 whereby the president was empowered to penalize imports from Latin American countries that did not afford reciprocal treatment to American exports. At this time 87 percent of exports from Latin America entered the United States free of duty. Tariff reciprocity was an instrument of diplomacy and one that worked all the better for not attracting domestic comment and confrontation. The outgoing president, Grover Cleveland, had revived the idea of a conference for nations in the Western Hemisphere, and under Harrison the conference of eighteen countries convened in Washington on October 2, 1889. Sitting until April 19, 1890, it resulted in the founding of the Commercial Union of American States but produced no tangible economic advantages.

Although Blaine was called "Jingo Jim," he exercised a moderating influence on foreign policy. On October 18, 1891, a party of rowdy sailors from the cruiser Baltimore went on shore leave in Valparaiso, Chile, where they were attacked by a mob of Chileans who killed two and wounded seventeen others. There was great moral outrage and much saber rattling in the United States. The world press took much pleasure in criticizing "Yankee imperialism." But Blaine defused the situation, and the crisis passed on January 28, 1892, after Chile capitulated to American demands for an indemnity.

HAWAII AND SAMOA

Between America and Asia two groups of islands had special strategic importance, Hawaii in the North Pacific and Samoa in the South Pacific.

The Hawaiian Islands, (or the Sandwich Islands) discovered by Captain Cook in 1778, lay 2,300 miles southwest of California and served as a merchant base between America and Asia. By 1840 the capital, Honolulu, was an established port of call for American merchant ships and whalers. On January 30, 1875, Hamilton Fish concluded a treaty of friendship with Hawaii in which each nation gave the other exclusive trading privileges and the United States guaranteed Hawaiian independence. On January 20, 1887, the Senate agreed to the renewed and expanded form of the 1875 treaty of friendship with Hawaii negotiated by Secretary of State Thomas F. Bayard (1885–89). Bayard had secured a new concession, permission to establish a naval base at Pearl Harbor on the island of Oahu.

The treaties of 1875 and 1887 encouraged the production of sugar fivefold. In 1890, 99 percent of Hawaiian sugar exports went to the United States. Hawaiians believed that increasing American involvement would end in annexation. They disliked increasing Hawaiian economic dependence on the United States. The McKinley Tariff of 1890, which raised the duty on sugar by 2 cents a pound, devastated the Hawaiian economy. The price of its sugar fell from $100 to $60 a ton. Sugar plantations lost their former value. American planters and investors now concluded that annexation was absolutely essential. The turning of Hawaii into a territory would give its sugar the status of American sugar and restore it to its former place in the American market.

In 1887 the dissolute old king of Hawaii, Kalakua, had been prevailed upon to accept a reform constitution restricting his power and making both cabinet and assembly more responsible. But on January 29, 1891, he was succeeded by his sister, Liliuokalani, who was determined to reassert the monarchy. Her policy prompted a counterrevolution by American expatriates supported by the American minister, John L. Stevens, and achieved by marines from the USS *Boston*. A committee of safety, consisting largely of the planter sons of American missionaries, deposed Liliuokalani on January 17, 1893, and established a provisional government under Chief Justice Sanford B. Dole. He opened negotiations for annexation with John Stevens, and President Benjamin Harrison accepted his terms on February 14, 1893.

However, on his return to office, Grover Cleveland would not countenance annexation. "I mistake the Americans," he declared, "if they favor the odious doctrine that there is no such thing as international morality; that there is one law for a strong nation and another for a weak one." He withdrew the treaty from the Senate on March 9, 1893, and dispatched a special commissioner, James H. Blount, to Hawaii, who reported on July 17, 1893, that Stevens had instigated the revolution on behalf of American businessmen. Thinking that the provisional government would fall, Cleveland renounced American interests. But he could not remove the provisional government and was eventually obliged to recognize the Republic of Hawaii on August 17, 1894. Cleveland's successor as president, William McKinley, had no qualms about annexation, especially since the rising power of Japan was a potential threat to American interests in the Pacific. Because supporters of annexation could not muster a vote of two thirds in the Senate, they and the president agreed to a joint resolution requiring only a simple majority in both houses. On August 12, 1898, Hawaii became part of the United States, and on April 20, 1900, it was awarded full territorial status.

On January 17, 1878, the Samoan Islands (or Navigators' Islands), located 4,100 miles from the coast of California, granted the United States trading rights and permission to build a coaling station at Pago Pago on the island of Tutuila. This concession made Britain and Germany jealous. For ten years the three powers competed for superior concessions, each supporting rival chieftains who were expected to promote the special interests of their sponsor state. German intentions of taking the islands with a force of seven warships were destroyed when a hurricane in Apia Harbor sank six of their ships on March 15 and 16, 1889.

On June 14, 1889, the United States entered into a tripartite protectorate with Britain and Germany over the Samoan Islands, ratified by the Senate on February 4, 1890. The powers agreed to regulate the arms and liquor traffic and the sale of land. Secretary of State Walter Q. Gresham (1893–95) observed later that this apparently insignificant treaty represented "the first departure from our traditional and well established policy of avoiding entangling alliances with foreign powers in relation to objects remote from this hemisphere."

In the past the United States, Britain, and Germany, for their own ends, had each promoted rival claimants to the throne of Samoa. Their discredited strategy now caught up with them as their former royal clients continued to quarrel despite the new tripartite protectorate. The upshot was a prolonged civil war. The three great powers eventually realized they could only secure lasting peace in Samoa if they ended the joint protectorate. They now decided to partition the island outright. The United States and Germany divided the islands between them on December 2, 1899 (ratified on January 16, 1900). Britain was compensated by the acquisition of the Solomon Islands.

Anglo-American relations were no more settled in the Gilded Age than they had been in the Civil War. On February 29, 1892, Britain agreed to accept arbitration in a fisheries dispute between Canada and the United States over extermination of the seal, hunted for its fur in Alaskan waters. A tribunal found legally in favor of Canada but morally in favor of Blaine's attempt to save the seal from extinction.

In 1895 a long-standing dispute between Britain and Venezuela over the boundary of British Guiana came to a head after the discovery of gold in both Latin American countries. Britain had previously refused to accept American arbitration; and Cleveland, supported by Congress, made it clear in a message of December 17, 1895, that if Britain would not accept arbitration voluntarily he himself would define and enforce the boundary. Venezuela's claim was based on historical grounds and was supported by an

American syndicate, which it proposed to reward with a lucrative concession. Cleveland's ultimatum was a deliberate ploy to distract the American electorate from divisions in the Democratic ranks and was recognized as such by commentators, who referred to it as another case of "twisting the lion's tail." This message provoked more saber rattling in the United States. However, a catastrophic fall in American stocks on world markets chastened the American plutocracy. Britain and Venezuela agreed in a treaty of Washington of February 2, 1897, to accept arbitration by an independent commission. On October 3, 1899, it upheld most of the British claims.

CHAPTER EIGHT

THE CLOSING OF
THE FRONTIER

IN 1890 the Bureau of the Census announced that the frontier was closed, that is, there was no longer any discernible demarcation between frontier and settlement.

Up to and including 1880 the country had a frontier of settlement, but at present the unsettled area has been so broken into by isolated bodies of settlement that there can hardly be said to be a frontier line. In the discussion of its extent, its westward movement etc., it can not, therefore, any longer have a place in the census reports.

Westward expansion was now complete. Manifest Destiny had been fulfilled. Realization that the Golden West was no longer open had a considerable psychological effect on native Americans and immigrants alike. In 1893 historian Frederick Jackson Turner, then a professor at Wisconsin and subsequently at Harvard, wrote his brief but seminal article, "The Significance of the Frontier in American History," which was published by the American Historical Association in 1894. He argued that the development of the New World had run a very different course from that of the Old because of "The existence of an area of free land, its continuous recession, and the advance of American settlement westward." The frontier acted as a safety valve for the East and helped to make American society more fluid than European. Outposts stimulated the spirit of individualism and inventiveness, putting a special premium on democracy and versatility. American society, moreover, owed to the frontier its special characteristics of earthiness and practicality.

The final settlement of the West was one of the most dramatic stories of the Gilded Age. According to the map little changed. The continental boundaries of the United States were almost the same in 1901 as they had been in 1865. Yet in 1865 there were very few settlements between the Mississippi Valley in the Midwest and California and Oregon on the Pacific—apart from a few pioneers around Santa Fe in New Mexico and the Mormons in Utah. The great prairies between Kansas and Nebraska in the East and the Rocky Mountains in the West had previously been considered unsuitable for settlement. They were sometimes called the Great American Desert on account of their inhospitable terrain and climate. These central plains had the most extreme temperature range in the United States from Bismarck, North Dakota, where the mean temperature fell to minus 45 degrees Fahrenheit in winter, to Phoenix, Arizona, where the temperature was 117 degrees in summer.

Nevertheless, this last frontier of nineteenth–century America was invaded by three successive waves of pioneers—miners, ranchers, and farmers. In three decades they settled more land in America than their eastern predecessors had done in 250 years. Between 1607 and 1870 409 million acres of land had been settled and 189 million acres were cultivated, but between 1870 and 1900, 430 million acres were settled and 225 million acres were cultivated. The foundation of this final settlement was new technology, which improved communications and the laying of transcontinental railroads (q.v.).

The settlers were both native Americans from the states of the Mississippi Valley and the Old Northwest and immigrants from Europe. Native Americans moved West because they felt that the pressure of increasing population in the East was narrowing their opportunities. The immigrants, as we have seen, were attracted by advertising campaigns run by states and steamship companies. They were dispersed throughout the West by railroads and labor bureaus. Indeed, it was the revolutions in transportation and com-

From June 1876 when he experienced a remarkable vision after enacting
the Sun Dance for two days, Tatanka Iyotake ("Sitting Bull"), chief of
the Hunkapapa or Western Sioux, was regarded as a remarkable shaman.
Bleeding profusely from the wounds to his shoulders and arms where
he had torn off and given away 100 pieces of skin, he saw white soldiers
falling from the skies upon the Sioux. Thus he prophesied the destruction
of the Indian way of life: thus it was to be. (Library of Congress).

munication of railroad and telegraph that made possible the superhuman endeavor of taming a wilderness.

MINING AND RANCHING

It was not agriculture but mining that first provided the incentive for settling the mountains and desert and ranching that led to the opening of the Great Plains. In 1859 gold was discovered in Pike's Peak, Colorado, and silver in Nevada. The gold rush of 1859 soon died away, for the precious lodes in Colorado were particularly heavy and required special, expensive machinery for the extraction of ore. However, silver was a different proposition, and the rush to exploit the Comstock Lode reached its climax in the Big Bonanza of 1873. Between 1859 and 1880, $292 million of silver bullion was mined. Silver and copper were also discovered in Montana at Butte in 1875 and 1876. The mines of Colorado yielded gold and silver at Silverton (1873), Leadville (1873), Ouray (1875), and Cripple Creek (1878). Idaho yielded gold in the Caribou Mountains in 1870; gold at Bonanza in 1875; and silver, lead, and zinc at Couer d'Alene from 1882. Nevada yielded gold, copper, and lead in Eureka from 1872. In Arizona mines were opened at Prescott (1862), Lordsburg (1870), Globe (1873), and Tombstone (1879) for the extraction of gold, silver, and copper. Most dramatic of all, prospectors discovered gold in the Black Hills of (South) Dakota in 1874. In 1876 the Homestake mine was opened. It became the largest gold mine in the Western Hemisphere.

As to miners' methods, prospectors used placer mining, collecting pans (or cradles) of sand and gravel from the bed of streams and shaking (or rocking) them in running water. The heavier gold nuggets and dust sank to the bottom of the pan while the lighter sand was washed away. Lode mining was more complex and involved the use of stamp mills to pulverise veins of quartz containing gold. Gold was extracted after mercury had been poured into the pulverised material and formed an amalgam with it. Lode mining on federal lands necessitated the use of heavy machinery and more permanent occupation than placer mining. Accordingly, in the Mineral Land Act of 1866 (amended 1870 and 1872), Congress granted miners property rights for $5 an acre along lodes no more than 1500 feet by 600 feet. It also allowed miners to claim a patent for placer mining of deep gravel deposits, old river beds that had dried out and risen, at $2.50 an acre for no more than 40 acres and no less than 10.

Since the prospectors were usually migrants from the Pacific Coast, the mining frontier moved from west to east. This transient society was almost exclusively made up of men working in remote areas without their families. They wanted to make a lucky strike and then enjoy their new wealth back home. The usual local community was a rowdy camp that sometimes became a ghost town, deserted after a local mine had proved barren. Fortunes were made and lost by individuals who struck lucky and squandered their money. Sandy Bowers was one who discovered silver and used the earnings of his mine to build a splendid house costing $407,000 and to take his wife on a tour of the world. On their return to Nevada they threw open their home and entertained parasites in a most lavish way. When their mine petered out, they had nothing to fall back on. Sandy returned to prospecting, and his wife took in washing to sustain them.

Mark Twain, who spent a couple of years in Virginia City, provided the most memorable account of the silver boom in *Roughing It* (1872). The rude manners of the frontier are illustrated in an anecdote about Jim Baker, a western scout. He was not used to city spittoons and simply spat out his tobacco on the carpet of a hotel lobby in Denver. Each time the porter moved the cuspidor closer to his range, he spat in a different direction. Finally the porter placed the spittoon right under his nose. Jim looked up and said, "You know, if you keep movin' that thing around I'm li'ble to spit in it."

At the end of the Civil War the ranching frontier was based in Texas. Its climactic conditions were ideal for raising cattle and its land policy suited the owners. Texas had never ceded its public domain to the federal government and now it allowed ranchers to acquire land for grazing at 50 cents an acre. This generous policy encouraged mammoth ranches such as the XIT Ranch in the Texas Panhandle which contained over 3 million acres. The staple breed of cattle was the Texas longhorn which was so numerous and extensive as to threaten crops growing in Arkansas and Missouri as it roamed or was being driven north to market. In 1867 Joseph McCoy devised a route whereby cattle would be driven north from southern Texas to Abilene, Kansas, along Chisholm's trail to the west of any settlement. The journey was known as the long drive. From Abilene the Kansas and Pacific Railroad transported cattle to the slaughterhouses of Chicago. Between 1866 and 1885 a total of 5.71 million cattle went north by this route.

In 1868 Philip D. Armour established a meatpacking business in Chicago, and he was followed by Gustavus Swift and Nelson Morris. Meatpacking made use of the assembly-line process long before it was adopted in industry. Each worker had a particular task on the line. In the Armour plants each part of the animal was processed. Besides meat the hogs and cattle provided glue, sausage casings, fertilizer, and pepsin. Armour once claimed, "I like to turn bristle, blood, bones and the insides and outsides of pigs and bullocks into revenue."

After the Civil War it seemed that ranching was one route to fortune. Calves bought for $5 or $10 each in Texas and raised on the northern plains could fetch above $25 when they were sold. The grass they ate cost nothing, and the expense of the drive was estimated at less than a cent per head per mile. But the long drive was not really cost-effective. Many cattle lost weight or died. Indians obstructed drives and sometimes charged levies for passage through the Indian Territory. Ranchers discovered that the more northern plains were rich in grass and that their cattle could, after all, withstand the hazards of the winter there. Thus, by the early 1870s, the open range had replaced the long drive in Kansas, Nebraska, and Wyoming. By the end of the decade it had spread to Montana and Dakota. This, too, was a passing phase in livestock farming. Herds multiplied quickly and ranges became overcrowded. The winters of 1885 and 1886 were especially severe. In January 1887 the West from the Dakotas to Texas experienced its worst blizzard to date with a temperature of minus 68 degrees. Ranchers could not round up their cattle, and thousands died.

During the heyday of the long drive and open range cowboys were kings of the road. They were itinerant workers whose striking clothes were really a protective uniform for their work. The wide-brimmed hat shielded head and eyes from the glare and heat of the sun and served as a bucket at waterholes. The bandanna around his lower face masked the cowboy's mouth and nose from the dust raised by cattle on the move. Chaps (chaparajos) or leather leggings around his denim trousers guarded him from the stings and thorns of brush and cactus, and high-heeled boots gave him a firm grip in stirrup and on sand. His most precious possession was not a gun but a saddle. It was often said that a cowboy rode a "forty-dollar saddle on a ten-dollar horse."

Because there were no boundaries and cattle wandered freely, the open range led to various problems of ownership that were resolved by branding cattle. Herds were rounded up in the spring and fall and divided among their owners. The calves, which followed their mothers, were then branded in special pens. Roundups were the most celebrated and arduous of the cowboys' duties, with work lasting twelve or fifteen hours a day in grueling heat. The great freeze of 1887 ended the open range. Ranchers returned to more traditional methods of raising livestock, restricting their herds and fencing them in.

THE FARMING FRONTIER

The third wave of pioneers, the farmers, survived numerous catastrophes and were, as a group, perhaps the most permanent settlers. The Homestead Act of 1862 allowed prospective farmers, on payment of a small registration fee, to settle on a plot of 160 acres (a quarter of a section). They were granted full title to the land after five years of continuous farming. However, whereas a farm of 160 acres in the Ohio Valley would be large enough to sustain a family, it would be insufficient for ranching or farming in the trans-Mississippi West. Nevertheless, at the end of the Civil War pioneers began moving from Kansas, Nebraska, and Missouri along rivers and streams with rich soil and timber and, after 1870, ever westward across the plains on land opened up by railroad routes and by the rout of the Indians.

New inventions and new processes made it possible to farm where no crop had ever been raised before. Although the soft winter wheat farmed in the East died on the Great Plains, scientists discovered that two varieties of hard wheat could be grown there:

spring wheat from northern Europe was sown in Dakota and Minnesota; Turkey Red wheat from the Crimea was grown in Kansas and Nebraska. However, the traditional American method of milling soft wheat would not do for hard wheat. In 1870 E. W. Croix, a Frenchman, invented a machine to recover the rich glutinous part of the wheat kernel, or middlings. This "gradual reduction" process was perfected by Washburn Mills of Minneapolis in 1871. It improved the quality of flour and made it possible to use spring wheat more widely than before. As a result, wheat production in areas where the crop could be killed by harsh weather, such as Montana and (North) Dakota, expanded greatly and led to a bonanza of farm settlement along the Red River Valley. Between 1880 and 1887 wheat production in the Dakotas increased from 3 million to 62 million bushels.

A new method called dry farming made use of water below the soil in arid territory. By plowing a deep furrow that loosened the upper soil, the farmer brought water to the surface by capillary attraction. After it had rained he harrowed the field to create a mulch that slowed down the process of evaporation. In 1878 John F. Appleby invented the "twine binder." Historian T. N. Carver explains, "It was the twine binder more than any other machine or implement that enabled the country to increase its production of grain, especially wheat."

The results of the new expanded agriculture were truly phenomenal. American production of wheat increased from 211 million bushels in 1867 to 599 million bushels in 1900. The Department of Labor calculated that whereas it took 35 hours of labor in 1840 to produce 15 bushels of wheat, it took only 15 hours in 1900. American wheat exports rose from 6 million bushels in 1867 to 102 million bushels in 1900.

A simple invention, barbed wire, patented by Joseph F. Glidden of Illinois in 1874, in the absence of timber to make fences, made it possible to define ownership of land in the West. In 1876, in cooperation with an eastern wire manufacturing firm, he produced and sold 3 million pounds of barbed wire. In 1880 he sold 80 million pounds. The invention made the development of the ranching and farming frontiers somewhat smoother than it might otherwise have been because it greatly reduced disputes over territory.

The expansion of agriculture was recognized by Congress as being as important a development as the Industrial Revolution. All kinds of legislation were passed to assist western settlement. The Timber Culture Act of 1873 granted 160 acres to any settler who undertook to plant a quarter of his land with trees within ten years. The Desert Land Act of 1877 awarded 640 acres of land at 25 cents an acre to any settler who attempted to irrigate some of it within three years. Once the land was irrigated, the settler could gain full ownership on payment of $1 an acre. The Timber and Stone Act of 1878 allowed a settler to buy 160 acres at $2.50 an acre for the sake of its timber and stone provided the land contained no valuable minerals.

The federal government also promoted agricultural research. By the two Morrill Acts of 1862 and 1890, Congress granted land to the states for the establishment of agricultural and mechanical colleges and then began to provide them with regular financial assistance. In the Hatch Act of 1887 it provided federal funds for a national system of agricultural research stations. In 1889 the Department of Agriculture was established and given cabinet status.

No matter how great was the assistance pioneers received from government and industry, their lot was arduous in the extreme. Their homes were primitive. Settlers first made a dugout by excavating a hole in the side of a hill and building an outer wall with blocks of turf and sod. Later they would erect a sod house from strips of thick turf around a wooden frame. These crude homes were warm in winter, cool in summer, and safe from fire. But they were open to flood and damp from floor and roof. For fuel settlers used wood and hay and buffalo dung. Their water came from local streams, handmade wells, and rainwater stored in barrels. It was often the toughness and resourcefulness of their womenfolk that saw the settlers through. It was the wife who had to provide everything the family needed in the primitive home, preserving enough fresh meat in summer to last all winter and boiling down fat to make soap.

Pioneer farmers started under difficult circumstances, and adverse weather often turned their only security into a liability. Editor William Allen White writes of climactic conditions in Kansas in the 1880s:

The pioneers had seen it stop raining for months at a time. They had heard the fury of the winter blast as it came whining across the short burned grass and cut the flesh from their children huddling in the corner. These movers have strained their eyes, watching through the long summer days for the rain that never came. . . . They have tossed through hot nights, wild with worry, and have arisen only to find their worst nightmares grazing in reality on the brown stubble in front of their sun-warped doors.

Plagues of grasshoppers sometimes came in clouds, obscuring the sun and devouring the vegetation until there was nothing left of the farm but the mortgage. In 1874 the worst invasion ever devastated the plains from Dakota to Texas. Prairie fires in summer and fall also devastated farms and property. Autumn storms swept across the prairies, their raging winds whipping everything outdoors. Winter blizzards penetrated houses, leaving furniture and food covered by icicles and snow. The heads of cattle grew so great with ice they had to be lowered to the ground. To protect their precious livestock pioneers opened their family homes to horses and calves, poultry and pigs, for weeks on end.

The 1880s were years of dramatic westward expansion supported by eastern investors who reckoned farms in the Golden West were the safest form of investment. The panic of 1873 and the subsequent depression had discredited banks and industry. Nevertheless, an expanding population needed to be fed. Between 1875 and 1877 investors launched scores of mortgage companies to capitalize on the rising price of farmland. Farmers and prospective farmers responded with alacrity to the temptations of mortgages at 6 or 8 percent interest. The historian of westward expansion, Ray Allen Billington, explains, "Few farmers could resist the pressure. Newcomers to the West mortgaged their homesteads to buy farm machinery, mortgaged the farm machinery to provide money until the first crop was harvested, mortgaged the first crop to carry the family through the winter." In Kansas, Nebraska, Minnesota, and Dakota there was at least one mortgage for every family. In Kansas alone mortgage debts tripled between 1880 and 1887. The price of land did rise just as investors had predicted. In Kansas land that cost $15 an acre in the early 1880s was sold for $270 an acre at the end of the decade. In one year alone town lots in Omaha, Wichita, and elsewhere rose from $200 to $2,000. In 1887 forty-two sections of prairie outside Wichita were sold for a total of $35 million.

What was the sum total of these three waves of settlement? The mining districts were accepted as territories shortly after the first strikes, but apart from Nevada in 1864 and Colorado in 1876, none was admitted as a state until 1889. In 1880 both Kansas, which had been admitted as a state in 1861, and Nebraska, which had been admitted in 1867, were settled as far west as the 98th meridian. Kansas claimed a population of almost 996,000; Nebraska, more than 452,000.

Owing to unusually clement weather, bumper crops, and railroad penetration by the Illinois Central to Sioux City, Dakota Territory (organized in 1861) enjoyed a boom of settlement from 1868 to 1873. Each additional line to touch the territory—the Chicago and Northwestern at Watertown, the Northern Pacific at Bismarck, and the St. Paul at Wahpeton, attracted and distributed settlers in ever greater numbers. Thus, in 1870 Dakota had a population of about 12,000. The discovery of gold in the Black Hills led to a gold rush of 10,000 prospectors to Dakota in 1875. But the second boom began in earnest with the success of Oliver Dalrymple, a wheat farmer from Minnesota, hired by the Northern Pacific Railroad to prove that Dakota was fertile. Using new methods Dalrymple cultivated eighteen sections of land in the Red River Valley, harvesting 25 bushels of wheat per acre at a cost of only $9.50 and making a profit of more than 100 percent at market prices. Roused by Dalrymple's successful experiment, eastern investors from 1878 began to put their capital in bonanza farms along the Red River Valley. This led to the second Dakota boom of 1878 to 1885, which was furthered by the advance of two railroads across the territory—the Chicago, Milwaukee and St. Paul, and the Chicago and Northwestern.

In 1879 James J. Hill organized the Great Northern Railroad, which laid track to Devil's Lake in 1883 and from there to Seattle in 1893. Because the Great Northern had no land grant, Hill ran it on a strictly commercial basis, which encouraged genuine settlement rather than land speculation. Homestead grants rose from 213,000 acres in 1877 (before the second boom) to 1.37 million in 1878 and then successively to a peak of 11.08 million acres in 1884. By 1885 all Dakota east of the Missouri was settled. Between 1880 and 1890 its total population rose four times, to 540,000.

Mountain regions developed more slowly. In 1867 speculators made towns of Cheyenne and Laramie in Wyoming, confident that they would become stations of the projected Union Pacific. In 1868 Wyoming became a territory. However, farmers were deterred from settling there because of its mountainous and arid terrain, and when it finally became a state in 1890, Wyoming had only a sparse population of 62,255. Farmers settled in Montana to feed and service the prospectors in Butte and other mining towns, and their path of settlement followed the tracks of the Northern Pacific. In 1890 Montana had a population of 143,000.

The rapid settlement of Dakota, Montana, and Wyoming prompted these new territories to seek admission to the Union as states. Their demands were resisted by Democrats in Congress because all three were Republican. But the election of 1888 gave the Republicans a slender majority in Congress, which they decided to use to their future electoral advantage by passing an omnibus bill in 1889 that admitted North Dakota and South Dakota as separate states on November 2, Montana on November 8, and Washington on November 11. Not to be overdone, Idaho and Wyoming devised constitutions and demanded statehood in 1890, which they were awarded, respectively, on July 3 and July 10. In Utah, which became a territory in 1850, the population was 211,000 in 1890. The Mormons formally abandoned polygamy in 1890 and devised a constitution and the territory was received into the Union as a state in 1896.

The admission of these new, sparsely populated states affected the composition of the Senate, to which every state—no matter how tiny its area or how small its population, sent two representatives—and, to a lesser extent, the House. Some argued that the Golden West was thus afforded a disproportionate influence in the federal government, which emphasized agrarian interests at the expense of the urban masses.

THE TRAGEDY OF THE AMERICAN INDIAN

Westward expansion contained as bitter a tragedy as any in the New South. Indians and bison were eliminated together. There were two subspecies of bison: the plains buffalo (*Bison bison bison*); and the larger, woods buffalo (*Bison bison athabascae*), sometimes called the mountain buffalo because they took to the mountains in the winter. In the sixteenth century they roamed across North America from what became Mexico to what became Canada. They were massive shaggy creatures with humped shoulders and dangerous horns. They looked clumsy but could sprint at 30 miles per hour for a quarter of a mile. Indians ate their meat fresh in summer and smoked in winter, using the hides of the bulls for tents, the hides of the cows for robes, and the hair of both for ropes.

At the end of the Civil War there were about 15 million bison west of the Mississippi. An observer reckoned that there were 4 million in a single herd by the Arkansas River in 1871. A train crossing the Great Plains was once delayed for eight hours while a huge herd crossed the track. In the interests of speed and efficiency, expanding railroads decided to eliminate the bison. The laying of the Union Pacific Railroad by 1869 divided the herd in two. In 1871 a tannery in Pennsylvania discovered that bison hides could be used commercially. Every bison was now worth between $1 and $3. Bison offered the hunter, free from the Union army but well equipped, a tempting opportunity. He served the railroads and commercial interests in exterminating the buffalo. Within four years about 3.7 million bison had been killed. By 1875 the entire southern herd had been destroyed. The northern herd was more isolated and took longer to eliminate, yet ten years later this had been accomplished. In 1886 a member of the Smithsonian Institution had the greatest difficulty in tracing and rounding up 25, the last that remained.

The main tragedy of the Indians had taken place before 1865. From the sixteenth century they had been swept ever westward by the advance of whites. What happened in the Gilded Age was a final catastrophe, perhaps more harrowing than earlier elimination because the Indians were now fighting for survival without hope. The successive removal of Indians from the East onto the Great Plains had already made the Indian community as a whole less dependent on farming for food and more dependent on the bison. Thus, the decimation of the bison had a political purpose. With their source of food gone, Indians would be obliged to settle down and accept rations on a federal reservation.

In 1866 the United States extorted new treaties from the Five Civilized Tribes of the Cherokees, Creeks, Seminoles, Chickasaws, and Choctaws. This was in retaliation for their enforced cooperation with the Confederacy during the Civil War. Their reservations in the Indian Territory were reduced in size. They were also obliged to admit Plains Indians to their land and to permit railroads access through it. Between 1865 and 1889 the central Indian Territory received at least twenty-five different tribes. The reservation was undermined from without by white rapacity and from within by shortages of food and medicine.

The Plains Indians farther west resented the invasion by white miners of Colorado, and during the Civil War attacked their camps. The most notorious white reprisal was the massacre by Col. J. M. Chivington, a Methodist minister, of about 500 Cheyenne men, women, and children in a surprise attack on their camp at Sand Creek on November 28, 1864. In their barbarity militia and frontiersmen clubbed children and disemboweled pregnant women. Miraculously, the Cheyenne leader, Black Kettle, survived. In Denver, Chivington later showed a collection of 100 scalps as a vaudeville act at a local theater. He was hailed as a public benefactor.

Partly in revenge, northern Sioux then massacred a small detachment of soldiers on the Bozeman Trail, a wagon route devised by John Bozeman from the Platte River to the mines of Montana. On December 21, 1866, Capt. William J. Fetterman and eighty men were lured from Fort Phil Kearney, Wyoming, and overwhelmed by Red Cloud and the Oglala Sioux. The Fetterman massacre led to an emotional outburst from eastern reformers who blamed the disasters on the contradictory nature of government policy regarding the Indians, especially the division of federal authority between the Departments of Interior and War.

The Interior Department, created in 1849, had charge of Indian

The notorious slaughter of bison on the Kansas Pacific Railroad. In 1865 there were fifteen million bison west of the Mississippi; by 1886 all but twenty-five had been exterminated. The Indians took part in the slaughter and thus precipitated their own further decline. Wood engraving after Ernest Griset. (Library of Congress).

affairs but always relied on the army to execute its unpopular, poorly planned policies. It was staffed by ignoramuses. Sometimes they had not even set eyes on an Indian until they took up their posts at some remote spot. They received a pittance of only $1,500 per annum but had every expectation of a sound political future. Graft, corruption, and theft were rife among Indian agents. One agent sold the government blankets and material supplied for Apaches to local merchants and stole government cattle for his own ranch. Another devoted his energy to his mine at San Carlos and used federal funds to improve and extend it.

Because of mounting public pressure Congress proposed a more responsible Indian policy. The Indian Act of 1867 established a peace commission of four civilians and three generals to end the Sioux War. The commission was instructed to persuade Indians to abandon the life of nomadic hunters for a protected existence on reservations. By October 1867 the commission had completed arrangements for the southwestern tribes to settle on various reservations. Yet war continued in the midst of peace. In 1868 Black Kettle and the Cheyenne who had survived the Sand Creek massacre of 1864 were defeated by Gen. Philip H. Sheridan and his rising officer, Col. George Armstrong Custer, by the Washita River in Indian Territory. Black Kettle was slain. In the north Chief Red Cloud of the Sioux signed a peace treaty at Fort Laramie, Wyoming, on November 6, 1868. It recognized the Black Hills or *Paha Sapa* of Dakota as a giant Sioux reservation. The government now decided to pretend that the Indian problem no longer existed. On March 3, 1871, Congress forbade further treaties with tribes in a law declaring that henceforth "no Indian nation or tribe . . . within the United States shall be acknowledged or recognized as an independent nation, tribe or power."

There followed a final generation of Indian wars before the extermination of the bison, the coming of the railroad, and the introduction of rapid-fire weapons put an end to the vicious cycle of attacks and retribution. The Kiowa, Comanche, Arapahoe, and Cheyenne fought the Red River Wars of 1874 and 1875 in which Quanah Parker, the son of a Comanche war chief and a white captive, led an abortive attack on bison hunters in the Battle of Adobe Walls in Texas, on June 24, 1874. But, after his defeat in

1875, he decided to persuade the Comanches to enter reservations and thus was instrumental in bringing peace to the plains of the Southwest. The fearless Apache leader Geronimo, who emptied much of Arizona of whites, also sued for peace in 1875. By then his force, reduced to 36 braves, was hopelessly outnumbered by 5,000 federal soldiers. Whites also defeated the Modocs and the Nez Percés under Chief Joseph. All accepted small and undesirable reservations.

The Indians' ability to survive the final onslaught of predatory whites was undermined by their own chronic internecine warfare. Nevertheless the chiefs, in conducting the wars of the Great Plains, managed to persuade Cheyenne and Comanche to join forces with Arapahoe and Kiowa in what might have been a successful guerrilla retaliation had it not been for the decimation of their food supply, the defection of many of their people to the enemy as soldiers and scouts, and the superior resources of the federal army.

In 1876 the Sioux, Cheyenne, and Arapahoe astounded white society with an overwhelming attack on George Armstrong Custer and 266 men of the Seventh Cavalry. Despite the treaty of 1867, white prospectors had invaded the Indian lands of Dakota in their search for gold. Custer was the miners' self-appointed protector. He and his small force were annihilated by Sitting Bull and Crazy Horse and their people at Little Big Horn on June 25, 1876. This was Custer's last stand. Despite their victory, the Indian braves were intimidated by the arrival of increased numbers of federal troops. Sitting Bull and his followers retreated into Canada. Crazy Horse and the Oglala Sioux surrendered at Fort Robinson in May 1877. To prevent his escape his captors bayoneted him to death in a guardroom that September. The other Indians were assigned to reservations.

Ulysses S. Grant's policy of allowing religious denominations to supervise reservations was called a "Peace Policy." It failed. The churches fell out and disputed their rights with one another. The agents they appointed as managers were often incompetent or corrupt. Moreover, their attempts to convert Indians to Christianity crushed Indian culture. Christian missionaries not only tried to convert Indians to their religion but also insisted on adherence to their standards of social behavior. In particular, they

The vainglorious Colonel George A. Custer who, with 266 other whites, met his death on the Little Big Horn on June 25, 1876, at the hands of the Sioux. The battle was the final move in a well-planned strategy by Sioux military genius Crazy Horse who had defeated General Crook at the Battle of Rosebud ten days earlier. (Library of Congress).

wanted Indians to give up hunting for farming. The quality of Christianity on the frontier was no inducement. As an Indian remarked to Bishop Henry Benjamin ("Straight Tongue") Whipple of the Episcopalians when he heard him speak against alcoholism and adultery among Indians, "My father, it is your people, who you say have the Great Spirit's book, who bring us the fire-water. It is your white men who corrupt our daughters. Go teach them to do right, and then come to us and I will believe you."

Several organizations promoted the Indian cause, including the National Indian Association in Philadelphia; the Indian Citizenship Committee of Boston; and the Indian Rights Association, founded in Philadelphia by Herbert Welsh and Henry S. Pancoast. The National Indian Defense Association, organized by Dr. T. A. Bland, was different from the others. It opposed policies of white acculturation aimed at destroying Indian tribes. The most effective propaganda was by Helen Hunt Jackson in two remarkable books, *A Century of Dishonor* (1881) and *Ramona* (1884).

As a result of these various efforts, the government was shamed into financing Indian education. In 1870 Congress appropriated funds for Indian schools, and by 1899, $2.5 million was being spent each year on 148 boarding and 225 day schools for 20,000 children. Indian schools emphasized industrial and agricultural skills. In 1879 Capt. Richard H. Pratt, who favored assimilation, established the most famous Indian school at Carlisle, Pennsylvania. In 1878 Congress appropriated funds for an Indian police and Courts of Indian Offenses, not only to maintain law and order on the reservations, but also to assist in acculturation. The Indian police and judges were expected to conform to white standards of behavior and to act as a counterweight to the power of the traditional tribal chiefs.

In 1887 the Indians still held some 138 million acres of land. Although the system of landholding on Indian reservations worked well enough, conservatives and reformers alike were agreed on a policy of severalty—dividing tribal areas among families as private property. The Dawes Severalty Act of February 4, 1887, named after Senator Henry L. Dawes of Massachusetts, gave legal form to a piecemeal practice of many years' standing. It allowed the president discretion to allot reservation land to Indians to be held in trust for them for twenty-five years. Heads of families were to receive 160 acres of land; other Indians were to be awarded smaller amounts. The act conferred American citizenship on those Indians who accepted the allotment. The idea was not humanitarian. The plan was to turn nomadic hunters into sedentary farmers and to break up the tribes once and for all. But the policy was doomed to failure at a time of agricultural depression. Besides, no care was taken to provide Indians with arable land. After the awards had been made the surplus land was sold commercially. Most Indians had little understanding of what the act entailed, since the idea of private property was strange to their culture. Those who did understand the act recognized the snares inherent in the scheme and protested against it. In 1891 an amendment to the Dawes Act ended the policy of awarding 160 acres to heads of families. In the future individual Indians, regardless of status, were to be allotted 80 acres each.

After the Dawes Act conditions on remaining reservations deteriorated to the extent that they became scandalous. As Indian historian Alvin M. Josephy, Jr., attests:

Indian life was marked by poverty, squalor, disease, and hopelessness. In general, Indians received little or no education and were still treated as wards, incapable of self-government or making decisions for themselves. Whatever revenues the tribes received from land sales were dissipated, with virtually none of them going to assist the Indians to create sound foundations for the development of the human and economic resources of the reservation.

For a time Indians sought bizarre consolation in religious cults. The most important were the Peyote cult and the Ghost Dance movement. The Peyote cult was the consumption of a mild narcotic found in the roots and buttons of a certain cactus. It induced hallucinations, and some Peyote groups used it in Christian services. The Ghost Dance religion was a further disillusioning experience for those Plains tribes crushed by the extermination of the bison. It was led by Wovoka, or Jack Wilson, a Paiute of Nevada. He was an Indian medicine man. In 1888 he recovered from a serious illness and claimed he had received a message from the Great Spirit who had appointed him prophet. He prescribed fastings, dances, and songs (the Ghost Dance) and encouraged secret ceremonies to herald the appearance of a messiah who would revive the bison. Ironically, the movement was spread through the South and West by the universal medium of white education. Apprehensive whites interpreted it as a prelude to another Indian rebellion. They were confirmed in their erroneous suspicions by a visit paid by Kicking Bear, a Sioux chief, to Wovoka. Moreover, Sitting Bull had returned from Canada in 1881. Indian police decided to arrest him to prevent him from becoming leader of the supposed insurrection. Sitting Bull had long believed that he would die at the hands of his own people, the Sioux. On the night of December 14, 1890, forty Indian police were assigned to dispatch him. He was shot dead by a Sioux, Red Tomahawk.

The death of Sitting Bull did not, of course, result in an Indian uprising. Three hundred Teton Sioux did leave a reservation at Standing Rock but mainly as a conservative protest against the Ghost Dance movement. They were overtaken by the Seventh Cavalry. Some refused to surrender their arms. The troops then fired without provocation and either killed outright or wounded fatally the pathetic band of travelers. This was the notorious massacre at Wounded Knee, South Dakota, of December 29, 1890. According to *Historical Statistics* (1975) the Indian population in 1890 was only 190,682—a fragment of the number before white contact.

There now remained but one last "unsettled" territory in the West. The first designs on the Indian Territory were shown by railroads, which began petitioning Congress to open some lands for extra lines as early as 1874. In 1879 the Missouri, Kansas and Texas hired a malcontent Cherokee, Elias C. Boudinot, to claim in the *Chicago Times* that there lay 13 million undesignated acres within the territory, which by rights really belonged to the American people. This encouraged squatters from Kansas and Missouri to stake claims in the Oklahoma district. In 1880, led by David L. Payne of Kansas, a former homesteader and Indian fighter, they invaded the territory and were repulsed. He founded an Oklahoma colony in Kansas pledged to open the territory. After a series of unsuccessful forays into Oklahoma, he died in November 1884 and was succeeded as leader by W. L. Couch, who continued his policy of invasion and withdrawal. On March 3, 1885, Congress authorized the Indian Office to terminate Indian claims to the empty Oklahoma district and Cherokee outlet in the territory. But the Indian agents realized that any white settlement in the Indian Territory would soon lead to the collapse of the entire reservation. They decided to do nothing. But Congress could not withstand increasing demands for homesteads, and in January 1889 it obliged the Creeks and Seminoles to waive their rights to the land in return for $4.19 million. On March 23, 1889, President Benjamin Harrison declared that Oklahoma district would be opened to settlers on April 22 that year.

Prospective settlers gathered at the boundary and sped into Oklahoma by horse and wagon, by train and on foot as soon as rifle fire announced that it was noon. Ray Allen Billington describes the scene:

At last the revolvers barked, and along the line pandemonium broke loose. Men whipped up their horses, wagons careened wildly forward, horses freed from overturned vehicles galloped slowly about—all was hurrah and excitement. The Sante Fe trains, steaming slowly forward at a regulated pace which would not give their passengers an undue advantage, disgorged riders along the route as men leaped from roofs or platforms and rushed about in search of a claim. Noise and confusion reigned as the shouts of successful "Boomers," the crash of hammers on stakes, the clatter of wagons, the crash of overturned vehicles, and the curses of disappointed homesteaders mingled to create a bedlam unique in the annals of the nation.

That day 1.92 million acres of Oklahoma district were settled.

On May 2, 1890, Congress granted the new settlement the status of a territory. In the following years it extended its lands by opening up successive reservations under the terms of the Dawes Act: in September, 1891, 900,000 acres of the Sauk, Fox, and Potawatomi; in April 1892, 3 million acres of the Cheyenne and Arapahoe; in September 1893, 6 million acres of the Cherokee.

The Dawes Act of 1887 did not apply to the Five Civilized Tribes living in Indian Territory for whom separate provision was made by a special senatorial commission of 1893. By this time it was perfectly clear that the severalty policy had been, at best, a terrible mistake. At worst, it was another white betrayal. Where land was of no interest to whites, such as the desert of the Southwest, Indians were not forced to accept severalty. Elsewhere, whites exploited Indian innocence by systems of leaseholding and guardianship that reduced the rightful owners to paupers. Whites did not always get the best of the bargain, however, as the following anecdote suggests. In 1897 a Blackfoot chief in Montana asked for a bank loan in Great Falls so that he could go to Washington and urge the treaty rights of his tribe. The cashier agreed to the loan only when he discovered that the chief owned at least 3,000 horses, which could be accounted as collateral. He was, nevertheless, reluctant to hand over the money and suggested instead that the chief open a deposit account and use a checkbook. He reckoned without his client's sarcasm, "Hunh, how many horses you own?"

THE WILD WEST

To many the Golden West was really the Wild West. In the absence of established law and order crime was rife in the West, especially rustling horses and cattle and armed robbery of trains and stagecoaches. There were three types of law officer: town marshals appointed by town councils; county sheriffs elected in state counties and appointed by governors in territories; and United States marshals appointed by the federal government to police territories and prevent crime. They were supplemented by the private operatives of Pinkerton's National Detective Agency and the Wells Fargo Express Company and, in Texas, by the state Rangers. Picturesque characters among the lawmen included Sheriff Frank Canton of Wyoming; Marshal Henry Brown of Caldwell, Kansas; Marshal Long Jim Courtwright of Fort Worth; and Tom Threepersons, a Cherokee who was an expert shot. Posterity has not been kind to some of the semiofficial groups of vigilantes formed to protect local interests against raids by outlaws. In 1884 cattlemen in Montana, determined to eradicate cattle rustling, went on the rampage and killed thirty-five people, several of whom were undoubtedly innocent. Some said the vigilantes' real motive was

If western theater could not stay abreast of the fashions in classical drama it was not behind the times when it came to variety shows as this somewhat fanciful drawing of an auditorium in Cheyenne suggests. (Library of Congress).

to move legitimate smallholders off their own ranches to make way for the big cattlemen.

The outlaws themselves have passed into picaresque legend. The mass media have turned desperadoes into heroic individuals combating the encroaching power of the state. The most famous were William H. Bonney, "Billy the Kid," originally from New York who was put down by Sheriff Pat Garrett in 1881; Joaquin Murieta of New Mexico; Robert Leroy Parker ("Butch Cassidy"), leader of the Wild Bunch, which included Harry Longabaugh ("The Sundance Kid") and Harvey Logan ("Kid Curry"); and Belle Starr. This woman outlaw was no beauty, yet it was said that she had more lovers than a dog has fleas.

Two characters of the Golden West, who became legends in their own lifetime, turned the fact into commercial advantage. William F. Cody ("Buffalo Bill") was an army veteran who began to work as an actor in 1872 when he appeared in a lurid melodrama, *Buffalo Bill, the King of the Border Men*, staged for him in New York. In 1883 he toured the country with his own Wild West Show, a carnival of stage effects involving cowboys and Indians. One of his most popular stars was crack shot Annie Oakley of Ohio. She could hit the thin edge of a playing card in midair and shoot a cigarette from the lips of her husband and manager, Frank Butler. In 1887 the show went to London and she won a contest with Grand Duke Michael of Russia, a famous marksman, to discover who could smash the most glass balls thrown in the air. She hit forty-seven out of fifty to the duke's thirty-five. On this occasion her target in the cigarette trick was the German emperor. Because she could perforate a playing card five times in midair her name was used to describe any punched theater ticket. Sitting Bull, during a brief period of favor with the authorities in the mid 1880s, was another of Buffalo Bill's artists.

The official closing of the frontier emphasized the physical fact that the supply of virgin land had come to an end, that the population had increased, and that the supply of natural resources had decreased. No longer could one escape the pressures of the East by going west. The romantic legend that while there was free land every man had the opportunity to make his fortune died with the frontier. The realization of frontiersmen that they were not truly free of the East was a factor leading to the Populist revolt that shook American politics in the 1890s.

The federal government had freely disposed of unoccupied land in a period when few people were ready to admit that the supply was not endless. However, the admission of the new western states to the Union spurred on a conservation lobby. It believed Americans had already wasted precious natural resources by their reckless extraction of minerals, their careless cutting of forests, and their exploitation of arable, and even semi arid, land. In 1891 it urged on Congress the Forest Reserve Act. This gave the president authority over "public lands wholly or in part covered with timber." Thus he could protect them from sale or homesteading by setting them aside as forest reserves. Accordingly, Cleveland turned 25 million acres of the San Joaquin forest in California into a national forest. Harrison withdrew 13 million acres and McKinley 7 million acres from the public domain. Where western land was barren the problems were different. If the plains were to be successfully settled it was essential that water was brought to the land. Private cooperative projects were clearly insufficient to irrigate a whole desert and in 1894 Congress passed the Carey Act. It authorized the president to allow western states to sell up to 1 million acres of public lands to raise funds for irrigation projects. However, it was left to Theodore Roosevelt, who made conservation a subject of his first annual message to Congress when he became president in 1901, to improve and expand these policies.

CHAPTER NINE

GATES OF SILVER AND
BARS OF GOLD

How the west was to be won was an American dream. How it *was* won became a myth. The tales of free and fertile soil, handsome harvests and plentiful profits on the farms that circulated in the East obscured part of the truth. Scores of settlers were far from successful; they were isolated pioneers eking out an existence in discomfort and disillusion. They were cheated of prosperity, not only by unreliable nature, but also their own limitations and inabilities as farmers. Yet the drudgery and disappointments, the hardships and hard knocks of life out West remained hidden behind the facade of the frontier myth. And the myth was as much a means of self-justification for the settlers as it was a celebration of the land. After all, their own flight from Europe or eastern cities was an irreversible fact. The myth attracted more and more settlers. It also hid the truth from those already there. As English historian Andrew Sinclair suggests in his *Prohibition* (1963), "their hatred of the past only grew. For the settlers were the disinherited of the cities . . . those displaced by industry. They fled to an agricultural myth which told them that their exclusion was a successful repudiation of wealth and aristocracy and luxury."

The Golden West had already begun to lose some of its glamor before the official closing of the frontier. The severe winters of 1886 and 1887 and the harsh summer of 1887 ended the ideal, fertile climactic conditions prevailing since the mid 1870s. In some parts of the West and South the soil had been exhausted by wasteful, exploitive methods of farming." In Marcus Lee Hansen's striking phrase, "The land was mined, not farmed." Farms failed; mortgages were foreclosed; and farmers were put out of house and home. In the four years from 1888 to 1892 half of the population of western Kansas moved on, as did 30,000 people from South Dakota. Wagons carried the ominous legend, "In God We Trusted, in Kansas We Busted." In the course of the nineteenth century Iowa had more than 2,000 abandoned settlements.

Because American farmers had committed themselves to service the industrial market they became vulnerable to its economic oscillations. The depressions of 1873 and 1893 were as devastating to them as to industrial artisans. After 1885 American wheat could no longer enter overseas markets on such advantageous terms as in the twenty years after the Civil War. European countries built tariff walls to protect their own agriculture. Other countries, such as Argentina and Russia, expanded their wheat crop and began to compete with the United States for sales. The average price of American wheat fell from $1.05 per bushel in the period from 1866 to 1875, to 92 cents between 1876 and 1885, and then to 67 cents between 1886 and 1895. Although the American yield per acre increased more than 250 percent in this period, the actual value of the crop was less than 50 percent higher in 1895 than it had been in 1870.

In their fight for survival farmers declined from owners to tenants as they accepted the harsh terms of loan sharks and corporations. By 1890, 25 percent of farmers in Kansas were tenants or sharecroppers; in Nebraska, 17 percent; in South Dakota 11 percent. Farm tenantry in the country as a whole increased as the century drew to a close from 25 percent in 1880 to 28 percent in 1890 and 36 percent in 1900. The high cost of credit weighed heavily on a class composed largely of debtors. Farmers who had been encouraged to borrow during a boom required additional money to withstand a depression. When they were refused they turned on their creditors, accusing them of betrayal.

In the past, pioneers had been isolated and bore their hardships and poverty in secret. But once farmers were far more numerous, and better informed by improved communications, they united in common protest at the wearisome round and gross injustices of their hard lot. Eastern voices told them that the world was suffering from an agricultural surplus. Western voices said that the cause of the problem was not overproduction in the West but underconsumption in the East. They reasoned that consumption was low because retail prices were too high. "Thieves in the night," among whom were numbered bankers, railroads, and grain elevators, exploited farmers and stole their profits.

The West was most scandalized by the costs of transportation. It considered railroads the principal villains because of their discriminatory rates. In 1877 it cost 95 cents to ship a ton of farm produce east of Chicago on the Pennsylvania Railroad; but it cost $3.20 to ship a ton of produce west of the Missouri on the Burlington Railroad. Railroads' replies that traffic in the West was more expensive to run did not satisfy western farmers, who understood the predatory nature of monopolies and were convinced that the true beneficiaries of an unfair system were eastern capitalists.

A second target of farmers' complaints were grain elevators. Grain elevators were giant storage bins located in railway sidings to distribute grain to the freight cars in the adjacent station. Western railroads forbade farmers from loading their grain on cars directly themselves and laid sidings for only one grain elevator in each station. Consequently, farmers either had to sell their grain to local elevator operators or use their services for a fee. In either case, the operators had a monopoly of the business. The operators were supposed to pay for the grain according to standard rates established in Chicago with different prices for grain of different qualities. However, in the remote West, unscrupulous operators took advantage of farmers' isolation by misgrading or mixing grain and paying less for it than the standard price.

Farmers resolved to retaliate against the creeping power of the trusts by launching new political parties to redress their economic grievances. In 1867 Oliver Hudson Kelley, a clerk in the Department of Agriculture, founded the National Grange of the Patrons of Husbandry. At first his aims were social and cultural, and the Grange grew slowly. But the agricultural depression of the 1870s led to sudden expansion as discontented farmers recognized the

The Granger movement conferred dignity on discontented farmers of the West, emphasizing that their contribution to the American economy—providing food—was the most valuable of all as this chromolithograph of 1875 suggests. Later posters paid tribute to the real grievances of farmers by altering the central caption to "And I pay for all!" (Library of Congress).

Grange as a forum for political debate. In 1872, 1,105 lodges were founded; in the panic of 1873, 8,400 more; and in January and February 1874, another 4,700. The Grange comprised 1.5 million members, a potent political force. In 1873 and 1874 it succeeded in electing representatives throughout the South and West and held the balance of power in Illinois, Iowa, Minnesota, and Wisconsin.

By pooling their economic resources, farmers in local lodges could afford the newest and most efficient equipment. They also appointed agents to barter directly with manufacturers and get prices reduced. For example, they acquired reapers for $175 instead of $275 and wagons for $90 instead of $150. The system of co-operative buying not only reduced manufacturers' prices to farmers but also compelled local merchants to lower their prices. The Grange also encouraged farmers' cooperatives in production. They founded or acquired mills, elevators, and plants for production, and insurance companies and banks for finance. In Iowa they even entered industry in 1874 to manufacture reapers and plows. When cooperatives failed, it was usually because of mismanagement. Inexperienced farmers expanded them too quickly and ran into bitter price-cutting competition from traditional wholesalers and retailers whose resources could outlast theirs.

When it comes to the gross abuses practiced by the railroads that, more than anything else, had united western farmers in the Grange, the lodges realized that they could not go into open competition with the great railroads and lay rival lines. The West was so sparsely settled that the only economic form of transportation must be an efficient railroad with a monopoly of business. They therefore focused on state regulation—seeking laws to establish the maximum rates that railroads and elevators could charge. The first regulatory laws passed by the state legislatures of Illinois and Minnesota in 1871 were ineffective and declared unconstitutional in state courts in 1873. But farmers in Illinois responded that fall with a new law establishing a commission to decide rates for passengers and freight alike. In 1874 Minnesota, Iowa, and Wisconsin followed suit with similar laws. However, in these three states the laws were soon repealed. Railroads had retaliated by raising all rates to the legal maximum and withdrawing some services.

In Illinois the law was better defined and more difficult to subvert. Thus railroads appealed to the courts, charging that the Illinois law violated the Fourteenth Amendment, which forbade any state from depriving a person of life, liberty, or property. Their argument was that a state commission that set railroad and elevator rates was denying the companies the free use of their property. There were eight *Granger* cases. *Munn* v. *Illinois*, which went to the Supreme Court in 1876, was the most crucial. There were only fourteen warehouses in Chicago to store the grain from seven states, and the Court had to decide whether the owners had the right of unrestrained control over millions of farmers. Munn's argument was that the fixing of rates by Illinois was confiscatory. However, as we know, Chief Justice Morrison R. Waite, speaking for the majority of 5 in the *Munn* decision, given in 1877, said otherwise. On the very same day the Supreme Court also sustained Granger laws establishing maximum rates in three other cases: *Peik* v. *Chicago and Northwestern R. R.; Chicago, Burlington and Quincy R. R.* v. *Iowa*; and *Winona and St. Peter R. R.* v. *Blake*.

Both its successes and its failures contributed to the decline of the Grange. In Illinois farmers thought the battle with monopolies was over after they had won the *Munn* case. In Iowa those who lost financially when the cooperatives failed became disillusioned. In Wisconsin railroads intimidated farmers by discriminating against them. Thus, for a variety of reasons, members abandoned the Grange, which survived only as a social club for farmers. Some discontented farmers then entered the Greenback party (q.v.) that, despite massive support in the Midwest in the elections of 1878, remained a tool of eastern interests committed to a policy of inflation. Its success was short-lived, and in 1880 its enlightened presidential candidate, James Baird Weaver, received only 308,578 votes.

POPULISM

However, the agrarian revolt continued and culminated in Populism. A recent historian of the movement, Lawrence Goodwyn, has challenged the dismissive analyses of earlier historians in two remarkable accounts, *Democratic Promise* (1976), and a shorter version, *The Populist Moment* (1978). It is his contention that it was the crop lien system in the South, rather than general agricultural depression, which first generated the movement. Perhaps the most succinct description of the crop lien system is that of the historian of the South, C. Vann Woodward, in one of his contributory chapters to the general survey history, *The National Experience* (1981):

> The farmer pledged an unplanted crop for a loan of an unstipulated amount at an undesignated but enormous rate of interest averaging about 60 percent a year. Trapped by the system, a farmer might continue year after oppressive year as a sort of peon, under debt to the same merchant and under constant oversight. The lien system imposed the one-crop system for the merchant would advance credit only against cash crops such as cotton or tobacco. . . . The system not only impoverished farmers but stifled their hopes and depleted their incentive.

With masterful use of statistics on agrarian debts in the South Lawrence Goodwyn explains that it was the crop-lien system and the merchants' manipulative use of it for their own advantage that first led to keen agrarian discontent in the region. It spread rapidly elsewhere when displaced Southern farmers moved West in the 1870s.

The immediate predecessor of Populism was the Farmers' Alliance. The Farmers' Alliance, originally founded by Texas cattlemen in 1874 against horse thieves, superseded the Grange as the forum for discontented farmers in the Southwest in the 1880s. The pivotal leader was S. O. Daws of Mississippi, a compelling lecturer, who exhorted his audiences to join the Alliance and form trade stores. Among his converts was William Lamb of Tennessee who had organized more than a hundred suballiances by October 1885. The Alliance had then 50,000 members.

At this crucial moment the Great Southwest Strike of militants among the Knights of Labor (q.v.) erupted against Jay Gould. It divided the Alliance between those who wanted to become more involved on behalf of the strikers and those who wanted to withdraw from labor disputes altogether. Among those who deplored the Alliance's hesitation was William Lamb. In January 1886 he dared Alliance president Andrew Dunlap to acknowledge that farmers were not middle class yeomen independent of the commercial system but ordinary workers like industrial artisans. He wanted intervention on behalf of the Knights and against Gould to take the form of a secondary boycott. S. O. Daws was unable to moderate between Lamb and Dunlap but he succeeded in persuading the Texas Alliance to accept an aggressive program of seventeen political objectives in May 1886. They included radical ideas on agriculture and labor, railroads and finance. A special convention of members meeting in Cleburne, near Dallas, in August 1886 accepted the proposals by the rather narrow vote of 92 to 75.

At a special meeting in Waco, Texas in January 1887, a new leader, Dr. Charles W. Macune from Wisconsin, proposed, and had accepted, two ideas which transformed the Alliance: the creation of the Farmers' Alliance Exchange, a statewide cooperative for the marketing of cotton crops; and a merger of the large Texas Alliance and the much smaller Farmers' Alliance of Louisiana into a new organization, the National Farmers' Alliance and Cooperative Union, of which he became president. It was, moreover, part of Macune's strategy to divert potentially dissident members into a massive recruitment campaign. Between 1887 and 1891 it sent lecturers into forty-three states and territories. Thus, by 1889 the Alliance had established branches as far apart as Florida, Missouri, Oklahoma Territory, Colorado, and Maryland and claimed a total of 3 million members.

The Farmers' State Alliance of Kansas, organized in December 1888, was particularly vital—including among its members Henry Vincent, editor of the *American Nonconformist*, and Ben Clover, who became its president. The pivot of their activities was the Winfield Co-operative Mercantile and Manufacturing Association in Cowley County.

However, the cooperative venture encountered considerable difficulties. The hostility of the commercial establishment to anything that threatened its own profits drove Alliance leaders to political action. Charles Macune and the Texas Alliance sought alternative means of support for cooperatives to those provided by ordinary banks. Accordingly, Macune devised the joint-note plan for the Southern Alliance in late 1887 and, when it failed in midsummer 1888, the sub-treasury plan. This would have allowed

Eugene Debs, leader of the American Railway Union, who organized a secondary boycott of railway workers during the Pullman strike of 1894. When his adversaries proved stronger and the strike collapsed, Debs became convinced social justice could only proceed from socialist politics and founded the Socialist Party of America. (Library of Congress).

farmers to borrow money from the state government for up to 80 percent of the value of their crops stored as collateral in special government warehouses. The idea was to provide the farmer with an easy source of credit at a low rate of interest (1 percent), while allowing him to withhold his crop from the market for a year if prices were depressed. Thus could he escape the crop lien system.

Macune's search for sound financial backing for farmers' cooperatives independent of regular banks and his solutions had already led to intense discussion at the Alliance's second national convention in Meridian, Mississippi in late 1888. Radical lecturer H. S. P. ("Stump") Ashby had previously called a meeting of farmers and laborers to Waco in May 1888 which adopted a six point platform including the abolition of the existing banking system. It led to the formation of a Texas Union Labor Party at Fort Worth on July 4, 1888. This was the embryo of a new third party.

Meanwhile, in the upper plains, Milton George, editor of the *Western Rural* of Chicago, had launched a Northwestern Farmers' Alliance in 1880. It grew steadily until the winter of 1886 and, during the prolonged agricultural depression which followed, it was, perhaps, most active in Illinois, Dakota, and Minnesota. By 1887 the Farmers' Mutual Benefit Association in Illinois had 2,000 members. In Dakota farmers Henry Loucks and Alonzo Wardall organized a territory-wide cooperative marketing exchange which included the distinctive feature of crop insurance at a premium of between 21 and 25 cents an acre. With the assistance of novelist and critic Ignatius Donnelly they also revived the defunct Minnesota Farmers' Alliance in 1889. Black farmers united in the Colored Farmers' National Alliance and Cooperative Union, founded by a white Baptist minister, R. W. Humphrey, at Lovelady, Texas in 1886. In 1890 he claimed 1.2 million members in sixteen states. This was a gross exaggeration. A more probable estimate is a quarter of a million.

Macune, now living in Washington, had struck up a personal and professional friendship with Terence Powderly, grand master of the Knights of Labor, and was planning an amalgamation of the National Alliance (now called the Farmers' and Laborers' Union of America) with the Knights. He recognized that in one fatal particular the farmers were not united. There still remained a wide

Samuel Gompers, leader of the Cigar Makers' Union and president of the American Federation of Labor, was committed to tangible economic gains for craft workers and opposed political activists for discrediting the labor movement. (Library of Congress).

gulf between the West and the South because of the smoldering prejudices of the Civil War. The South was solidly Democratic; the West was Republican. Nevertheless, in December 1889 delegates of the Northern and Southern Alliances convened at St. Louis in an abortive attempt to merge. Macune's emphasis on the sub-treasury plan divided, rather than united, the delegates at St. Louis. However, they agreed that their fundamental platforms were similar. Both wanted a graduated income tax, federal ownership of railroads, laws against land speculation, greater economy in government, and the use of greenbacks as currency.

The cooperative movement had stirred new political sensibilities. From Washington Macune organized a National Reform Press Association to distribute material to over 1,000 newspapers across the country and launch official newspapers of the Alliance in small towns. In the early 1890s there were more than 1,000 Alliance (or Populist) journals, notably the *People's Party Paper,* *The Progressive Farmer,* and the *Southern Mercury.* They were all members of the National Reform Press Association which included other papers sympathetic to their cause such as the Vincent family's *American Nonconformist* and Julius Wayland's *Appeal to Reason.*

By 1890 the Alliance was sufficiently confident in some states to field its own candidates in the congressional and state elections that year. In Kansas, the geographic center of the states and now the eye of the political storm, the Agrarian party elected five congressmen (Jerry Simpson, William Baker, John Otis, John Davis, and the Alliance state president, Ben Clover), and they gained a majority of 96 to 29 in the lower house of the state assembly. As the People's Independent party in Nebraska they took both houses of the state assembly and elected Omar Kem to Congress. In addition they proved themselves a potent political force in Georgia, Tennessee, South Dakota, Indiana, Michigan, and Minnesota.

Nevertheless, close analysis of the 1890 election results suggests that traditional party machines remained intact and the control of crucial committees in the state assemblies which included alliancemen still rested with politicans serving business. The most outspoken supporters of the Cleburne Demands of 1886, such as Evan Jones and H.S.P. Ashby, were disillusioned. They believed the

Booker T. Washington, principal of the Tuskegee Institute and prominent spokesman on black affairs. His so-called Atlanta Compromise of
1895 was regarded by black activists as a capitulation to white racism.
(Library of Congress).

infant third party was failing nationally and in the states and they now attributed its failure to the Alliance's undue emphasis on the cooperative movement. They thought it had diverted farmers' energies from far-reaching political goals to limited, short-term economic remedies. In Georgia, radical allianceman and congressman Tom Watson challenged Alliance state president Lon Livingston to support the sub-treasury plan and lead an exodus of members from the Democratic party. He propounded his ideas in the *People's Party Paper*, a journal which first appeared on October 1, 1891. It declared, "Georgia is ready for a third party and will sweep the state with the movement."

Roused by Lamb, Watson, and other leaders 1,400 delegates, mainly from the Southern Alliance, met first in Cincinnati in May 1891 and then again in St. Louis on February 22, 1892, to launch the People's party, or Populists. The party chose Leonidas Lafayette Polk of North Carolina as its president. He was a forceful speaker and it was common opinion that he was the only Populist leader capable of enticing Southern alliancemen away from the Democrats. But on June 11, 1892, he died in Washington after a short illness.

The center of agrarian discontent had moved westwards from the states of the Mississippi Valley to the plains. Historian Wilfred E. Binkley has shown in *American Political Parties* (1943) how the price of wheat was a barometer of agrarian discontent. When wheat fell from $1.50 a bushel in 1865 to 67 cents in 1868, the Grange was founded. After climbing back above the $1.00, it then fell to 87 cents in 1874 when the Anti-Monopoly, Independent, Reform, and National Greenback parties appeared. By the time the price of wheat rose again, to $1.05 in 1877, the Granger movement had run its course. Then a fall to 80 cents by 1878 produced the Alliance, which had 3,000 lodges or sub-alliances by 1887 when the average price of wheat was only 68 cents. It later climbed again. But it fell from 85 cents in 1891 to 49 cents in 1894, and it was during this period that the Populists nominated a presidential candidate.

The most important agrarian movements, the Granges of the early 1870s and the Populists of the early 1890s, were born in depression. Both movements amounted to revolts. They were

William Jennings Bryan of Nebraska, the most eloquent public speaker of his day and unsuccessful Democratic candidate for the presidency in 1896, 1900, and 1908. His campaign of 1896 gave the two parties their first genuine political difference since the Civil War as the "Battle of the Standards" between gold and silver unleashed a generation of pent-up emotions about the nature of American capitalism. (Library of Congress).

most intense in the South and West where staple crops, respectively cotton and wheat, were grown for world markets and thus subject to fluctuating prices. Farm protest moved westward with the production of wheat, so that the focal point of the Granger movement was in Illinois, Iowa, Minnesota, and Wisconsin, the "older" wheat area. That of Populism was in Kansas, Nebraska, and North and South Dakota, the "newer" wheat area. By the 1890s the older area was becoming like the Northeast in its concentration on fruit, corn, hogs, and dairy farming. Rather than side with the Populists, they blamed the West, with its easy and cheap production of wheat, for their troubles. The Northwestern Alliance disintegrated by 1892.

The Populists' convention of 1,300 delegates meeting at Omaha, Nebraska on July 4, 1892, drafted a reform platform based on the premise "wealth belongs to him who creates it." The Omaha platform, which had its origins in the Cleburne Demands of 1886 and successive Alliance planks, became the symbol of Populism. The preamble was a plaintive emotional appeal written by Ignatius Donnelly and first delivered at St. Louis in February that year. He reviewed the ills of America in the early 1890s.

We meet in the midst of a nation brought to the verge of moral, political and material ruin. Corruption dominates the ballot box, the Legislatures, the Congress, and touches even the ermine of the Bench. The people are demoralized; most of the States have been compelled to isolate the voters at the polling places to prevent universal intimidation and bribery. The newspapers are largely subsidized or muzzled; public opinion silenced; business prostrated, our homes covered with mortgages, labor impoverished, and the land concentrating in the hands of the capitalists. . . . The fruits of the toil of millions are boldly stolen to build up colossal fortunes for a few, unprecedented in the history of mankind, and the possessors of these in turn despise the Republic and endanger liberty. From the same prolific womb of governmental injustice we breed the two great classes—tramps and millionaires.

The Omaha platform specifically called for the free and unlimited coinage of silver at the ratio of 16 to 1, a currency of at least $50 per person in circulation, a graduated income tax, postal savings banks, federal ownership of telegraphs and railroads, and reclamation of lands held by railroads and other corporations for

Ignatius Donnelly who drafted the Populist platform of 1892. (Library of Congress).

speculation. When Populists, furthermore, demanded immigration restriction, an eight-hour day on government works, an end to the use of injunctions against labor, and the outlawing of the Pinkerton mercenaries, they were simply including traditional labor demands. All these proposals had been made, at different times, by the National Labor Union, the Knights of Labor, and the American Federation of Labor. Populists certainly recognized the importance of urban labor. It was a catchment area they could not afford to ignore. Their platform of 1892 included a self-conscious appeal to artisans. "The urban workmen are denied the right of organization for self-protection, imported pauperized labor beats down their wages, a hireling standard army, unrecognized by our law, is established to shoot them down, and they are rapidly degenerating into European conditions."

Thomas Watson of Georgia met the vexed questions of race relations and civil rights in the South head on. Although he recognized that if Populists made allies of black Republicans they ran the risk of antagonizing white Democrats further, he grasped the nettle, telling both races they were the victims of institutionalized racism:

You are kept apart that you may be separately fleeced of your earnings. You are made to hate each other because upon that hatred is rested the keystone of the arch of financial despotism which enslaves you both. You are deceived and blinded that you may not see how this race antagonism perpetuates a monetary system which beggars both.

On the surface it seemed that a new third party had arisen with a massive base of support. But its hold was shallow and it could not sustain what Goodwyn calls "a culture of reform." For example, the American labor movement was not ready for the sort of politics the Populists proposed. Organized labor was not truly cohesive. The Knights was in decline. Samuel Gompers, leader of the growing AFL (q.v.), was hostile to any working class movement which he thought would either distract his members from their immediate economic goals or discredit the working class as a whole. Furthermore, Catholic artisans in the urban ghettos tended to maintain solidarity with their ethnic machines and vote Democratic.

Deprived of their strongest candidate for president by the death of Leonidas Polk, the Populist nominated General James Baird Weaver of Iowa. Weaver's radical credentials were impeccable. For that very reason, however, he was not likely to appeal to the public at large. Nevertheless, the campaign of 1892 was distinguished by the impact made on national politics by various charming and eloquent Populists leaders. Mary Ellen Lease, "the Kansas Pythoness," was a lawyer and a vigorous orator who had spoken 160 times in the campaign of 1890. She was also a most plagent singer. She was a militant suffragist, a violent Anglophobe, and was resolutely opposed to big business. It was she who told Kansas farmers to raise less corn and more hell. She was but one of many energetic women who seized the political opportunity offered by Populism to urge an expanded political role for women. Ignatius Donnelly, the "Sage of Nininger," was editor of the *Anti-Monopolist*, a radical Minnesota newspaper, and author of *Caesar's Column*, a lurid revolutionary novel. Jeremiah or Jerry ("Sockless Socrates") Simpson was the epitome of the bucolic radical who inveighed against the advocates of hard money as "pie-bellied hypocrites." Senator William Peffer of Kansas was a committed prohibitionist whose extraordinarily long beard was a gift to cartoonists. These leaders were good copy and captured newspaper headlines but they could not persuade Americans to change their traditional political allegiances. Weaver took 1,029,846 votes, 8.5 percent of the total, and an absolute majority in three states. Of these he carried Kansas by a most narrow margin but gained more than 40 percent of the votes in Nebraska and North Dakota.

In the state contests the Populists were openly swindled. For instance, in the Alabama state elections of 1892, Reuben Kolb, candidate for governor of the "Jeffersonian Democrats," took a plurality of votes and carried the state, but was deprived of his victory by the party machine of the incumbent governor, Thomas Jones, which invented a massive black vote to defeat him in the final tallies. In Georgia, eyes and ears were concentrated on the campaign of Representative Thomas Watson for reelection to the tenth congressional district. His attacks on Republicans and Democrats in Congress had made him known across the nation and so his success or failure in an intense and bitter election campaign would be taken as a portent of the national fortunes of the People's party. When it became clear that black Americans would hold the balance of power in Georgia, conservative Democrats perpetrated a series of murders of black citizens to terrify the others. On election day, Democratic managers indulged in bribery, stuffing ballot boxes, and fraudulent counting to have Watson's opponent, Major James Black, elected. The total vote returned by election judges was twice the number of qualified voters. Thus did the Democratic party hold Georgia intact.

But election to office was no guarantee of a change in government. Some successful Populists discovered the cards were stacked against reform. A joint Populist and Democratic candidate, Davis H. Waite, a radical editor from Aspen, Colorado, was elected governor of the state in 1892. The state assembly, however, remained in the hands of the Republicans, and refused to pass his bill to regulate the railroads. By 1893 he was thoroughly exasperated and declared, "It is better, infinitely better, that blood should flow to the horses' bridles rather than our national liberties should be destroyed." Thus he earned the nickname "Bloody Bridles" Waite.

Populist leaders expected to do better in the elections of 1894 and 1896 than they had in 1892. Their hopes fed on disasters: continuing agricultural depression; adverse weather on the plains; indisputable mismanagement of political and economic affairs by Congress and administration before, during, and after the panic of 1893. They were well aware that the various crises of the mid 1890s gave them a special chance to break the traditional mold of American politics. But it was not to be. Four western states (Kansas, Colorado, North Dakota, and Idaho), in which the Populists had scored successes in 1892, went Republican in 1894. In Kansas the new party had fused with the Democrats in 1892. But when Populist candidates won that year it was on account of Democratic votes, and the Democratic party expected compensation in the way of patronage. Confirmed Populists could not countenance this compromise. In 1894 they chose to contest the elections alone and their candidates were defeated. The Republicans elected their entire state ticket, seven of eight congressmen, and 91 of 124 assemblymen.

It was not, however, a case of decline everywhere. Notwithstanding widespread intimidation, bribery, and ballot-rigging practiced by the Democrats in Texas, the Populist vote rose there from 23 percent in 1892 to almost 40 percent in 1894. The mixed results of the 1894 elections were difficult to interpret and lent respectability to support for the sort of coalition of Populists and Democrats that had existed in Nebraska since 1890 even though in certain parts of the South Populists and Democrats were at loggerheads.

In state after state cooperatives starved for lack of credit. In the three years, from the election of 1892 to the end of 1895, the strongest constituencies of traditional Populism remained the three states of Texas, Kansas, and Georgia. In the western states the agrarian revolt was transformed by the emergence of silver as a political issue.

BIMETALLISM

The new movement on behalf of the mining interest was most striking in Nebraska where it was promoted not by independents but by a low tariff faction of the Democrats whose most zealous spokesman was Congressman William Jennings Bryan. His understanding of the monetary system was rudimentary. In 1892 he cheerfully confessed, "The people of Nebraska are for free silver and I am for free silver. I will look up the arguments later." Silver mine owners had launched the American Bimetallic League in 1889 but not until the depression of 1893 could they hope to make free silver a major issue in national politics. Their campaign was buttressed by editorial support in such diverse papers as the *World Herald* of Omaha, the *Commercial-Appeal* of Memphis, and the *Evening Star* of Washington. In the mining states of the West, Populism now attracted support solely on account of its proposals for monetary reform involving the coinage of silver at a ratio of 16 to 1 from which the miners hoped to gain more work. Given its geographic origins, the silver movement was, perhaps, an inevitable, even a natural, successor to the ineffectual Northwestern Farmer's Alliance. It had little in common with the enterprising

National Farmers' Alliance of the Southwest. Nevertheless, as prohibitionist Dr. D. Leigh Colvin, put it, "The silver movement represented far more than merely free coinage. It was a complex of pent-up feelings against the excessive power of great wealth."

The dissent that culminated in the conflict between gold and silver was brought about by three specific elements: a decrease in the supply of gold, an increase in the supply of silver, and variations in the amount of currency in circulation. Underlying what became known as the Battle of the Standards was a need for a flexible currency that could grow with the population and the economy—specie that was specific and not specious.

As we have noted, world production of gold had decreased between 1865 and 1890 whereas the production of industry, mining, and agriculture had increased. Moreover, the population also increased: in the United States in 1890 it was almost twice that of 1865. The increase in the number of people and the decline in gold production was the root cause of third parties proposing an expansion of the currency. In the same period the production of silver in America had increased greatly—by about 1 thousand times between 1855 and 1890. In 1855 the value of production was $52,000; in 1865, $11.64 million; in 1890, $57.24 million. It was W. H. Harvey's simplistic and misleading *Coin's Financial School* (1894) that made the silver cause accessible to millions across the country.

William Allen White, then the young editor of the Emporia *Gazette*, compared the fervor of the silver movement to the fanaticism of the Crusades. "Indeed, the delusion that was working on the people took the form of religious frenzy. Sacred hymns were torn from their pious tunes to give place to words which deified the cause and made gold—and all its symbols, capital, wealth, plutocracy—diabolical." Agrarian communities earnestly believed that when they had elected a silver legislature it would, by proclamation, produce the millenium of bimetallism. "It was a season of shibboleths and fetiches and slogans. Reason slept; and the passions—jealousy, covetousness, hatred—ran amuck; and whoever would check them was crucified in public contumely."

To conservatives the proposed reform was abhorrent, threatening to undermine the economy, isolate the United States from Europe, and increase governmental interference in business. Reformer Henry Demarest Lloyd, who was sympathetic to the People's party, described the free silver movement as the cowbird of reform. A cowbird took over the nests of other birds, threw out their eggs, and laid its own in their place.

Leading Populists also disapproved of the new emphasis on the silver issue in Populism. They considered it a superficial formula and thought it dangerous for the new party. However, a month after the 1894 federal elections the new party chairman, Herman Taubeneck of Illinois, declared the party should abandon the rest of the Omaha platform of 1892 in favor of a single platform of free silver for 1896. Thus, before the election of 1896 the People's party was riven by faction between political trimmers who wanted to fuse with the Democrats, and mid-roaders who wanted to chart a separate course. Those intent on office and victory at all costs included Senators William Allen and Marion Butler and radicals James Weaver and Jerry Simpson. They reasoned that although the People's party was supported by between 25 and 45 percent of the electorate in twenty states, this was not enough to elect congressmen. And only after election could the Populists enact their proposals. As far as they were concerned silver was popular with the public and represented a real chance of electoral victory.

Those who had been long identified with the Alliance and opposed political trimming included Tom Watson, Thomas Nugent, and E. M. Wardell. They were supported by most of the reform press. Committed alliancemen concluded that free silver would destroy the essence of their movement. Concentration on this one plank precluded debate and promulgation of others. Free silver would not change the existing system of commerce and banking which supported the dominant plutocracy. Furthermore, free silver was a political irrelevance amid ever mounting public discussion about the accelerating trend towards industrial monopolies, the concentration of capital they represented, and the political corruption they sustained. The adoption of free silver would simply allow the railroad lobbies to corrupt legislatures with silver instead of gold. In the words of editor, diplomat, and poet James Russell Lowell, it was a case of

> "With gates of silver and bars of gold
> Ye have fenced my sheep from their father's fold."

And Judge Thomas Nugent of Texas declared that silver coinage would "Leave undisturbed all the conditions which give rise to the undue concentration of wealth. The so-called silver party may prove a veritable trojan horse if we are not careful."

When Taubeneck tried to convince a mass audience at St. Louis in December 1894 of the need to narrow the Omaha plank to the coinage of silver at a ratio of 16 to 1, he was unsuccessful. It was the same when representatives of the National Press Association and the National Farmers' Alliance convened at separate meetings in early 1895. Both groups denounced the idea of a one-plank platform. Taubeneck replied that their attitude was clear proof of socialist subversion within the party. This led to outright attack on Taubeneck and Weaver by editors like Thomas Byron of Iowa in the *Farmer's Tribune*. Taubeneck had proved himself nothing better than a political broker. Ignatius Donnelly decided, "Narrow Populism to free silver alone and it will disappear in a rat hole."

Nevertheless, the silver lobby managed to infiltrate the new party. Its eastern journal, the *Silver Knight*, was managed by J. H. Turner who was also a member of the national executive committee of the People's party. In 1893 Weaver was active in the American Bimetallic League and presided over its convention. Silver interests also penetrated the Democratic party. The American Bimetallic League sponsored conferences to promote free silver which were attended by Democratic politicians such as one of June 1895 at Memphis at which Governor Ben Tillman of South Carolina, with his one eye on the main chance, was present.

The Democratic party was shaken to the core by the depression of 1893, Cleveland's inability to raise it, and the agrarian revolt which had robbed it of congressional seats in the elections of 1892 and 1894. Those concerned for the future of the party—not to mention their own careers—concluded that Cleveland's adherence to the gold standard (q.v.) was undermining their electoral basis in the South and West. Unless the president's policies could be reversed radical prophecies of a basic realignment of the parties might be fulfilled in 1896 at the Democrats' expense. The stampede of Democratic congressmen from the West to the silver cause convinced Populist mid-roaders they were on the right track.

THE ELECTION OF 1896

In 1896 three candidates presented themselves for consideration by the Republicans: former President Benjamin Harrison, disgraced by his defeat in 1892; "Czar" Thomas B. Reed, whose appeal was limited to New England and Congress itself; and William McKinley, coauthor of the tariff of 1890 and governor of Ohio. McKinley had the advantage of an amiable personality, and he could put on a show of personal dignity. Although he was identified with a controversial subject, the tariff, his record on silver was sufficiently ambiguous to appeal to both gold and silver interests in the party.

McKinley owed his success at the Republican National Convention, meeting in St. Louis on June 16, 1896, to the skill of his ally and manager, Marcus Alonzo Hanna, a prosperous businessman from Cleveland, anxious to play a decisive part in national politics. He was committed to a high tariff, but in other respects his attitudes to industrial problems were advanced. He held liberal views on the troubling subject of labor relations. It was widely known through the press that Hanna had urged Pullman to submit the labor dispute of 1894 (q.v.) to arbitration. Furthermore, McKinley, as governor of Ohio, had supported labor legislation and contributed to relief funds in the depression. Hanna's strategy in gaining the nomination for McKinley was for them both to visit small towns in the South and West and court there the sort of local celebrities who would become delegates to the nominating convention. In this way they planned to take the sting out of the Populists' tail in these sectors. Hanna urged McKinley to remain silent in the West on the subject of silver in order not to antagonize silver interests there. At their convention the Republicans adopted an unequivocal platform in favor of gold by an overwhelming majority.

The Democratic response, at their convention meeting in Chicago on July 6, resulted in one of the few elections (those of 1964 and 1972 are among the others) when the two parties, instead of blurring the issues that separated them, actually took different sides. As late as July 10, 1896, the *New York World* prophesied that in the forthcoming election, "The Silverites will be invincible if united and harmonious; but they have neither machine nor boss. The opportunity is here; the man is lacking." That very day William Jennings Bryan with a single speech made himself the missing leader. He did so against considerable odds. Ben Tillman of South Carolina had made the opening speech of the convention in favor of silver and was jeered. He commented ruefully, "There are only three things in the world that can hiss—a goose, a serpent, and a man."

Yet when it was his turn to speak all ears were fastened on Bryan who was, by now, widely known and well rehearsed. Everyone knew what he had to say, but he galvanized the convention with his ringing defense of agrarian discontent. His "cross of gold" speech became the most famous oration since Lincoln's Gettysburg Address and second inaugural. It was not impromptu but a final revision of a speech Bryan had delivered scores of times in the Midwest. His first point was that the usual definition of a businessman was too limited. All who worked and contributed to the common wealth were engaged in business. His second point was that agriculture, rather than industry, was the true basis of civilization, without which industry itself could not survive. He concluded with ringing rhetoric. "Having behind us the producing masses of this country and of the world, supported by the commercial interests, the laboring interests and the toilers everywhere, we will answer their demand for a gold standard by saying to them, 'You shall not press down upon the brow of labor this cross of thorns, you shall not crucify mankind upon a cross of gold.'"

On July 10, 1896, the *New York Sun*, a paper hostile to Bryan, carried this account of Bryan at the Democratic National Convention:

From all parts of the convention hall a great roar went up for Bryan, Bryan, Bryan. These cheers were continued and rolled on and on. . . . Mr. Bryan is a smooth-faced man of early middle life and his dark hair is long and wavy. . . . His rhetoric and English and his oratorical gestures were almost superb. . . . His voice is clear and resonant, and his bearing graceful. He is the idol of the silver camp, and if a vote could have been taken immediately after he had finished, he would, without the slightest doubt, have been nominated for President by acclamation.

Hearing Bryan's voice in a convention hall was an emotional experience for many delegates comparable to audiences hearing opera singers like Adelina Patti in the theater. Bryan won the nomination on the fifth ballot and ousted the other leading contender, Congressman Richard ("Silver Dick") Bland of Missouri. Outraged conservatives seceded and formed their own National Democratic party pledged to uphold the gold standard.

Bryan had taken the wind out of the Populists' sails. They could respond only by submerging their identity, and at their convention in St. Louis, they nominated Bryan as their presidential candidate. Besides, Taubeneck was determined the convention would support a platform built around the demand for free silver. He had ensured a system of apportionment of delegates to the convention which overrepresented the silver interests. The mid-roaders made a last sustained attempt to make their voice heard. As their price for accepting Bryan they persuaded the convention, after pandemonium on the floor of the hall, to nominate Tom Watson of Georgia for vice president against the wishes of fusionists and, probably, of Bryan himself.

With the nomination of Bryan by the People's party the agrarian revolt was over before the election campaign had begun in earnest. Not only were the most charming and attractive political characters for several decades dismissed in the orthodox press as cranks but their ideology was also roundly denounced by those who thought it subversive of American morals and politics. On August 15, 1896, William Allen White, wrote in the *Emporia Gazette* a series of leaders to be used by printers during his absence on vacation. One carried the striking title, "What's the Matter with Kansas?" and was brought to the attention of Herman Kohlsaat, publisher of the *Chicago Times-Herald*, who arranged for it to be syndicated across the country. It was immediately recognized as a pithy and pungent repudiation of Populism. White rounded on malcontents as professional failures who condemned the American system of government and finance simply because they could not cope with it.

What's the matter with Kansas? We all know; yet here we are at it again. We have an old mossback Jacksonian who snorts and howls because there is a bathtub in the State House. We are running that old jay for governor.

We have another shabby, wild-eyed, rattle-brained fanatic who has said openly in a dozen speeches that "the rights of the user are paramount to the rights of the owner." We are running him for chief justice, so that capital will come tumbling over itself to get into the State. We have raked the ash-heap of failure in the State and found an old human hoop-skirt who has failed as a business man, who has failed as an editor, who has failed as a preacher, and we are going to run him for congressman-at-large. . . . Then we have discovered a kid without a law practice and have decided to run him for attorney-general. Then for fear some hint that the State had become respectable might percolate through the civilized portions of the nation, we have decided to send three or four harpies out lecturing, telling the people that Kansas is raising hell and letting the corn go to weeds.

There was, however, much more to the Populist movement than White was ready to admit. It had awakened American politics from slumber and transformed the election of 1896 into a high tide of radical dissent and a final flow of the controversy over the currency. Thus were the forces arrayed for the election of 1896, the political climax of the Gilded Age. On one side the forces of reform representing mass discontent with two party politics based on the sectionalism of North and South and plutocratic management of the Industrial Revolution. They were led by stump orators and the radical press. On the other side were the politicos and plutocrats, hostile to any innovative economic theories that threatened their supremacy, and supported by party bosses and their machines, and by banking and the orthodox press.

The actual campaign was unusual in many respects. For the first time ever a candidate toured the country. Bryan spoke to millions in twenty-one states. Some considered his campaign an act of vulgar barnstorming unworthy of a presidential candidate. In the first part of the campaign Bryan, whose financial support was limited, was obliged to travel on scheduled commercial trains. Rather than arrive at meetings dusty and sweating, he used alcohol to rub himself down. Thus, although he never drank liquor, he would meet his audiences reeking of gin.

For his part, McKinley remained at his home in Canton where he received delegates on his front porch. However, he was neither lazy nor complacent. His receptions were planned down to the last detail. The visitors submitted speeches in advance, which

McKinley scrutinized, and sometimes revised, before they were read aloud and replied to in public for the benefit of the press. He offered generally compromising, moderate answers to all and sundry while displaying his double-barreled shotgun—the protective tariff and the gold standard—to any who wanted to see if their man was really hard.

Mark Hanna quite exceeded the lavish expenditure of Matthew Quay for Harrison in 1892. He openly urged banks to donate a quarter of 1 percent of their assets to the campaign and spent money like water on Republican literature in English and other languages. He had 120 million campaign documents distributed and circulated 275 different pamphlets to provide the press with copy to promote the cause. McKinley was the "Advance Agent of Prosperity" who would "Fill the Dinner Pail." When the campaign was over the Republican National Committee admitted to having spent $3 million; whereas the Democrats had spent only a tenth of that. Hanna's imaginative techniques and style of campaigning were unprecedented. They set a standard of penetration of the electorate for all presidential campaigns in future.

The morale of the Populists expired and the movement almost collapsed. The cooperatives were defunct and the party was practically penniless. Ironically, Bryan, who had acquiesced in the destruction of the people's movement before the election, was actually taken as a symbol of it.

The election results reaffirmed the Republican's recently won position as the majority party. Sensing the hostility of the cities to silver, Hanna remarked of Bryan, "He's talking silver all the time, and that's where we've got him." Of the eighty-two cities with a population of at least 45,000 only a dozen supported Bryan, and seven of these were in the Solid South and two in the silver states. McKinley received 7,102,246 popular votes to Bryan's 6,492,559, the first undisputed majority since 1872 but only 51.1 percent. In the electoral college he had 271 votes to Bryan's 176. Bryan, who carried twenty-one states, did not take one outside the South or east of the Mississippi. The twenty-two great industrial states of the North and East and Oregon voted decisively for McKinley. Bryan lost his own state, his own city, even his own precinct.

The conflict over the currency had been more dangerous politically than economically. It represented a challenge by the agrarian West and South against political control by the industrial Northeast. But neither the single nor the bimetallic policy would have led to economic disruption. Some of the Populists' demands of 1896 were realized later, such as the establishment of postal savings banks, the direct election of senators, statehood for remaining territories, ballot reform, and a graduated income tax. Yet the idea of structural reform of government was defeated with Bryan.

Bryan's emphasis on one issue had made the campaign simple enough for ordinary people to understand. But his argument rested on the known scarcity of gold. However, during the 1890s, gold production was increasing throughout the world, rising from $118.84 million in 1890 to $202.25 million in 1896. In 1896 India, which sold wheat in exchange for silver, had a poor harvest, whereas the United States produced wheat in abundance. The price of wheat rose. The price of silver fell. Gold production continued to rise. In 1898 it was $286.87 million, more than twice the amount of 1890. The increase was accelerated by new discoveries in Australia, South Africa, and the Klondike and by the invention of the cyanide process by MacArthur and Forrest, which extracted more gold from the same amount of ore. At the same time, production of silver increased only slightly from $163.03 million in 1890 to $218.57 million in 1898. Moreover, in 1897 the flagging fortunes of farmers began to revive and the prices of corn and wheat rose. On March 14, 1900, Congress passed an act making gold the single standard of currency. Silver was a dead issue.

Bryan was at the height of his powers in 1896 when he was thirty-six. He became a professional speaker on the Chautauqua circuit and was called the Great Commoner, the Peerless One, and the Boy Orator of the Platte. His daughter collected his anecdotes and one may suffice as an example of his wit.

A minister was delivering a sermon upon perfection and, illustrating the fact that no human being was perfect, said: "If there is a perfect person in this audience please rise." A dead silence ensued. . . . Having reached his climax, he thundered, "Now, if anybody in this church has ever heard of a perfect person, please rise." To the amazement of both minister and congregation a timid little woman in the back of the sanctuary arose. . . .

"And who may this perfect person be," inquired the minister. "My husband's first wife."

The story was not new. Lincoln had used it forty years earlier. But it makes its own ironic comment on Bryan, a man whose steady decline from youthful perfection was to become increasingly obvious to his public as his fixed convictions led him to bigotry. As Thomas B. Reed remarked at the turn of the century, "Bryan would rather be wrong than president."

CHAPTER TEN

WORLD ON FIRE

T HE DECADE beginning in 1890 had a most distinct historical character. For one thing, its chronological boundaries were marked by crucial historical events. The year 1890 saw the rise of the People's Alliance, the McKinley Tariff, the Sherman Anti-Trust Act, the official closing of the frontier, and the massacre at Wounded Knee. At the turn of the century, in 1901, Morgan bought out Carnegie, Robert La Follette became governor of Wisconsin, and Theodore Roosevelt became president.

The significance of these events was not lost on those who lived through them. There were several attempts to characterize the decade in terms of a color. The "Yellow '90s" was the description of Stuart P. Sherman. The "Mauve Decade" was the epithet of Thomas Beer. However, no one drew parallels with the London art of Aubrey Beardsley and Oscar Wilde and called it "the decayed decade." Other titles were "Electric" by H. L. Mencken, "Romantic" by Richard Le Gallienne, and even "Moulting" by W. L. Wittlesey.

The central events of the early 1890s certainly suggest political dissolution and public disillusion. The Sherman Anti-Trust Law was invoked, not against corporations, but against labor unions. The Homestead Strike of 1892 ended in the rout of the strikers. The Pullman strike of 1894 was crushed without mercy by the federal government in league with railroad barons. The panic and depression of 1893 scarred society, and the silver panacea of the

A New Bird for Thanksgiving.—Spain's goose is cooked, and William McKinley is the man who cooked it.

President William McKinley succeeded in defusing the debate about gold and silver in the lightning war with Spain of 1898 by which the United States acquired the Philippines, Puerto Rico, and Guam, and the right to intervention in Cuba. His military successes and the raising of the depression made him the most popular president of the Gilded Age. (Library of Congress).

Democrats and Populists was rejected in the election of 1896. But the accession of William McKinley to the presidency in 1897 revealed a marked change in America's self-regard. Expansion overseas now served to divert and defuse national tensions. Despite its horrors, the Spanish-American War of 1898 was even described by the new secretary of state, John Hay, as a "splendid little war."

McKinley was the last veteran of the Civil War to become president and the first from a family engaged in heavy industry. His wife, Ida, suffered from epilepsy and phlebitis. McKinley did not want it said of Ida that none dared sit beside her at the White House. He became expert at throwing a handkerchief over her face when she had a seizure during receptions. It is a myth that McKinley was the tool of conservative, northeastern businessmen. He hailed from the Midwest and headed a diverse coalition of interests. Fourteen years in Congress had taught him the arts of compromise, and he was determined, unlike his predecessor, Grover Cleveland, not to antagonize senators by high-handed actions. Assistant Secretary of the Navy Theodore Roosevelt was one of those who mistook McKinley's caution for cowardice. He said, "McKinley has no more backbone than a chocolate éclair." It was not true. McKinley was one of those leaders who knew how to listen. He was openly patient, secretly stubborn, and inwardly resentful of undue political pressure. Roosevelt later realized his mistake. He then remarked of the basic motive underlying the surface veneer of McKinley's charm, "He treats everyone with equal favor, their worth to him is solely dependent on the advantages he could derive from them."

CUBA

The election of 1896 had determined the outcome of the most controversial issue of the day. In 1897 the problem of Cuba replaced silver as the most troublesome question. In the late nineteenth century the Spanish colony of Cuba was in an almost continuous state of rebellion. Despite attempts at enticement by the Cuban rebels and intense provocation by the Spanish rulers, President Ulysses S. Grant and Secretary of State Hamilton Fish avoided American involvement in the Ten Years' War of 1868 to

1878. In 1878 Spain ended one rebellion with a paper peace but would not relinquish control of its island possession. America had $50 million invested in Cuban sugar and mining. Its trade with Cuba was worth more than $100 million in 1893. But guerrilla warfare took its toll of these lucrative investments. Between 1890 and 1896 Cuban trade had dwindled to a third of its former size.

The Cuban revolt of 1895 was conducted with great savagery on both sides and was, therefore, ideal copy for tabloids like the *New York World* and *New York Journal*, which were engaged in their own bitter war for circulation and survival. Spanish officials seized and searched ships at sea and ignored the rights of Cubans who had taken American citizenship. They destroyed fields of sugar-cane, butchered livestock, and dismantled mills—especially those belonging to foreigners. American sympathy for the Cubans deepened to outrage when the Spanish governor general, Valeriano Weyler, proclaimed a policy of "reconcentrado," the herding of peasants into towns before laying waste to the countryside. On April 4, 1896, Cleveland's secretary of state, Richard Olney, had formally warned Madrid "That the United States cannot contemplate with complacency another ten years of Cuban insurrection, with all its injurious and distressing incidents, may certainly be taken for granted."

When McKinley became president on March 4, 1897, his range of options toward Cuba and Spain was already quite narrow. In his inaugural address he declared, "We want no wars of conquest; we must avoid the temptation of territorial aggression." But he was well aware of the depth of public antipathy to Spain. He also knew that it had been fomented by newspapers interested in sensationalism and indifferent to historical perspective. He believed that the press would keep up the pressure on the public and that the public would continue to pressure Congress. He recognized that the basis of his popular support was, in one sense, wider than the Republicans but, in another, narrower. Formerly he had appealed not only to a single party but also the public at large. If he could not resolve the problem before the next election, he would be abandoned by both public and party. However, some eloquent Republicans were openly advocating expansion through war. They included congressmen from the Atlantic states, prominent publisher Whitelaw Reid, and self-seeking publicists like Theodore Roosevelt and Alfred Mahan. These Americans had different solutions to the Cuban problem. Some wanted the United States to expel Spain from the island, then take possession of it and gain control to the approaches of the projected isthmian canal in Central America. Some wanted to establish a Cuban republic.

The American consul in Havana, Fitzhugh Lee, was committed to the rebels but responsible in his conduct of consulate affairs. In 1897 McKinley appointed a New York lawyer, Stewart Woodford, known for his tact and determination, to the American ministry in Madrid. Furthermore, in June 1897 McKinley sent a special investigator, William J. Calhoun of Illinois, to report on Cuba. Calhoun's report of June 22, 1897, reaffirmed what McKinley had suspected. Of the notorious scorched-earth policy Calhoun concluded, "The country was wrapped in the stillness of death and the silence of desolation."

McKinley tried to convince Spain that its preferred solution should be gradual reform. On June 26, 1897, he advised Madrid to end the policy of reconcentration, introduce programs of relief for refugees, restore law and order, and concede Cuban autonomy. Underlying his request was an implicit warning. If Spain continued to fight simply to avoid political humiliation, then the rebels would prolong the war in order to ensure foreign intervention. Moreover, McKinley openly stated that Cuba had a special relationship with the United States. This last part of his message was no more than a thinly veiled threat. In its reply of August, Spain repudiated the whole notion of a special relationship between America and Cuba and reserved its imperial right to repress the rebellion.

However, the assassination of the reactionary prime minister, Antonio Cánoras del Castillo, in Madrid and the accession to power of a more liberal administration led to compromise. The new ministry recalled Gen. Valeriano Weyler and agreed to assist refugees and form a plan for Cuban autonomy. The queen regent, Maria Christina, promulgated the plan in November 1897. But it was rejected by the rebels, who realized that Spain would still retain the reins of power and maintain a formidable army of occupation on the island. Spain clung obsessively to the usual belief of an imperial power fighting an impossible guerrilla war that increased resources and a final sustained campaign would result in the defeat of the enemy. Moreover, Spanish *peninsulares* and officers on the island resented the very idea of autonomy and were committed to subverting it even after it became official Spanish policy. On January 12, 1898, a mob of veterans and hoodlums attacked the property of Havana businessmen who supported autonomy. These riots undermined American trust in Spain's ability to carry out its declared policy. Both sides in Cuba preferred war to reform, and the rebels declared for full independence.

On February 9, 1898, the *New York Journal* carried a facsimile of a purloined letter written by the Spanish minister in Washington, Enrique Dupuy De Lôme, to a friend in Cuba. In it De Lôme reviewed the prospects for a peaceful solution. He characterized McKinley as a weakling interested only in his own popularity, and he advised Spain to court American friendship by proposing a reciprocal tariff. What the letter implied was more damaging to the Spanish case than what it actually said. A year of diplomacy had produced nothing more from Spain than a stream of patently false promises.

On February 15, 1898, the *Maine*, an American ship paying a courtesy visit to Havana, exploded in the harbor with the loss of 266 sailors. It was widely assumed that the ship had been blown up by Spanish agents. Without a scintilla of proof, Assistant Secretary of the Navy Theodore Roosevelt announced, "The *Maine* was sunk by an act of dirty treachery on the part of the Spaniards." It is, however, difficult to see what Spain could have hoped to gain by exploding the *Maine*. The ship's commanding officer, Captain Sigsbee, asked the administration to suspend judgment. The suspicion remains that it was the work of Cuban agents provocateurs designed to discredit Spain and force America's hand. Nevertheless, McKinley secured a defense appropriation of $50 million from Congress, in part to prepare for war, in part to indicate to Spain the gravity of the situation.

A common charge of radical historians has been that America was bent on war for blatant commercial advantage. However, in *Expansionists of 1898* (1936) Julius Pratt reviewed the business press of the 1890s to demonstrate that the majority of businessmen believed that war would disrupt trade and argued against it. McKinley's mentor, Mark Hanna, was among those businessmen utterly opposed to war because of its inevitable financial and human cost. He spoke against it on March 26, 1898, at a private Gridiron dinner. Theodore Roosevelt replied, "We will have this war for the freedom of Cuba, Senator Hanna, in spite of the timidity of commercial interests." He was already intriguing against his superior, Secretary of the Navy John D. Long, with various orders for naval preparedness. It seemed that Roosevelt believed in war as social therapy.

While a commission of American experts examined the wreck in Havana, the State Department proposed a final compromise whereby Spain was to grant an armistice, end reconcentration, provide relief, and accept arbitration from McKinley. This ultimatum convinced the Spanish government that America was serious about Cuban independence. On March 31, 1898, it agreed to autonomy, relief, and redress for the *Maine*. In the meantime, American experts had attributed the ship's destruction to an unspecified "external cause." But the Spanish government refused arbitration and withheld recognition from the rebels. Supposedly in response to papal overtures, however, it granted an armistice on April 9. McKinley was not deceived by what he correctly interpreted as yet another example of Spanish obfuscation and delay. He saw only two possible outcomes to the catastrophe. Either Spain would continue to prosecute the war indefinitely and devastate the island in the process or the United States could intervene, expel Spain from the hemisphere, and establish peace. He believed that compromise would be futile and would simply prolong tragedy.

On March 17, 1898, the prudent Senator Redfield Proctor of Vermont, recently returned from Cuba, treated the Senate to a scathing account of Spanish misrule on the island. On April 6, 1898, six European ambassadors called on McKinley and asked him, in the interests of humanity, to refrain from intervention. He turned their request upside down by replying that any intervention would itself be in the interests of humanity. And this was the basis of his message to Congress on April 11, 1898, when he declared that "in the name of civilization, in behalf of endangered

American interests, which give us the right and the duty to act, the war in Cuba must stop." He asked Congress for authority to deploy military and naval forces "to secure a full and final termination of hostilities between the government of Spain and the people of Cuba." He was most dismissive of Spanish attempts at compromise and conciliation.

Both houses accepted an extra article proposed by Senator Henry M. Teller of Colorado to the war resolution of April 20, 1898, that "the United States hereby disclaims any disposition or intention to exercise sovereignty, jurisdiction, or control over said Island except for the pacification thereof, and asserts its determination, when that is accomplished, to leave the government and control of the Island to its people."

THE WAR OF 1898

The war of 1898 was the shortest in American history, lasting 100 days from April to August. Because this was to be an overseas war it was essential to paralyze the main Spanish fleet at the outset. Commodore George Dewey, commander of the American Asiatic fleet, sped from his base in Hong Kong to Manila in the Spanish Philippines where he penetrated the defenses of a Spanish armada at dawn on May 1, 1898. He then gave his famous order, "You may fire when ready, Gridley." Five times he maneuvered the American fleet around the Spanish armada, bombarding it without mercy, before giving the counterorder to "draw off for breakfast." Although it became obvious when the smoke cleared that the Spanish fleet was lost beyond hope, the Spanish military governor, Basilio Augustin, mistook the American withdrawal for retreat and sent a message to Madrid that Spain had won a great victory.

To the world outside the Philippines the issue was in doubt for several days until the *New York World* and the *Chicago Tribune* carried a scoop of Dewey's success on May 8, 1898. To America the week's suspense had been unbearable, and when definite news finally came the country was caught up in a great wave of patriotic fervor. Dewey, however, was not carried away with his success and waited for the arrival of enough troops to make a victory on the islands complete and secure. He also encouraged Emilio

To celebrate Admiral George Dewey's defeat of the Spanish fleet during the war of 1898 Eugene ("Ironquill") Ware, a Kansas lawyer, provided the *Capital* of Topeka with an absurd ditty which was syndicated across America and sung everywhere. (Library of Congress).

Aguinaldo, leader of the Filipinos opposed to Spanish rule, to renew their war of independence. In September the insurrection established an alternative government widely accepted on the islands.

After the Battle of Manila Bay, McKinley confessed in private that he had only a vague idea of where the Philippines were. Yet although he had declared in December 1897 that the seizure of territory was "criminal aggression," five months later he was maintaining, "while we are conducting the war and until its conclusion we must keep all we get; when the war is over we must keep what we want."

Success on land in Cuba was by no means assured for the United States. The army of 26,000 men lacked adequate supplies and equipment, and the War Department led by Secretary Russell A. Alger was incompetent. Fortunately for America, Spain was even more inefficient. It had a superior land force of 200,000 troops in Cuba but deployed only 13,000 at Santiago where the Americans landed, and eventually defeated, the Spanish. Rather than surrender without a fight, Adm. Pascual Cervera led his inferior fleet out of Santiago Harbor on July 3 to certain defeat against a superior American force of four battleships. Gen. Nelson A. Miles's campaign to take Puerto Rico, another Spanish island in the Caribbean, between July 21 and August 12 passed off more smoothly. It was in this feverish atmosphere of imperial expectation, and to protect the Philippines, that Hawaii was annexed by a joint resolution of Congress that passed the House on June 15, 1898, and the Senate in July (q.v.).

The war was over on August 12 when McKinley, as commander-in-chief of the armies and navies, signed a protocol by which Spain was ordered to evacuate Cuba, to cede Puerto Rico and an island in the Marianas (Guam) to the United States, and to allow America to occupy Manila until a peace treaty had determined the future of the Philippines. The protocol thus set an entirely constitutional precedent for an extension of presidential power. Moreover, McKinley's words implied that a war begun in the name of liberty for Cuba should end in territorial acquisition for the United States. McKinley dispatched a carefully selected commission to oversee the peace conference in Paris, including his most trusted associate, Assistant Secretary William R. Day; publisher Whitelaw Reid; and Senators William P. Frye of Maine, Cushman K. Davis of Minnesota, and George Gray of Delaware.

McKinley was genuinely concerned for the future safety of the Filipinos. He recognized their inexperience in government and also dreaded the predatory intentions of other powers toward the islands. But he was equally eager to secure extra trade and new trading routes for the United States. Thus, from a mixture of interested and disinterested motives, he instructed the commission to demand the entire archipelago. Later McKinley recorded his reasoning:

We could not give them back to Spain—that would be cowardly and dishonorable; we could not turn them over to France or Germany—our commercial rivals in the Orient—that would be bad business and discreditable; we could not leave them to themselves—they were unfit for self-government—and they would soon have anarchy and misrule over there worse than Spain's was; and there was nothing left to do but to take them all, and to educate the Filipinos, and uplift and civilize and Christianize them, and by God's grace do the very best we could for them, as our fellow-men for whom Christ also died.

The idea of converting the Filipinos to Christianity was, of course, eyewash. The Philippines, named after a religious fanatic, Philip II, had been Catholic for centuries

McKinley began to work for public support for his policy of retaining the Philippines. He did not expect to secure Senate ratification of the proposed treaty without a contest. His opponents inside and outside Congress were a motley but formidable crew. Their arguments were as varied as their personalities. Some said it was unconstitutional to rule territories acquired in war without the consent of the people concerned. Senator George Frisbie Hoar of Massachusetts welcomed the annexation of Hawaii but opposed the acquisition of the Philippines because he believed the Hawaiian peoples were in favor of annexation and the Filipinos were opposed to it. The "little Americans," led by novelist Mark Twain, editor E. L. Godkin, and reform politician Carl Schurz, dreaded that imperial responsibilities would entail increased armaments and involve the United States in confrontation with rival powers. Steel tycoon Andrew Carnegie said that imperialism would encourage an American aristocracy and erode individualism. Thomas B. Reed represented a racist school of thought, aghast at the prospect of introducing people from the South Seas into the United States. Congressman Champ Clark of Missouri remarked of the Filipinos, "No matter whether they are fit to govern themselves or not, they are not fit to govern us." He ridiculed the idea of "a Chinese senator from Hawaii, with his pigtail hanging down his back, with his pagan joss in his hand," arguing in pidjin English with Henry Cabot Lodge.

Expansionists vehemently denied that the United States was about to engage in imperial competition with Europe and argued that their aims were limited to coaling stations and naval bases on strategic islands. They suggested an American naval line from the

Atlantic in the East to Cuba in the Caribbean to an isthmian canal and from there to Hawaii, Guam, and Manila in the Pacific. "McKinleyism," said its advocates, meant control of islands en route to Asia, not colonies on the continent itself.

In the Senate debate, those opposed to annexation concentrated their case on historical and constitutional grounds, that the acquisition of colonies was immoral. They argued that the United States could hardly uphold the Monroe Doctrine to protect the New World from the Old if it annexed remote territories across the Pacific. What remained unperceived by both the proponents and opponents of expansion were the responsibilities it involved.

The treaty was actually signed on December 10, 1898. To compensate Spain the United States paid $20 million for the Philippines, Puerto Rico, and Guam. When the Senate voted on the treaty on February 6, 1899, it was ratified by 57 votes to 27, only 2 votes more than the necessary two thirds majority.

It was followed by a Filipino revolt led by Emilio Aguinaldo that lasted two years and in which more people died than in the war of 1898. It ended with the capture of Aguinaldo on March 27, 1901. The American military government was replaced on March 4, 1901, by a civil commission of four members. William Howard Taft, a circuit judge, headed the commission to establish a civil government in the Philippines. The average weight of the commissioners was 227 pounds, and it was said the natives would find them "an imposing spectacle." Carnegie wrote to a friend in the cabinet, "You seem to have finished your work of civilizing the Filipinos; it is thought that about 8,000 of them have been completely civilized and sent to Heaven; I hope you like it."

The loss of American lives in the course of the Filipino revolt widened the debate about American imperialism. In February 1899, British poet Rudyard Kipling published his famous appeal to racial and patriotic duty:

> Take up the White Man's burden,
> Send forth the best ye breed . . .
> To wait in heavy harness,
> On fluttering folk and wild—
> Your new-caught sullen peoples,
> Half devil and half child.

His poem was generally taken as an address to America in the Philippines as well as to Britain in South Africa. Among the many parodies the most pithy was provided by the *New York Times*, which penetrated the moral myth to expose the material practice of imperialism.

> Take up the White Man's burden;
> Send forth your sturdy sons,
> And load them down with whiskey
> And Testaments and guns.
>
> Throw in a few diseases
> To spread in tropic climes,
> For there the healthy niggers
> Are quite behind the times.

In Cuba, Gen. Leonard Wood, as temporary governor general, devised the future form of the island's relations with the United States. In 1900, after Havana had been much improved by progressive methods of sanitation, over 1,400 people—mainly Spanish immigrants—died there in an epidemic of yellow fever. A commission of four army surgeons under Dr. Walter Reed believed the theory of Cuban physician Dr. Carlos Finlay that yellow fever was transmitted by the stegomyia mosquito. Unlike the 700 other species of mosquito, the stegomyia lives in houses and lays its eggs only in clean water. Their research was fatal for two members of the commission, Dr. James Carroll and Dr. Jesse W. Lazear, but proved Finlay's theory. Gen. William Crawford Gorgas, as chief sanitary officer in Havana, continued his campaign to cleanse the city, exterminate the stegomyia mosquito, and eliminate the disease.

Their efforts focused American attention on the responsibilities of the United States toward Cuba. William Allen White was quite typical of journalists when in the *Emporia Gazette* of March 20, 1899, he expressed a philosophy of racist supremacy.

Only Anglo-Saxons can govern themselves. The Cubans will need a despotic government for many years to restrain anarchy until Cuba is filled with Yankees. Uncle Sam the First will have to govern Cuba as Alphonso the Thirteenth governed it. . . . It is the Anglo-Saxon's manifest destiny to go forth as a world conqueror. He will take possession of the islands of the sea. . . . This is what fate holds for the chosen people. It is so written. . . . It is to be.

The president agreed. In his message of December 1899, McKinley argued that the new Cuba "must needs be bound to us by ties of singular intimacy and strength if its enduring welfare is to be assured." Underlying these sentiments was the president's design to turn the fledgling republic into an American protectorate. The Platt amendment to an army appropriation bill of March 2, 1901, allowed the president to end the occupation of Cuba after its government agreed to five conditions: never to make a treaty that would impair its independence; never to contract a debt it could not repay; to consent to American rights of intervention to preserve Cuba's independence and stabilize its government; to execute a sanitary program planned during American occupation; and to allow the United States a naval base on the island.

American imperialism was both a fulfillment and a betrayal of American traditions. It was a logical extension of the Monroe Doctrine, by which the United States claimed the right to preserve the New World from the Old, and a natural development of Manifest Destiny. Although the United States had acquired much of its continental territory, such as Florida and Alaska, by purchase, it had also acquired much by war—Texas, California, New Mexico, and Arizona from Mexico and the central plains and Great American Desert from the indigenous Indians. However, the notion of holding colonies was alien to the principles of the Revolution and the Constitution. And because the war of 1898 was fought overseas, it set precedents in strategy, tactics, and diplomacy.

The sudden acquisition of territories overseas, moreover, posed various constitutional questions about the civil rights of the peoples involved. In a series of test cases, the *Insular* cases, of which all but two were decided on May 27, 1901, the Supreme Court resolved the controversy with a sophistical distinction. By a majority of 5 to 4 it declared that the Philippines and Puerto Rico were territories appurtenant to, but not part of, the United States, and thus that their peoples were subjects, not citizens. The ar-

After a promising start to a career in politics Theodore Roosevelt suddenly withdrew from public life following the deaths of his beloved wife and mother on the same day in 1884. He retired to a ranch in the Badlands of Dakota. To publicize his activities, he had his photograph taken in 1885 in costume but in a photographic studio and thus added luster to his legend on his return to politics in 1886. (Library of Congress).

gument was not about theory but about tariff. According to the Court's decision, the United States could both acquire the islands and yet erect a tariff wall against their crops of sugar and tobacco that would otherwise compete as imports with its own produce in the domestic market. Mr. Dooley, the Irish American saloon keeper invented by Peter Finley Dunne at the turn of the century to satirize politicians, concluded his discussion of the *Insular* cases with, "no matter whether the constitution follows th' flag or not, th' Supreme Court follows th' illiction returns."

THE OPEN DOOR

McKinley planned to shape American economic growth by selling goods overseas, especially in Asia. He believed that it was necessary to cooperate with, rather than compete against, other European countries; and in order to ensure cooperation, he sought international tariff reciprocity. Although nations with highly developed industries considered that China was the natural market for expanding production, they paid little heed to the fundamental obstacles in the way. Few of the Chinese population of 400 million were either interested in, or rich enough to buy, Western goods; and most of the population lived in a vast and remote hinterland beyond the reach of existing transportation.

In the 1890s industrial goods accounted for 90 percent of American exports to China, rising in value from $3 million at the beginning of the decade to $13 million at the end. This dramatic increase suggested even greater capacity and profits if only the United States could penetrate China's social infrastructure and provide credit and expertise to develop its economy and transportation. This was recognized by a group of businessmen in cotton, mining, and railroads, who organized themselves as a Washington lobby, the Committee on American Interests in China, on January 6, 1898, and, on June 9, 1898, changed the title to the American Asiatic Association.

Secretary of State John Hay decided to lend diplomatic weight to such efforts. He wanted a so-called Open Door policy to supersede the existing spheres-of-influence policy, which meant, in practice, the partition of China by the great powers. Hay's Open

Door Notes to Britain, Germany, and Russia of September 6, 1899, and later to France, Italy, and Japan, sought their agreement on three subjects: that none of them would interfere with the trading rights of others in China; that Chinese officials should collect a tariff on all foreign imports; that none of the powers would charge the others discriminatory rates for the use of harbors and railroads in their sections of Chinese territory. Britain agreed on certain conditions, and Russia procrastinated. The remaining powers said they would concur provided all the others did so. On March 20, 1900, Hay decided to interpret these somewhat recalcitrant replies as "final and definitive" assent to his proposals. His biographer, Tyler Dennett, explains that the First Open Door Notes were essentially public announcements intended to crystallize public opinion.

However, as a historian of foreign policy, Richard Leopold, explains, "wishful thinking and unwarranted assumptions were not enough" to turn publicity into policy. Events undermined announcements. Chinese xenophobia found expression in the Boxer movement that on June 13, 1900, attacked foreign legations in the capital, Peking, killing 231 people. It was quelled by troops of the great powers on August 4, 1900. The great powers then exacted an outrageous indemnity of $333 million from China, of which $24 million went, temporarily, to the United States. The United States returned $10 million to China, which its government used to establish a trust fund for the education of Chinese youths in both China and the United States.

The Open Door was no longer even ajar. Hay decided to revise his First Notes. His Second Open Door Notes were, like the First, instructions to American envoys abroad. But this time they were unilateral. On July 3, 1900, Hay issued a circular diplomatic note extending American policy toward China, protecting trade rights of the Open Door, and seeking a solution to assure China of permanent safety and peace. Hay neither sought nor received any treaty or reply. Both the First and Second Open Door Notes represented an American attempt to persuade China to accept the United States as moderator in its relations with other powers. Moreover, both McKinley and Hay hoped that China would, in time, identify its economic interests with those of the United States.

McKinley's successful foreign policy symbolized America's newfound sense of national destiny. His compromises in domestic affairs were presented by his allies as the foundation of lasting stability with material benefits. His political and personal stature was now higher than that of any other president in the Gilded Age.

Thus in 1900 McKinley's rival, William Jennings Bryan, realized that he needed to retain the silver issue to recapture the Democratic nomination but that for the actual campaign he must replace it with something else. He decided to make imperialism the main issue of the campaign and called for the freeing of the new dependencies. Thus, the principal issue of the election of 1900 was annexation of territories overseas. Republicans referred to it as expansion; Democrats called it imperialism. Republican Senator George Frisbie Hoar of Massachusetts, an eloquent opponent of expansion, believed that Bryan's use of the issue to further his election campaign actually made the policy of imperialism much worse. Without Bryan's interference, Democratic senators opposed to expansion would have joined the Republicans in defeating the Philippines treaty. Instead, they were distracted and confused by his policies of liberation and voted for ratification subject to various conditions that were to involve America in needless expense.

George Dewey, the hero of Manila Bay, was under great pressure from newspapers and his ambitious second wife to challenge Bryan for the Democratic nomination. His announcement on April 3, 1900, that he would enter the race was received with regret by his admirers and ridicule by his opponents. It had been proposed in 1898 that Dewey's victory be commemorated by a classical arch of triumph to be paid for by public subscription and erected at the junction of Fifth Avenue and Twenty-third Street in New York City. To encourage subscriptions and provide a splendid focal point for Dewey's triumphal procession through New York in 1899 a full-scale model in wood and plaster was erected on the site. As Dewey's popularity waned, subscriptions lagged and the white paint and plaster peeled. The arch was now considered a dangerous nuisance. In December 1900 the grand design was abandoned. The model was demolished and carted away to the city dump. Mr. Dooley commented sourly, "When a grateful raypublic, Mr. Hinnissy, builds an ar'rch to its conquering hero, it should be made of brick, so that we can have something more convanyient to hurl after him when he has passed by."

PROGRESSIVISM

Just exactly what the United States had accomplished in the Gilded Age was assessed in 1897, somewhat caustically, also by Mr. Dooley:

I have seen America spread out from th' Atlantic to th' Pacific, with a branch office iv th' Standard Ile Comp'ny in ivry hamlet. I've seen th' shackles dropped fr'm th' slave, so's he cud by lynched in Ohio. . . . An' th' invintions . . . th' cotton-gin an' th' gin sour an' th' bicycle an' th' flyin'-machine an' th' nickel-in-th'-slot machine an' th' Croker machine an' th' sody-fountain an'—crownin' wurruk iv our civilization— th' cash raygister.

This emphasis on material progress without spiritual satisfaction was disturbing to many Americans. Moreover, it was not only countryfolk who felt displaced by the political and industrial changes of the Gilded Age. By 1900 middle-class Americans were responding to two challenges to social stability. One was the control of political and economic life by big business. The other was unrest and discontent among the lower classes, especially factory workers and immigrants. At the turn of the century the most important political issue was still monopolies popularly called "the trusts." In 1896 Charles B. Spaur estimed that 1 percent of the population owned more than half of the total national wealth. In 1897 the total value of all corporations individually worth $1 million or more was $170 million. In 1900 the total value was $5 billion. When Andrew Carnegie sold out to the House of Morgan in 1901 the bonds and stocks issued by Morgan for the United States Steel Corporation were valued at $1.41 billion (q.v.). At this time the average annual wage was between $400 and $500.

High society was at its most glamorous and glittering even as the Gilded Age drew to its close. The inauguration of President William McKinley and Vice President Theodore Roosevelt in 1901 was followed by a splendid ball amid the Corinthian columns of the Pension Building, Washington, D.C., designed by Montgomery C. Meigs and built between 1882 and 1886. (Library of Congress).

In these circumstances it is not surprising that historian Mark Sullivan, writing in 1925, should suggest that the average American had the feeling that he "was being 'put upon,' his horizons shortened by an unseen enemy whom he called the Invisible Government, the Money Interests, the Gold Bugs, Wall Street, the Trusts, and for Westerners, the East." In 1898 Mark Twain commented sarcastically of a fictitious "Blessings-of-Civilization Trust," "This world-girdling accumulation of trained morals, high principles, and justice cannot do an unright thing, an unfair thing, an ungenerous thing, an unclean thing."

The arguments of Henry Demarest Lloyd against the trusts and

Jacob Riis against the slums and those of William Harvey for silver and Edward Bellamy for utopia were debated in the country at large. Even Social Darwinism, the dominant philosophy of the Gilded Age, underwent a transformation at its close. Once it had simply been a justification of laissez-faire, favoring the survival of the most fit economically. At the turn of the century William James, John Dewey, and later, Thorstein Veblen and Charles Beard all argued in their different ways that man could direct and control the forces around him. Thus society could be improved. The new reformers, progressives, developed an inordinate trust in the beneficial results of a good political mechanism.

Progressives wanted to make government more representative and democratic by a whole series of devices—the secret ballot, the initiative, referendum, and recall, the direct primary, and the direct election of senators. The first direct primary election was held in Minneapolis in September 1900 on terms prescribed by the state assembly in 1899. In 1901 Governor Robert La Follette had the direct primary introduced in Wisconsin. Woman suffrage had made a beginning in four sparsely populated states of the West where there were even fewer women than men. It was adopted by Wyoming (1869), Colorado (1893), Utah (1896), and Idaho (1896).

Progressives were also determined to make government more efficient, not only by eradicating corrupt practices, but also by reforming the structure of local government. Missouri was the first state to give its cities home rule in 1875. We earlier noted how the hurricane in Galveston, Texas, in 1900 that destroyed the city offered progressives there an opportunity to devise new administrative agencies to ensure efficient government. Progressive leaders were urban and urbane. They came from northern European Protestant families. They were educated at colleges and entered professions or businesses that gave them social or economic status. As reform candidates they suddenly found they could beat the old party machine. When people were aroused they got a strong leader and overdue reforms. Bryan tried to identify himself with the new form of dissent, but he was tarnished because of his association with silver. It was, instead, Theodore Roosevelt who became the principal spokesman for the progressives.

Roosevelt was the scion of a wealthy New York family originally of Dutch extraction. His was the seventh generation to be
born in Manhattan. His father, Theodore, was a Lincoln Republican later committed to reform movements. His mother, Martha
Bulloch, was a southern belle who imparted to "Teedie" her love
of heroics and sense of humor. Roosevelt was frail and hyperac-
tive, suffering from violent attacks of asthma on Sundays and poor
eyesight on weekdays. But he did well at Harvard and entered
public life as an assemblyman in Albany in 1881 when he was
twenty-three. Both his beloved mother and first wife died within
hours of each other on February 14, 1884, in his house. For the
next two years he retired to the private life of a rancher in the
Badlands of Dakota Territory. His injunction to slow cowboys,
"Hasten forward there quickly," was much quoted in local saloons. He remarried and reentered public life, working as a civil
service commissioner from 1889 to 1895 and then as president of
the board of police commissioners in New York.

He served McKinley as assistant secretary of the navy, but during the war of 1898 resigned to get into the fighting. He assembled
a motley crew of soldiers, the Rough Riders, each seeking adventure and glory. The courageous and dexterous performance of
his regiment at San Juan Hill turned him into a legend. Subsequently Roosevelt described his wartime adventures in a best-sell-
ing book. Mr. Dooley's advice to the author was, "If I was him
I'd call th' book 'Alone in Cubia.'" He also suggested alternative
titles: "Th' Biography iv a Hero be Wan who Knows"; and "Th'
Darin' Exploits iv a Brave Man be an Actual Eye-Witness, th'
Account iv th' Desthruction iv Spanish Power in th' Ant Hills, as
it fell fr'm th' lips iv Teddy Rosenfelt an' was took down be his
own hands."

Although New York State was, at this time, held by the Republicans, the administration there had been discredited by extravagance and malpractice. The state boss, Senator Tom Platt,
recognized that the only way the Republicans could retain power
was by fielding a truly popular and untarnished candidate for governor in the state elections of 1898. Roosevelt was the obvious
choice. But Platt was apprehensive that, as governor, Roosevelt
would act as independently and aggressively as he had throughout

his public career. His fears were justified after Roosevelt won the election and took office in 1899. Roosevelt refused to appoint to public office the party hacks nominated by Platt. Furthermore, he initiated independent social legislation of a kind that was anathema to the Old Guard on such subjects as conservation, labor, industrial safety, workmen's compensation, and tenement dwellings.

Roosevelt then proposed a franchise tax to make street railways pay taxes on the true value of their franchises. He wanted to erode the outrageous profits of these traditional Republican supporters. Beside himself with rage, Platt had the speaker of the state legislature tear up Roosevelt's message on the subject rather than read it to the assembly. Roosevelt responded by dispatching a second message on April 28, 1899, rallied his supporters, and had the bill passed over the unofficial veto of the boss. Platt realized that his days were numbered. If Roosevelt remained in office another two years, Platt reckoned he would destroy the entire boss system. Yet Roosevelt's popularity was such that Platt could not deny him renomination in 1900 without discrediting the Republicans and inviting people to vote for the Democrats.

Platt decided to remove his exasperating protégé by getting him nominated as vice presidential candidate at the Republican National Convention in June 1900. Roosevelt, like others ambitious for the presidency itself, regarded his proposed elevation as a relegation. He told his confidant Henry Cabot Lodge, "I should be simply shelved as Vice President." Not since Martin Van Buren in 1836 had an incumbent vice president been elected president. Lodge was the only one of Roosevelt's friends who advised him to accept the nomination. But Roosevelt's growing popularity in the country at large and especially in the West worked against his initial inclination and for Platt. As far as Roosevelt's many admirers were concerned, being vice president was better than being governor of New York. Mark Hanna liked Roosevelt and what he represented no more than Platt did. As national boss he could refuse Platt's suggestion and wanted to do so. But he realized that Roosevelt's presence on the ticket would strengthen McKinley's chances of reelection very considerably.

McKinley was duly renominated on June 19, 1900, in Philadelphia. And Roosevelt gave in to the Republican elders. The *New*

ROOSEVELT'S IDEA OF REORGANIZATION.

As governor of New York Theodore Roosevelt initiated progressive legislation independent of, and opposed to, the party machine of Senator Tom Platt. Platt realized that if Roosevelt remained in office much longer the days of the old guard would be numbered and determined to be rid of his exasperating protégé by having him elected vice president. (Library of Congress).

York Journal carried a cartoon showing Platt as a cowboy astride a pony. He has thrown his lariat and caught Roosevelt by the foot and is ready to tie him up like a wild steer. It was Roosevelt who did the active campaigning, visiting twenty-four states and making about 700 speeches. McKinley simply repeated his front porch campaign of 1896. Americans were urged: "Don't haul down the flag" now that the Republicans had provided a "Full Dinner Pail."

Bryan was unanimously renominated at the Democratic National Convention in Kansas City on July 5. The Populists had already divided into two feuding factions. "The Spanish war finished us," stated Tom Watson, "The blare of the bugle drowned the voice of the reformer." In 1900 they once again fused with the Democrats.

In the election of 1900 McKinley took 7,218,491 votes to Bryan's 6,356,734, a majority of 51.7 percent. He carried twenty-eight states to Bryan's seventeen and with them 292 votes in the electoral college to Bryan's 155. When Platt was asked if he would attend the inauguration, he replied, "Yes, I am going to see Theodore Roosevelt take the veil."

On September 6, 1901, McKinley attended the Pan American Exposition in Buffalo. In the Temple of Music he bent forward to give his customary red carnation to a little girl. He was shot at close range by an unemployed artisan and self-styled anarchist, Leon Czolgosz. "I didn't believe that one man should have so much service and another man should have none," he told his captors afterwards. Like Garfield before him, McKinley did not die immediately of the gunshot wounds in his stomach but of gangrene, which set in and killed him eight days later. Roosevelt was on a hunting trip in the Adirondacks when the news came that McKinley was dying. He set out for Buffalo and arrived after McKinley had died. On September 14, 1901, Roosevelt took the oath of office in the same house where McKinley lay dead. The Gilded Age was over. The Age of the Titans—Roosevelt, Bryan, and Woodrow Wilson—had begun. As Walt Whitman remarked, "Produce great persons: the rest follows."

CHRONOLOGY

AMERICA IN THE GILDED AGE, 1865—1901

1865 Appomattox
Lincoln assassinated;
   Andrew Johnson becomes president
Reconstruction
13th Amendment: slavery abolished
Black Codes

1866 Civil Rights Act
Fetterman massacre
National Labor Union organized

1867 Reconstruction Acts
Tenure of Office Act
Indian Act
National Grange of the Patrons of Husbandry founded
Christopher Sholes invents typewriter
Alaska purchase

1868 14th Amendment: freedom of individual
Johnson impeached
Refrigerator car invented
Grant defeats Seymour

1869 Central Pacific and Union Pacific transcontinental railroad completed
      "Black Friday" gold crisis
      Knights of Labor founded
      Westinghouse air brake invented

1870 15th Amendment: equal rights
      First Enforcement Act
      Standard Oil Company of Ohio organized
      Tweed Ring broken

1871 Second and Third Enforcement Acts
      Chicago fire
      Alabama claims settled

1872 Grant defeats Greeley
      Crédit Mobilier scandals

1873 Salary Grab Act
      Collapse of Jay Cooke and Co;
          Panic and Depression

1874 J. F. Glidden invents barbed wire
      Red River War begins

1875 Resumption Act
      Strike of the Molly Maguires
      Civil Rights Act
      Whiskey Ring broken

1876 Disputed election
      Cruikshank Opinion
      National Independent (Greenback) party founded
      Custer's Last Stand
      Alexander Graham Bell invents telephone
      Centennial Exhibition

1877 Hayes ends Reconstruction
Desert Land Act
Great Railroad Strike
Munn v. *Illinois*

1878 Bland-Allison Silver Purchase Act
Timber and Stone Act

1879 Return to specie payments
Thomas Edison invents incandescent lamp

1880 James Bonsack invents cigarette making machine

1881 Garfield assassinated; Chester A. Arthur becomes president
Star Route Frauds
Helen Hunt Jackson, *A Century of Dishonor*
Henry Demarest Lloyd, *The Story of a Great Monopoly*
Henry James, *Washington Square* and *The Portrait of a Lady*

1882 Chinese Exclusion Act
Trusts devised by Standard Oil

1883 Pendleton Civil Service Act
Civil Rights cases
Northern Pacific Railroad completed;
Atchison, Topeka and Santa Fe Railroad completed
Standard time adopted by railroads

1884 Cleveland defeats Blaine
Mark Twain, *Huckleberry Finn*

1885 Combine harvester invented

1886 Haymarket riot
AFL founded
Wabash case
Statue of Liberty

1887   Interstate Commerce Act
Dawes Severalty Act
Hatch Act
Hawaii cedes Pearl Harbor to U.S.

1888   Edward Bellamy, *Looking Backward*
Harrison defeats Cleveland

1889   Oklahoma opened
Jane Addams opens Hull House
Commercial Union of American States

1890   Closing of frontier
Massacre of Wounded Knee
McKinley Tariff
Sherman Anti-Trust Act
Sherman Silver Purchase Act
Mississippi constitution and poll tax

1891   Forest Reserve Act
People's Party (Populists) meets at Cincinnati

1892   Homestead strike
Cleveland defeats Harrison

1893   Great Northern Railroad completed
Panic and Depression
Repeal of Sherman Silver Purchase Act
Frederick Jackson Turner's "frontier thesis"
Chicago School of Architecture

1894   Carey Irrigation Act
Pullman strike
Coxey's Army

1895   *E.C. Knight and Co.* v. *U.S.*
Pollock v. *Farmers' Loan and Trust Co.*
Cuban revolt
Anglo-American dispute in Venezuela

1896   *Plessy* v. *Ferguson*
      Guglielmo Marconi invents wireless telegraphy
      McKinley defeats Bryan

1897   Maximum Freight Rate Case
      William James, *The Will to Believe*

1898   Spanish American War: U.S. takes possession of Philippines,
         Guam, and Puerto Rico
      Annexation of Hawaii

1899   Hay's Note on Open Door
      Three-nation protectorate of Samoa
      Frank Norris, *McTeague*

1900   Second Note on Open Door
      Gold Standard Act
      Galveston devastated by hurricane

1901   McKinley assassinated; Theodore Roosevelt becomes president
      Platt amendment
      Morgan buys out Carnegie

SOURCES

Notwithstanding the special interest of such individual collections of papers as those of Thomas Edison at Menlo Park and Jane Addams at Swarthmore College, the Library of Congress offers the widest horizon in primary sources in the Gilded Age. It houses the papers of all the presidents except Hayes; their secretaries of state; and other leading actors on the political scene, including Horace Greeley, Carl Schurz, William Jennings Bryan, and James G. Blaine. These collections also contain a wealth of personal material, such as the fragment of a moving account by Mrs. James Blaine of Garfield's assassination. Such documents allow us to peer into the personalities behind the policies. The papers of the Pinkerton family, for example, reveal a bitter heritage of hatred and envy in the relationships between father and sons that gives personal substance to the notorious legend of implacable defiance of the rights of the public for the sake of private interests. The Library of Congress also has, among those of the robber barons, the papers of Andrew Carnegie, and, among the inventors, those of Alexander Graham Bell and his family. They, too, throw light on the consuming ambition and dexterous professional skill of these pivotal entrepreneurs.

The two most crucial novels for interpreting the period are complementary: the satire, *The Gilded Age*, by Mark Twain and Charles Warner (Boston, 1873); and the utopian *Looking Backward 2000–1887* by Edward Bellamy (Boston, 1888).

The memoirs of Blaine (1884–86), Sherman (1895), Powderley (1890), and Gompers (1925) provide a fund of insight into society and politics, as do those of Carnegie (1920), Booker T. Washington (1900), and Jane Addams (1910). Other valuable primary sources include the plangent polemics of social critics in a series of classic exposures that have influenced all subsequent interpretations of the period. They include Henry George, *Progress and Poverty* (New York, 1879); Henry Demarest Lloyd, *Wealth Against Commonwealth* (New York, 1894); and Ida M. Tarbell, *A History of the Standard Oil Company* (New York, 1904).

Primary sources are not limited just to literature. We can learn much about the Gilded Age from two pioneers in the visual arts whose work changed the character of American cities. By his photographs Jacob A. Riis sharpened the perception of the middle class about the urban environment. They are held in the Jacob A. Riis collection of the Museum of the City of New York and, also, the Library of Congress. A hundred are reproduced in the modern Dover edition of *How the Other Half Lives*, edited by Charles A. Madison, (New York, 1971). By his architectural designs Louis Sullivan transformed the facade and skyline of American cities. His ideas can be studied directly from his drawings collected in *The Drawings of Louis Henry Sullivan* edited by Paul Edward Sprague (Princeton, 1979). The magnificent collection of superb contemporary photographs of people and places by Frances Benjamin Johnston in the Library of Congress is another indispensable visual source.

The Bibliography is, like the book itself, intended as a basic guide to students new to the history of the period. It gives greater emphasis to factual accounts of the years from 1865 to 1901 than to more sophisticated interpretations that cover a wider span of time and require of their readers much detailed knowledge. Thus it does not include works on the search for order, the mind of the South, the transformation of the school, or virgin land. Many historians of the Gilded Age, or of special topics within it, have been most prolific. To include all the books of such excellent writers as H. Wayne Morgan on politics and imperialism; Alfred Dupont Chandler, Jr., on business; C. Vann Woodward on the South; Maldwyn Jones on immigration; Alexander B. Callow on cities;

Ray Allen Billington and Frederick Merk on the West; Lawrence Goodwyn on Populism; John Hope Franklin on blacks; and Carl Degler on social history would make the whole list very long indeed. The bibliography, therefore, mentions only the truly seminal works of these and other authors. Without the benefit of their research and insight my task would have been harder.

The most comprehensive single bibliography of the period is Vincent P. DeSantis, *The Gilded Age, 1877–1896* (Northbrook, Illinois, 1973). Other useful bibliographies include David L. Smith, *The American and Canadian West* (Oxford, 1980) and David L. Brye (editor), *European Immigration and Ethnicity in the United States and Canada* (Oxford, 1983).

Statistics given in this book on population, immigration, agricultural and industrial production, and election returns are from the United States Bureau of the Census, *Historical Statistics of the United States 2* vols., (Washington, D.C., 1975). Those on gold and silver production and the currency are from the United States Bureau of the Census, *Statistical Abstract of the Census* (Washington, D.C., 1922). A useful abridged version of the bicentennial edition is Ben J. Wattenberg (ed.), *The Statistical History of the United States From Colonial Times to the Present* (New York, 1976).

BIBLIOGRAPHY

GENERAL

Carl N. Degler, *The Age of the Economic Revolution, 1876–1900* (Glenville, Ill., 1967)

Howard Wayne Morgan, *Unity and Culture: The United States 1877–1900* (London, 1971); ed., *The Gilded Age: A Reappraisal* (Syracuse, N.Y., 1963; revised, 1970)

Robert Higgs, *The Transformation of the American Economy, 1865–1914: An Essay in Interpretation* (New York, 1971)

Thomas C. Cochran and William Miller, *The Age of Enterprise: A Social History of Industrial America* (New York, 1942)

John A. Garraty, *The New Commonwealth 1877–1890* (New York, 1968)

Robert H. Walker, *Life in the Age of Enterprise, 1865–1900* (New York, 1967, 1971)

Richard Guy Wilson, Dianne H. Pilgrim, and Richard N. Murray, *The American Renaissance, 1876–1917* (New York, 1979)

INVENTIONS

John W. Oliver, *History of American Technology* (New York, 1956)

H. J. Habakkuk, *American and British Technology in the Nineteenth Century* (Cambridge, UK, 1962)

Waldemar B. Kaempffert, *A Popular History of American Invention* (New York, 1924)

Robert E. Conot, *A Streak of Luck—Edison* (New York, 1979)

Robert V. Bruce, *Bell: Alexander Graham Bell and the Conquest of Solitude* (Boston, 1973)

Siegfried Giedion, *Mechanization Takes Command* (New York, 1948)

1876

John Maas, *The Glorious Enterprise: The Centennial Exhibition of 1876 and H. J. Schwarzmann, Architect in Chief* (New York, 1973)

William Pierce Randal, *Centennial: American Life in 1876* (Philadelphia, 1969)

Dee Brown, *The Year of the Century, 1876* (New York, 1966)

RAILROADS

John F. Stover, *The Life and Decline of the American Railroad* (New York, 1970); *The Railroads of the South, 1865–1900* (Chapel Hill, N.C., 1955)

George R. Taylor and Irene D. Neu, *The American Railroad Network, 1861–1890* (Cambridge, Mass., 1956)

Robert W. Fogel, *Railroads and American Economic Growth: Essays in Econometric History* (Baltimore, 1964)

Edward G. Campbell, *The Reorganization of the American Railroad System, 1893–1900* (New York, 1938)

Alfred Dupont Chandler, Jr., *The Railroads, Pioneers in Modern Management* (New York, 1979)

Thomas C. Cochran, *Railroad Leaders, 1845–1890* (Cambridge, Mass., 1953)

INDUSTRY AND CORPORATIONS

Rendigs Fels, *American Business Cycles, 1865–1897* (Chapel Hill, N.C., 1959)

Alfred Dupont Chandler, Jr., *The Visible Hand: The Managerial Revolution in American Business* (Cambridge, Mass., 1977)

Glenn Porter and H. C. Livesay, *Merchants and Manufacturers: Studies in the Changing Structure of Nineteenth Century Marketing* (Baltimore, 1971)

George H. Evans, Jr., *Business Incorporation in the United States, 1800–1943* (New York, 1948)

Edward C. Kirkland, *Industry Comes of Age: Business, Labor and Public Policy, 1860–1897* (New York, 1961); *Dream and Thought in the Business Community, 1860–1900* (Ithaca, N.Y., 1956; Chicago, 1964)

Sidney Fine, *Laissez-Faire and the General Welfare State: A Study of Conflict in American Thought, 1865–1901* (Ann Arbor, Mich., 1956)

Richard Hofstadter, *Social Darwinism in American Thought, 1860–1915* (Philadelphia and London, 1944 and 1945)

ROCKEFELLER AND OIL

Allan Nevins, *Study in Power: John D. Rockefeller, Industrialist and Philanthropist* (New York, 2 vols., 1940, 1953)

Ralph W. Hidy and Muriel E. Hidy, *Pioneering in Big Business, 1882–1911: A History of the Standard Oil Company, New Jersey* (New York, 1955)

Jules Abels, *The Rockefeller Billions: The Story of the World's Most Stupendous Fortune* (New York and London, 1965)

Bruce Bringhurst, *Antitrust and the Oil Monopoly: The Standard Oil Cases, 1890–1911* (Westport, Conn., 1979)

CARNEGIE AND STEEL

Joseph F. Wall, *Andrew Carnegie* (New York, 1970)

Louis M. Hacker, *The World of Andrew Carnegie, 1865–1900* (Philadelphia and New York, 1968)

T. A. Wertime, *The Coming of the Age of Steel* (Chicago, 1962)

MORGAN AND FINANCE

Andrew Sinclair, *Corsair: The Life of J. Pierpont Morgan* (Boston, 1981)

Cass Canfield, *The Incredible Pierpont Morgan: Financier and Art Collector* (New York, 1974)

Frederick Lewis Allen, *The Great Pierpont Morgan* (New York, 1949)

George Wheeler, *Pierpont Morgan and Friends: The Anatomy of a Myth* (New York, 1973)

ROBBER BARONS

Anna Rochester, *Rulers of Americas: A Study of Finance Capital* (London and New York, 1936)

Matthew Josephson, *The Robber Barons* (London, 1962)

Stewart H. Holbrook, *The Age of the Moguls* (New York, 1953)

W. Lloyd Warner and J. Abegglen, *Big Business Leaders in America* (New York, 1955)

Arthur D. H. Smith, *Commodore Vanderbilt: An Epic of American Achievement* (New York, 1927)

William Letwin, *Law and Economic Policy in America: The Evolution of the Sherman Anti-Trust Act* (New York, 1965)

IMMIGRATION

Maldwyn A. Jones, *American Immigration* (Chicago, 1960)

Marcus Lee Hansen, *The Immigrant in American History* (Cambridge, Mass., 1948)

Oscar Handlin, *Race and Nationality in American Life* (Boston, 1957); *The Uprooted* (Boston, 1952)

Leonard Dinnerstein and David Reimers, *Ethnic Americans: A History of Immigration and Assimilation* (New York, 1975)

Thomas J. Archdeacon, *Becoming American: an ethnic history* (New York, 1983)

Charlotte Erickson, *American Industry and the European Immigrant, 1860–1885* (Cambridge, Mass., 1957)

Philip A. M. Taylor, *The Distant Magnet: European Emigration to the U.S.A.* (New York, 1971)

Alan M. Kraut, *The Huddled Masses: the immigrant in American society, 1880–1921* (New York and London, 1982)

Barbara Solomon, *Ancestors and Immigrants* (Cambridge, Mass., 1956)

John Higham, *Strangers in the Land: Patterns of American Nativism, 1860–1925* (New Brunswick, N.J., 1955); *Send Them to Me: Jews and Other Immigrants in Urban America* (New York, 1975)

Jack Chen, *The Chinese of America* (New York, 1981)

Stuart C. Miller, *The Unwelcome Immigrant: The American Image of the Chinese, 1785–1882* (Berkeley and Los Angeles, 1969)

CITIES

Arthur M. Schlesinger, *The Rise of the City, 1877–1898* (New York, 1933)

Blake McKelvey, *The Urbanization of America, 1860–1915* (New Brunswick, N.J., 1963); *American Urbanization: A Comparative History* (Glenville, Ill., and Brighton, Sussex, 1973)

Alexander B. Callow, Jr., ed., *American Urban History: An Interpretative Reader with Commentaries* (New York, 1969)

Sam Bass Warner, Jr., *Streetcar Suburbs: The Process of Growth in Boston 1870–1900* (Cambridge, Mass., 1962); *The Urban Wilderness: A History of the American City* (New York and London, 1972)

Joy J. Jackson, *New Orleans in the Gilded Age: Politics and Urban Progress, 1880–1896* (Baton Rouge, 1969)

William Bullough, *Cities and Schools in the Gilded Age* (Port Washington, N.Y., 1974)

Laurence R. Veysey, *The Emergence of the American University* (Chicago, 1965)

David Burg, *Chicago's White City of 1893* (Lexington, Ky., 1976)

Harold M. Mayer and Richard C. Wade, *Chicago: Growth of a Metropolis* (Chicago, 1969)

ARCHITECTURE AND PLANNING

Vincent Scully, *American Architecture and Urbanism* (New York, 1969)

Carl Condit, *The Chicago School of Architecture* (Chicago, 1964)

Henry-Russell Hitchcock, *The Architecture of H. H. Richardson and His Times* (Hamden, Conn., 1961; first published, 1936)

Albert Bush-Brown, *Louis Sullivan* (New York, 1960)

BOSSES AND REFORMERS

Alexander B. Callow, Jr., ed., *The City Boss in America* (London, New York, and Toronto, 1976); *The Tweed Ring* (New York, 1966)

Seymour Mandelbaum, *Boss Tweed's New York* (New York, London, and Sydney, 1965)

Leo Hershkowitz, *Tweed's New York: Another Look* (New York, 1977)

Clifford W. Patton, *The Battle for Municipal Reform: Mobilization and Attack, 1875–1900* (Washington, 1940)

Roy Lubove, *The Pregressives and the Slums: Tenement House Reform in New York City, 1890–1917* (Pittsburgh, 1962)

Martin V. Melosi, *Garbage in the Cities: Refuse, Reform, and the Environment 1880–1980* (College Station, Tex., 1981)

Allen F. Davis, *American Heroine: The Life and Legend of Jane Addams* (New York, 1973); *Spearheads for Reform: The Social Settlements and the Progressive Movement, 1890–1914* (New York, 1967)

Charles H. Hopkins, *The Rise of the Social Gospel in American Protestantism, 1865–1915* (New Haven, Conn., and London, 1940)

P. J. Frederick, *Knights of the Golden Rule: The Intellectual as Christian Social Reformer in the 1890s* (Lexington, Ky., 1976)

LABOR

Henry Pelling, *American Labor* (Chicago, 1960)

Foster Rhea Dulles, *Labor in America, a History* (New York, 1949)

Philip Taft, *Organized Labor in American History* (New York, 1964)

Joseph G. Rayback, *A History of American Labor* (New York, revised, 1966; first published, 1959)

Sanford Cohen, *Labor in the United States* (Columbus, Ohio, 3d. ed., 1976; first published, 1960)

Philip S. Foner, *A History of the Labor Movement in the United States,* 4 vols. (New York, 1947–64); *Organized labor and the Black Worker, 1619–1973* (New York, 1974)

Albert Fried, ed., *Except to Walk Free: Documents and Notes in the History of American Labor* (New York, 1974)

Herbert Gutman, *Work, Culture, and Society in Industrializing America* (New York, 1977)

Barbara Wertheimer, *We Were There: The Story of Working Women in America* (New York, 1977)

Irvin Yellowitz, *The Position of the Worker in American Society, 1865–1896* (Englewood Cliffs, N.J., 1969)

NATIONAL UNIONS

Lloyd Ulman, *The Rise of the National Trade Union* (Cambridge, Mass., 1955)

Norman J. Ware, *The Labor Movement in the United States, 1860–1895* (New York, 1929)

Philip Taft, *The AFL in the Time of Gompers* (New York, 1957)

Stuart Bruce Kaufman, *Samuel Gompers and the Origins of the American Federation of Labor, 1848–1896* (Westport, Conn., 1973)

Bernard Mandel, *Samuel Gompers, a Biography* (Yellow Springs, Ohio, 1963)
Gerald N. Grob, *Workers and Utopia: A Study of Ideological Conflict in the American Labor Movement, 1865–1900* (Chicago, 1961, 1976)

LABOR DISPUTES

Samuel Yellen, *American Labor Struggles* (New York, 1969)
Jeremy Brecher, *Strike!* (Boston, 1979)
P. K. Edwards, *Strikes in the United States, 1881–1974* (New York, 1981)
Anthony Bimba, *The Molly Maguires* (New York, 1970)
Wayne G. Broehl, Jr., *The Molly Maguires* (Cambridge, Mass., 1964)
Robert V. Bruce, *1877: Year of Violence* (Indianapolis and New York, 1959)
David Henry, *A History of the Haymarket Affair* (New York, 1963)
Leon Wolff, *Lockout: The Story of the Homestead Strike of 1892* (New York, 1965)
William Carwardine, *The Pullman Strike* (Chicago, 1973)
Ray Ginger, *The Bending Cross: A Biography of Eugene Victor Debs* (New Brunswick, N.J., 1949)
Jerry M. Cooper, *The Army and Civil Disorder—Federal Military Intervention in Labor Disputes, 1877–1900* (Westport, Conn., 1980)
Michael Nash, *Conflict and Accommodation—Coal Miners, Steel Workers, and Socialism, 1890–1920* (Westport, Conn., 1982)

RECONSTRUCTION

Kenneth M. Stampp, *The Era of Reconstruction, America after the Civil War, 1865–1877* (New York and London, 1965)
John Hope Franklin, *Reconstruction after the Civil War* (Chicago, 1961)
Rembert W. Patrick, *The Reconstruction of the Nation* (New York and London, 1967)
James E. Sefton, *Andrew Johnson and the Uses of Constitutional Power* (Boston, 1980)
Harold M. Hyman, *A More Perfect Union: The Impact of the Civil War and Reconstruction on the Constitution* (New York, 1973)
William Gillette, *The Right to Vote: Politics and the Passage of the Fifteenth Amendment* (Baltimore, 1965)

RADICAL RECONSTRUCTION

William R. Brock, *An American Crisis: Congress and Reconstruction, 1865–1867* (London and New York, 1963)
Michael L. Benedict, *A Compromise of Principle: Congressional Republicans and Reconstruction, 1863–1869* (New York, 1974)
Fawn M. Brodie, *Thaddeus Stevens, Scourge of the South* (New York, 1959)

Hans Trefousse, *Impeachment of a President: Andrew Johnson, the Blacks, and Reconstruction* (Knoxville, Tenn., 1975); *Reconstruction: America's First Effort at Racial Democracy* (New York, 1971)

THE SOUTH DURING RECONSTRUCTION

Michael Perman, *Reunion without Compromise: The South and Reconstruction: 1865–1868* (Cambridge, England 1973)

Lawrence F. Litwack, *Been in the Storm as Long: The aftermath of Slavery* (New York, 1979)

James L. Roark, *Masters without Slaves: Southern Planters in the Civil War and Reconstruction* (New York, 1977)

Lawrence N. Powell, *New Masters: Northern Planters during the Civil War and Reconstruction* (New Haven, Conn., 1980)

William S. McFeely, *Yankee Stepfather: General O. O. Howard and the Freedmen* (New Haven, Conn., 1968)

Allen W. Trelease, *White Terror: The Ku Klux Klan: Conspiracy and Southern Reconstruction* (New York, 1971)

THE NEW SOUTH

Comer Vann Woodward, *Origins of the New South, 1877–1913* (Baton Rouge, La., 1951; with a critical essay in recent works by C. B. Dew, 1971)

Melvin L. Greenhut and W. Tate Whitman, eds., *Essays in Southern Economic Development* (Chapel Hill, N.C., 1964)

Paul H. Buck, *The Road to Reunion, 1865–1900* (Boston, 1937)

Paul M. Gaston, *The New South Creed: A Study in Southern Mythmaking* (New York, 1970)

John K. Winkler, *Tobacco Tycoon: The Story of James B. Duke* (New York, 1942)

BLACK AMERICA

Robert Higgs, *Competition and Coercion: Blacks in the American Economy, 1865–1914* (Cambridge and New York, 1977)

Roger L. Ransom and Richard Sutch, *One Kind of Freedom: The Economic Consequences of Emancipation* (Cambridge and New York, 1977)

Stanley P. Hirshson, *Farewell to the Bloody Shirt: Northern Republicans and the Southern Negro, 1877–1893* (Bloomington, Ind., 1962)

Rayford W. Logan, *The Betrayal of the Negro, from Rutherford B. Hayes to Woodrow Wilson* (New York, 1965; first published, 1954)

Vernon Lane Wharton, *The Negro in Mississippi, 1865–1890* (New York, 1947, 1965)

Comer Vann Woodward, *The Strange Career of Jim Crow* (New York, 1955; revised, 1974)

August Meier, *Negro Thought in America, 1880–1915: Racial Ideologies in the Age of Booker T. Washington* (Ann Arbor, Mich., 1963)

Louis R. Harlan, *Booker T. Washington: The Making of a Negro Leader, 1856–1901* (New York, 1972)

J. Morgan Kousser, *The Shaping of Southern Politics: Suffrage Restriction and the Establishment of the One-Party South, 1880–1910* (New Haven, Conn., 1974)

PARTY POLITICS

Leonard D. White, *The Republican Era, 1869–1901 A Study in Administrative History* (New York, 1958)

Robert D. Marcus, *Grand Old Party: Political Structure in the Gilded Age, 1880–1896* (New York, 1971)

David Rothman, *Politics and Power: The United States Senate, 1869–1901* (Cambridge, Mass., 1961)

Matthew Josephson, *The Politicos, 1865–1896* (New York, 1938)

Howard Wayne Morgan, *From Hayes to McKinley: National Party Politics, 1877–1896* (Syracuse, N.Y., 1969)

Frank Tariello, Jr., *The Reconstruction of American Political Ideology, 1865–1917* (Charlottesville, Va., 1982)

Morton Keller, *The Art and Politics of Thomas Nast* (New York, 1968)

HALF BREEDS, STALWARTS, AND REFORM

William S. McFeely, *Grant, a Biography* (New York, 1981)

Allan Nevins, *Hamilton Fish: The Inner History of the Grant Administration* (New York, 1936)

Glyndon G. Van Deusen, *Horace Greeley, Nineteenth Century Crusader* (Philadelphia, 1953)

Keith J. Polakoff, *The Politics of Inertia: The Election of 1876 and the End of Reconstruction* (Baton Rouge, 1973)

Kenneth E. Davison, *The Presidency of Rutherford B. Hayes* (Westport, Conn., 1972)

Donald Barr Chidsey, *The Gentleman from New York: A Life of Roscoe Conkling* (New Haven, Conn., 1935)

Allan Peskin, *Garfield, a Biography* (Kent, Ohio, 1978)

Thomas C. Reeves, *Gentleman Boss: The Life of Chester Alan Arthur* (New York, 1975)

Richard E. Welch, Jr., *George Frisbie Hoar and the Half Breed Republicans* (Cambridge, Mass., 1971)

John Sproat, *The Best Men: Liberal Reformers in the Gilded Age* (New York, 1966)

John M. Dobson, *Politics in the Gilded Age: A New Perspective on Reform* (New York, Washington, London, 1972)

Hans Trefousse, *Carl Schurz, a Biography* (Knoxville, Tenn., 1982)

Ari A. Hoogenbaum, *Outlawing the Spoils, a History of the Civil Service Reform Movement, 1865–1880* (Urbana, Ill., 1960)

Gordon Milne, *George W. Curtis and the Genteel Tradition* (Bloomington, Ind., 1956)

CLEVELAND AND BLAINE

Horace S. Merrill, *Bourbon Leader: Grover Cleveland and the Democratic Party* (Boston, 1957)

Rexford G. Tugwell, *Grover Cleveland* (New York, 1968)

J. Rogers Hollingsworth, *The Whirligig of Politics: The Democracy of Cleveland and Bryan* (Chicago, 1963)

David S. Muzzey, *James G. Blaine: A Political Idol of Other Days* (Port Washington, N.Y., 1934, 1962)

Harry J. Sievers, *Benjamin Harrison, Hoosier President: The White House and After* (New York, 1959)

WESTWARD EXPANSION

Ray Allen Billington with James Blaine Hedges, *Westward Expansion: A History of the American Frontier* (New York, 1974; first published, 1949)

Frederick Merk, *History of the Westward Movement* (New York, 1978)

Howard R. Lamar, *The Far Southwest, 1846–1912* (New Haven, Conn., 1966); *The Readers' Encyclopedia of the American West* (New York, 1977)

Lee Clark Mitchell, *Witnesses to a Vanishing America: The Nineteenth Century Response* (Princeton, 1981)

Earl S. Pomeroy, *The Territories and the United States, 1861–1890* (Seattle, 1969; first published, 1947); *The Pacific Slope* (New York, 1965)

William S. Greever, *The Bonanza West: The Story of the Western Mining Rushes, 1848–1900* (Norman, Okla., 1963)

Rodman W. Paul, *Mining Frontiers of the Far West, 1848–1880* (New York, 1963)

Walter von Richthofen, *Cattle Raising on the Plains of North America* (Norman, Okla., 1964)

Floyd Benjamin Streeter, *Prairie Trails and Cow Towns: The Opening of the Old West* (New York, 1963)

Robert R. Dykstra, *The Cattle Towns* (New York, 1976; first published, 1968)

Gene M. Gressley, *Bankers and Cattlemen* (New York, 1966)

FARMING

Fred A. Shannon, *The Farmer's Last Frontier: Agriculture, 1860–1897* (New York, 1945, 1961)

Gilbert C. Fite, *The Farmer's Frontier 1865–1900* (New York, 1966)

Allan G. Bogue, *From Prairie to Corn Belt* (Chicago, 1963)

Earl W. Hayter, *The Troubled Farmer, 1850–1900: Rural Adjustment to Industrialism* (De Kalb, Ill., 1968)

Paul W. Gates, *Landlords and Tenants on the Prairie Frontier: Studies in American Land Policy* (Ithaca, N.Y., 1973)

INDIANS

Henry C. Dennis, ed., *The American Indian, 1492–1970* (New York, 1971)

Angie Debo, *A History of the Indians of the United States* (Norman, Okla., 1970)

Francis Paul Prucha, *United States Indian Policy: A Critical Bibliography* (Bloomington, Ind., 1977); *Indian policy in the United States: Historical Essays* (Lincoln, Neb., 1981)

Wilcomb E. Washburn, *The Indian in America* (New York, 1975)

Alvin M. Josephy, Jr., *The Indian Heritage of America* (New York, 1968)

PLAINS WARS

Ralph K. Ardvist, *The Long Death* (New York, 1964)

Keith A. Murray, *The Modocs and Their War* (Norman, Okla., 1965)

James C. Olson, *Red Cloud and the Sioux Problem* (Lincoln, Neb., 1965)

John W. Bailey, *Pacifying the Plains: General Alfred Terry and the Decline of the Sioux, 1866–1890* (Westport, Conn., 1978)

Robert Utley, *The Last Days of the Sioux Nation* (New Haven, Conn., 1963)

Odie B. Fauk, *The Geronimo Campaign* (New York, 1969)

Dee Brown, *Bury My Heart at Wounded Knee* (New York, 1971)

INDIAN REFORM

Helen Hunt Jackson, *A Century of Dishonor* (New York, 1881)

Francis P. Prucha, *American Indian Policy in Crisis: Christian Reformers and the Indians, 1865–1900* (Norman, Okla., 1976)

Robert W. Mardock, *Reformers and the American Indian* (Columbia, Mo., 1971)

Henry E. Fritz, *The Movement for Indian Assimilation, 1860–1890* (Philadelphia, 1963)

Paul Wallace Gates, *The Rape of Indian Lands* (New York, 1979)

Leonard A. Carbon, *Indians, Bureaucrats, and Land: The Dawes Act and the Decline of Indian Farming* (Westport, Conn., 1981)

CLOSING OF THE FRONTIER

Ray Allen Billington, *The American Frontier Thesis* (Washington, 1971); *The American Southwest, Image and Reality* (Los Angeles, 1979); *Land of Savagery—*

Land of Promise: The European Image of the American Frontier in the Nineteenth Century (New York, 1980)

Carl Coke Rister, *Land Hunger: David L. Payne and the Oklahoma Boomers* (Norman, Okla., 1942)

FARMERS' MOVEMENTS

Fred A. Shannon, *American Farmers' Movements* (Princeton, 1957)

Theodore Saloutos, *Farmer Movements in the South, 1865–1933* (Berkeley and Los Angeles, 1960)

Solon J. Buck, *The Granger Movement* (Cambridge, Mass., 1913, 1963)

Irwin Unger, *The Greenback Era: A Social and Political History of American Finance, 1865–1879* (Princeton, 1964)

Allen Weinstein, *Prelude to Populism: Origins of the Silver Issue, 1867–1878* (New Haven, Conn., 1970)

Paul Kleppner, *The Cross of Culture: A Social Analysis of Midwestern Politics, 1850–1900* (New York, 1970); *The Third Electoral System, 1853–1892: Parties, Voters, and Political Cultures* (Chapel Hill, N.C., 1979)

R. J. Jensen, *The Winning of the Midwest: Social and Political Conflict, 1888–1896* (Chicago, 1971)

Roy V. Scott, *The Agrarian Movement in Illinois, 1880–1897* (New York, 1945)

G. H. Miller, *Railroads and the Granger Laws* (Madison, Wis., 1971)

Gabriel Kolko, *Railroads and Regulation, 1877–1916* (Princeton, 1965)

POPULISM

Lawrence Goodwyn, *Democratic Promise: The Populist Moment in America* (New York, 1976); *The Populist Moment: A Short History of the Agrarian Revolt in America* (New York, 1978)

John D. Hicks, *The Populist Revolt* (Minneapolis, 1931)

Norman Pollack, *The Populist Response to Industrial America* (Cambridge, Mass., 1976)

Robert W. Cherny, *Populism, Progressivism and the Transformation of Nebraska Politics, 1885–1915* (Lincoln, Neb., 1981)

Peter H. Argensinger, *Populism and Politics: William Alfred Peffer and the People's Party* (Lexington, Ky., 1974)

James E. Wright, *The Politics of Populism: Dissent in Colorado* (New Haven, Conn., 1974)

Comer Vann Woodward, *Tom Watson, Agrarian Rebel* (New York, 1938, 1963)

David D. Anderson, *Ignatius Donnelly* (Boston, 1980)

Carleton Beals, *The Great Revolt and Its Leaders: The History of Popular American Uprisings in the 1890s* (New York, 1968)

Samuel T. McSeveney, *The Politics of Depression: Political Behavior in the Northeast, 1893–1896* (New York, 1972)

Frank W. Taussig, *The Silver Situation in the United States* (New York, 1894; first published, 1892)

BRYAN, McKINLEY, AND THE ELECTION OF 1896

Harold Underwood Faulkner, *Politics, Reform, and Expansion, 1890–1900* (New York, 1959, 1963)

Robert F. Durden, *The Climax of Populism: The Election of 1896* (Lexington, Ky., 1965)

Stanley L. Jones, *The Presidential Election of 1896* (Madison, Wis., 1964)

Paul Glad, *McKinley, Bryan and the People* (Philadelphia, 1964)

Louis W. Koenig, *A Political Biography of William Jennings Bryan* (New York, 1972)

Paolo E. Coletta, *William Jennings Bryan*, vol. 1: *Political Evangelist, 1860–1908* (Lincoln, Neb., 1964)

Howard Wayne Morgan, *William McKinley and His America* (Syracuse, N.Y., 1963)

Herbert Croly, *Marcus Alonzo Hanna: His Life and Work* (New York, 1912)

FOREIGN POLICY

Milton Plesur, *America's Outward Thrust: Approaches to Foreign Affairs, 1865–1890* (De Kalb, Ill., 1971)

David M. Pletcher, *The Awkward Years: Foreign Policy under Garfield and Arthur* (Columbia, Mo., 1962)

John M. Dobson, *America's Ascent: The United States Becomes a Great Power, 1880–1914* (De Kalb, Ill., 1978)

Robert L. Beisner, *From the Old Diplomacy to the New, 1865–1900* (Arlington Heights, Ill., 1974).

Charles S. Campbell, *The Transformation of American Foreign Relations, 1865–1900* (New York, 1976); *Anglo-American Understanding, 1898–1903* (Baltimore, 1957)

William A. Russ, Jr., *The Hawaiian Republic, 1894–98, and Its Struggle to Win Annexation* (Selingsgrove, Pa., 1961)

Thomas J. McCormick, *China Market, America's Quest for Informal Empire, 1893–1901* (Chicago, 1967)

Paul A. Varg, *The Making of a Myth: The United States and China, 1897–1912* (East Lansing, Mich., 1968)

WAR OF 1898

David R. Trask, *The War with Spain in 1898* (New York, 1981)

Philip Foner, *The Spanish-Cuban-American War and the Birth of American Imperialism,* 2 vols. (New York, 1972)

Howard Wayne Morgan, *America's Road to Empire: The War with Spain and Overseas Expansion* (New York, 1965)

Julius W. Pratt, *The Expansionists of 1898* (Baltimore, 1936)

David F. Healy, *U.S. Expansionism: Imperialist Urge in the 1890s* (Madison, Wis., 1970); *The United States in Cuba, 1898–1902* (Madison, Wis., 1963)

Charles H. Brown, *The Correspondents' War: Journalists in the Spanish-American War* (New York, 1967); *Agents of Manifest Destiny: The Lives and Times of the Filibusters* (Chapel Hill, N.C., 1980)

Robert L. Beisner, *Twelve Against Empire: The Anti-Imperialists, 1898–1900* (New York, 1968)

Richard E. Welch, *Response to Imperialism: The United States and the Philippine-American War, 1899–1902* (Chapel Hill, N.C., 1979)

Stuart Creighton Miller, *"Benevolent Assimilation," The American Conquest of the Philippines, 1899–1903* (New Haven and London, 1982)

William B. Bean, *Walter Reed—A Biography* (Charlottesville, Va., 1982)

ROOSEVELT

Edmund Morris, *The Rise of Theodore Roosevelt* (New York and London, 1979)

David McCullough, *Mornings on Horseback* (New York, 1981)

G. Wallace Chessman, *Governor Theodore Roosevelt: The Albany Apprenticeship; 1898–1900* (Cambridge, Mass., 1965)

Mark Sullivan, *Our Times,* vol. 1: *America at the Turn of the Century* (New York, 1925)

Finley Peter Dunne, *Mr. Dooley's Opinions* (New York, 1901)

INDEX